REGULATION OF BLUE CROSS AND BLUE SHIELD PLANS

Robert D. Eilers

This volume is the first comprehensive treatment of the regulatory status of Blue Cross and Blue Shield plans in the United States. It presents a wealth of operating data and reflects opinions from most of the insurance commissioners throughout the country, as well as from Blue Cross and Blue Shield plan executives, officials of their national organizations, representatives of the insurance industry, and others involved in the field of medical care protection.

Introductory chapters discuss the organization and operations of associations, current coverage and benefits, inter-plan arrangements, and the significance of certain characteristics and goals of hospital and medical service associations. After considering the various methods by which plans are regulated, including both governmental supervision and self-regulation, the book proceeds to explore specific areas of regulation. Benefit structures, hospital reimbursement schedules, rate making procedures, reserve requirements, and the composition of boards of directors are among the areas which are analyzed. The traditional issue of plans' tax status is also evaluated.

The final section of the book considers additional problems of paramount importance for plans, including rising expenditures for medical care, catastrophic medical care protection, and coverage of the aged.

THE S. S. HUEBNER FOUNDATION FOR INSURANCE EDUCATION

Lectures

LIFE INSURANCE TRENDS AND PROBLEMS
LIFE INSURANCE TRENDS AT MID-CENTURY
INVESTMENT OF LIFE INSURANCE FUNDS
ACCIDENT AND SICKNESS INSURANCE
PENSIONS: PROBLEMS AND TRENDS
THE BENEFICIARY IN LIFE INSURANCE
LIFE INSURANCE SALES MANAGEMENT
ALL LINES INSURANCE

Studies

AN ANALYSIS OF GOVERNMENT LIFE INSURANCE
GROUP LIFE INSURANCE
GROUP HEALTH INSURANCE
GROUP ANNUITIES
THE ECONOMIC THEORY OF RISK AND INSURANCE
LIFE INSURANCE HOUSING PROJECTS
LIFE INSURANCE INVESTMENT IN COMMERCIAL REAL
    ESTATE
TOTAL DISABILITY PROVISIONS IN LIFE INSURANCE
    CONTRACTS
INSURANCE AND ECONOMIC THEORY
TRANSITION TO MULTIPLE-LINE INSURANCE COMPANIES
COMPULSORY TEMPORARY DISABILITY INSURANCE
    IN THE UNITED STATES
DEVELOPMENT OF COMPREHENSIVE INSURANCE
    FOR THE HOUSEHOLD
SAVINGS BANK LIFE INSURANCE
RIGHTS OF CREDITORS IN LIFE INSURANCE POLICIES
REGULATION OF BLUE CROSS AND BLUE SHIELD PLANS

REGULATION OF BLUE CROSS
AND BLUE SHIELD PLANS

by

ROBERT D. EILERS, PH.D.

*Assistant Professor of Insurance
and
Assistant Director, S. S. Huebner Foundation
for Insurance Education
University of Pennsylvania*

Published for

THE S. S. HUEBNER FOUNDATION
FOR INSURANCE EDUCATION
University of Pennsylvania

by

RICHARD D. IRWIN, INC., Homewood, Illinois

Library of Congress Catalog Card No. 63–10322
Manufactured in the United States of America

to my father and mother
Ben J. and Pearle L. Eilers

THE S. S. HUEBNER FOUNDATION
FOR INSURANCE EDUCATION

The S. S. Huebner Foundation for Insurance Education was created in 1940, under the sponsorship of the American Life Convention, the Life Insurance Association of America (then the Association of Life Insurance Presidents), and the Institute of Life Insurance, and operated under a deed of trust until 1955 at which time it was incorporated as a Pennsylvania nonprofit corporation. Its primary purpose is to strengthen and encourage insurance education at the collegiate level. Its activities take three principal forms:

a) The providing of fellowships and scholarships to teachers in accredited colleges and universities of the United States and Canada, or persons who are contemplating a teaching career in such colleges and universities, in order that they may secure preparation at the graduate level for insurance teaching and research.

b) The publication of research theses and other studies which constitute a distinct contribution directly or indirectly to insurance knowledge.

c) The collection and maintenance of an insurance library and other research materials which are made available through circulating privileges to teachers in accredited colleges and universities desirous of conducting research in the insurance field.

Financial support for the Foundation is provided by contributions from more than one hundred life insurance companies and proceeds from the sale of Foundation publications.

The program of activities is under the general direction of a Board of Trustees representing the life insurance institution. Actual operation of the Foundation has been delegated to the University of Pennsylvania under an administrative plan submitted by the University and approved by the Board of Trustees. The University discharges its responsibilities through an Administrative Board consisting of six officers and faculty members of the University of Pennsylvania and three academic persons associated with other institutions. Active management of the Foundation is entrusted to an Executive Director, appointed by the University of Pennsylvania.

vii

FOREWORD

The past quarter-century has witnessed a sharp and continuing increase in expenditures by the American people for health and medical care. This phenomenon reflects the combined influence of a significant rise in the unit cost of medical care and an equally notable upsurge in the rate of utilization of health and medical services. This has brought increasing recognition to the need for making advance provision for burdensome medical expenses.

In 1962 private health insurance provided protection to three-quarters of the United States population on a voluntary basis. It paid some $7 billion in benefits to individuals who incurred expenses from illness or injury. This voluntary approach to a major economic and social problem serves to bolster the free enterprise system. Blue Cross and Blue Shield associations play an important role in this endeavor.

The scope of Blue Cross and Blue Shield operations, however measured, is of such magnitude that the public interest is inevitably involved. Public interest is almost invariably accompanied by public supervision or surveillance. Thus, an inquiry into the nature and extent of regulation of Blue Cross-Blue Shield associations seems to be in order—if not long overdue. This volume represents the results of such an inquiry, the thoroughness and objectivity of which have been acclaimed by representatives of those groups, as well as by representatives of the insurance industry and regulatory agencies.

Mr. E. A. van Steenwyk, the late head of the Associated Hospital Service of Philadelphia and one of the pioneers in the Blue Cross movement, had the following to say:

Dr. Eilers' study is excellent and sets forth many facts and opinions which need to be in the literature. The discussion as to Blue Cross–Insurance Company differences is expertly handled.

ix

This worthwhile book will undoubtedly contribute significantly to our thought.

Mr. J. F. Follmann, Jr., Director of Information and Research, Health Insurance Association of America, stated that:

Dr. Eilers' study of the *Regulation of Blue Cross and Blue Shield Plans* reflects an incisive grasp of the subject. It, furthermore, contains considerable background information which can be helpful to an understanding of the rationale and concepts which underlie the regulatory pattern of Blue Cross and Blue Shield plans as it has evolved over the past twenty-five to thirty years. It is a work which will be of interest to a great many people and which will serve, for a long time to come, as a useful reference document.

This book is, in substance, the doctoral dissertation of Dr. Eilers. It is the fifteenth volume in the "Studies" Series and the twenty-third book in all to be published by the Foundation.

Dr. Eilers is a native of Iowa and a graduate of Drake University. After graduation from college he served three years in the United States Navy as a commissioned officer and is still an active participant in the reserve component of that branch of the military. Upon termination of his three-year tour of active duty, Dr. Eilers enrolled in the Graduate Division of the Wharton School, receiving his M.B.A. with a specialization in risk and insurance. For the next two years he was affiliated in a sales management capacity with a large eastern life insurance company. In 1959, having decided upon an academic career, he re-entered the University of Pennsylvania under the auspices of the S. S. Huebner Foundation for Insurance Education. Two years later he received his Ph.D. degree and joined the faculty of the Wharton School of Finance and Commerce as Assistant Professor of Insurance, a position he still holds. He also serves as Assistant Director of the Huebner Foundation.

The nature of the purpose for which the Foundation was created precludes it from taking an editorial position on controversial insurance theories or practices. It does not, therefore, detract in any wise from the quality of this volume to state that the findings of fact and conclusions derived therefrom are those of the author and not of the Foundation.

DAN M. MCGILL
Executive Director

Philadelphia
February, 1963

PREFACE

Although the birth of Blue Cross provided the cornerstone for the development of medical care coverages in the United States more than three decades ago, the significance of Blue Cross is based on much more than this historical fact. The current importance of the plans is documented, for example, by the impressive proportion of the population nationally, as well as in particular states and locales, which has come to rely upon the associations for hospital expense protection. The founding and growth of Blue Shield plans to finance surgical and medical expenses have been an interrelated development in the nonprofit service association movement during the last twenty years. Currently over one fourth of the citizens of the country are plan members, with Blue Cross enrollment exceeding fifty-six million and Blue Shield having more than forty-six million subscribers.

The expansion of Blue Cross and Blue Shield coverage has not been without competition. In fact the rivalry between plans and insurance companies has been so intense in recent years that many associations have been unable to maintain their proportional enrollment of those with medical care protection. Thus, associations have been making many important modifications to meet the challenge of providing more widespread coverage in terms of both benefits and insureds. These alterations present a number of crucial problems with respect to the regulatory procedures applicable to Blue Cross and Blue Shield plans. While the regulation of the associations has for sometime been a topic of lively interest among parties involved in the field of medical expense coverage, several of the current regulatory issues are of such significance that they not only affect the continued vitality of the plans themselves but may also be instrumental in shaping the structure of medical care protection in the United States. Despite the critical nature of the subject, there is a dearth of written material concerning the regulatory status of the associations. The bulk of the studies of Blue Cross and Blue Shield have been only statewide in scope and even then have generally not concentrated on the regulatory situation. The goal of the research upon which this volume is based was, therefore, to explore the regulatory status of Blue Cross and Blue Shield, consider the associated problems, and evaluate possible solutions. The resulting study involved virtually every facet of the associations and their operations.

The task of gathering and analyzing the data in connection with the study would undoubtedly have been insurmountable had not a prodigious amount of assistance been given by many individuals. As a result of this help, the research effort was actually a pleasant and invigorating experience. Throughout the project my wife, Dolores, was a constant source of aid and encouragement. Dr. Dan M. McGill, my faculty adviser, provided invaluable assistance from the inception of the research until the completed study was submitted to the publisher. It is with heartfelt gratitude that I acknowledge the assistance of these two individuals whose extensive contributions are not specifically mentioned in the text but whose help has been reflected throughout the entire volume.

The research for this study brought the author into contact with a great number of truly remarkable men who are intimately involved with medical care protection in the United States. Space limitations preclude mention of each of the insurance commissioners, Blue Cross and Blue Shield plan executives and national officials, members of trade and professional associations, executives of insurance companies, and educators who assisted in the research, gave freely of their opinions, and provided inspiration at many junctures.

I would be remiss not to mention specifically the early guidance of the late E. A. van Steenwyk, who gave a considerable amount of his time to counsel the author and provide background information which few others had firsthand. Mr. van Steenwyk also provided an extensive commentary on the entire manuscript after it was finished. The following men and members of their staffs also cooperated not only during the research but by reading and commenting at length on the completed manuscript: John W. Castellucci, Executive Vice President, National Association of Blue Shield Plans; J. F. Follmann, Jr., Director of Information and Research, Health Insurance Association of America; Walter J. McNerney, President, Blue Cross Association; J. Henry Smith, Underwriting Vice President, The Equitable Life Assurance Society of the United States; and the Honorable Frank Sullivan, Commissioner of Insurance for the State of Kansas and former President of the National Association of Insurance Commissioners. I am greatly indebted to each of these men for unselfishly sharing his time and wisdom. However, the general opinions expressed in the text should be ascribed to no one but the author, particularly since several of the gentlemen mentioned took at least qualified exception to some of the conclusions which were reached. In addition, any errors or omissions that may be found are the responsibility of the author and are not attributable to any of those who were kind enough to assist him in the research and writing.

The details in connection with the publication of the manuscript were handled in her usual, capable manner by Miss Mildred Brill, Administrative Assistant of the Huebner Foundation.

Finally, I am indebted to the S. S. Huebner Foundation for Insurance Education not only for publishing this volume, but also for the financial assistance I received as a Huebner Fellow during which time the manuscript was completed.

ROBERT EILERS

Philadelphia
January, 1963

CONTENTS

PART II. REGULATION

PART III. GROWTH PROBLEMS AND CONCLUSIONS

APPENDIXES

INDEX

LIST OF TABLES AND CHARTS

Part One

DEVELOPMENT AND DISTINGUISHING FEATURES

chapter I

INTRODUCTION

SCOPE

On the periphery of regulatory procedures applicable to health insurance companies, yet within the range of their influence, lies a group of insurance-type associations. These organizations use somewhat different approaches than do insurance companies in seeking to reduce the financial impact of accidents and illnesses on individuals and families.[1] The terms often used to identify such entities are "nonprofit hospital service associations" and "nonprofit medical service associations," in keeping with the dichotomy of services rendered by hospitals and physicians. Although generally under the purview of state insurance departments, hospital and medical service associations are exempt from many of the regulations which pertain to commercial carriers. At the same time, some regulatory procedures to which associations are subjected are more exacting than for insurance companies which offer competitive benefits. The differences in regulatory treatment of associations are as controversial as the techniques they use to deal with the medical care hazard.

This study is concerned with the regulation of Blue Cross and Blue Shield plans, which comprise the largest segment of the nonprofit associations in terms of numbers of persons

---

[1] Some organizations offer benefits on the occurrence of a contingency which is beyond the generally understood meaning of "accident" or "illness," e.g., dental and ocular expenses. There are about 125 dental care associations in this country, but they usually extend coverage only to special groups. Associations whose sole purpose is to provide "extra" benefits of this type will not be discussed.

covered, contributions paid in, and benefits paid out. Independent associations, which account for the remaining portion of these organizations, were excluded from the research on which this treatise is based. Less than 4 per cent of the hospital expense coverage in the United States at the end of 1960 was attributable to the independent associations.[2] While of particular importance in certain localities and industries, they have little significance on the national scene.[3] Since the regulatory statutes which apply to independent associations are usually identical to those which pertain to Blue Cross and Blue Shield, much of what is said concerning this formal type of regulation is also relevant to the former variety of organization. Nevertheless, the unqualified and uncapitalized word "associations" will hereafter refer only to Blue Cross and Blue Shield plans. If *national* associations are being considered, this fact will be specifically mentioned.

Many persons would argue that mutual insurance companies should be classified as nonprofit organizations. Regardless of the merits of the argument, the term "nonprofit," for the purpose of this treatise, will not include mutual insurers unless definite reference is made to them. This distinction is in consonance with state regulatory codes.

While the broad area of health insurance-type coverages as discussed above was subdivided by insurer type of organization—insurance companies, Blue Cross and Blue Shield plans, and independent associations—an equally logical categorization would be by type of benefits. The latter classification includes the broad divisions of income replacement benefits, and medical care expense benefits. Protection

---

[2] Health Insurance Institute, *Health Insurance Data, 1961* (New York, 1961), p. 12.

[3] The composition of independent plans in the United States at the end of 1960 was as follows (000 omitted):

	Hospital Expense	Surgical Expense	Regular Medical Expense
Total for all independent plans	5,542	6,573	6,773
Net total persons protected	131,962	121,045	87,541

against medical care expenses could be further subdivided into coverage for: hospital expenses, including room, board, and special services; surgical expenses; medical expenses, i.e., doctors' fees; and miscellaneous expenses which include nursing charges and other extra costs. Income replacement benefits are automatically excluded from consideration in this study as Blue Cross and Blue Shield plans do not provide this type of coverage.[4]

SUBJECT DEVELOPMENT

The development of the topic, "Regulation of Blue Cross and Blue Shield Plans," will be approached by first considering the current methods of handling medical care hazards. Blue Cross and Blue Shield benefits, organizations, and characteristics will be elaborated, after which the evolution of insurance regulation will be discussed. Specific regulatory areas applicable to Blue Cross and Blue Shield will then be examined. This latter section is the core of the book.

"Regulation" may be viewed as including those procedures which limit, guide, or govern the activities of individuals and groups of individuals to such an extent that the effect of the activities is in keeping with the desires and best interests of the society, as determined by the governing body.[5] The definition allows for the fact that regulation can take place through other than governmental organs. This is particularly true in the case of Blue Cross and Blue Shield

---

[4] The American Risk and Insurance Association has established a commission to clarify the definitions of insurance terms and to seek the adoption of the nomenclature which is selected. This Commission on Insurance Terminology has six active committees which are composed of scholars from industry, education, risk management, journalism, and other circles. Terms used in this study will agree with the majority opinion of the Committee on Health Insurance Terminology, where such information is known. "Health insurance" is an example. The committee's tenor of thought is that "health insurance" should be the broad term used to encompass coverages whose benefits at least partially offset the effects of reduced earned income or increased monetary outgo for medical care expenses which accompany accidents and illnesses.

[5] In conceiving this definition the author recognizes that there may be divergencies between the "desires" and the "best interests" of a society.

plans, a sizeable part of whose activities is subject to the purview, and often to the restraints, of medical and hospital societies, as well as to the organizational hierarchy in the Blue Cross and Blue Shield systems. Certain aspects of self-restraint imposed by associations, or the organizations to which they belong, are called "self-regulation." Since self-regulation, as well as governmental regulation, is included in this study, it has been necessary to cover some phases of Blue Cross–Blue Shield operations in detail. This will be observed in Chapters III and IV.

SOURCES OF INFORMATION

Much of the information underlying this study was provided by regulatory authorities for Blue Cross and Blue Shield in forty-four states. These officials responded with information to a questionnaire, contained in Appendix A. Personal interviews were conducted with the insurance commissioners and/or members of their departments in New York, Pennsylvania, and Illinois. Discussions were also held with many of the executive directors of associations in these states. Other plans in these areas, as well as those in California and locales of particular interest, were approached for information through correspondence. Interviews were conducted with officials of the Blue Cross Association, the National Association of Blue Shield Plans, the American Hospital Association, and others concerned with the medical care field.

While an effort has been made to portray the entire regulatory picture for Blue Cross and Blue Shield plans, the laws and procedures in New York, California, Pennsylvania, and Illinois have been relied upon heavily. These are the "Big Four" states population-wise as well as being the leading areas in numbers of persons covered by hospital, surgical and regular medical expense protection.[6] If the laws or regu-

---

[6] Health Insurance Institute, *op. cit.*, pp. 24–25. These four states account for approximately 34 per cent of the medical care coverage in the United

latory techniques applicable to Blue Cross or Blue Shield are changed in other states, it is quite possible that the alterations will be patterned after the standards and procedures used in these large jurisdictions.

States. They are also the states with the largest total premiums for health insurance. In terms of premiums for Blue Cross–Blue Shield and other hospital and medical plans, Michigan and Ohio rank ahead of Illinois. Persons with health insurance protection in New York, California, Pennsylvania, and Illinois received 35 per cent of the total health insurance benefit payments and 37 per cent of the total Blue Cross benefits in the United States in 1960. (*Ibid.,* pp. 24–25, 36–37, and 45–46.)

chapter II

HISTORY AND DEVELOPMENT
OF VOLUNTARY
MEDICAL CARE COVERAGE

THE EMBRYONIC STAGE OF
MEDICAL CARE PLANS

After 1900, bonds of kinship weakened and family ties loosened. As a result, the family unit became increasingly isolated, both socially and financially. Gregariousness and financial necessity stimulated the origination and expansion of groups which could, in certain respects, fill the relationships that had previously existed among families and in the community type of living. Fraternal societies flourished in the early part of this century among those having nationality, occupational, political, and religious bonds.

Insurance became enmeshed in the sociological change. The insurance mechanism offered a financial substitute for the former reliance on the family unit. In this scheme, individuals were brought together in an attempt to pool their common hazards.[1] As a part of the insurance system, a person became a member of a "family" gathered together for financial, and sometimes other, purposes.

---

[1] Insurance is "a formal social device for the substitution of certainty for uncertainty through the pooling of hazards." (C. A. Kulp, *Casualty Insurance* [3rd ed.; New York: The Ronald Press Co., 1956], p. 9.) As is to be expected, there is considerable argument among scholars as to the elements which are necessary in the insurance device. There is no need for this study to enter the conflict, as Dr. Kulp's definition suffices for purposes of illustration.

8

The grouping of individuals for the prepayment of medical care expenses is of more recent origin than the association of persons to pool their funds in order to provide loss-of-income or death benefits. Experiments in the advance payment of hospital care started in the late 1800's. After the turn of the century some group hospital insurance was available for employees. Several insurance companies sold hospital coverage as a part of their individual disability income contracts; these were not widely purchased, however. A typical provision was to pay additional income benefits if the insured was hospitalized.

There were isolated cases of occupational groups and a few nationality-type organizations "chipping in" in advance of the occurrence of a contingency requiring hospitalization, rather than contributing through sympathy after the event. Such organizations were characterized by local coverage and employee financing.

One of the earliest groups to be formed for the coverage of medical care expenses, as such, was the Northern Pacific Railway Beneficial Association, founded in 1882 by the railroad's employees.[2] Washington and Oregon were the sites of several early group-type medical care organizations, most of which made available only the services of a company-hired physician.

The usual pattern for the development of benefits by insurance companies was to have income replacement policies and subsequently—often not until the second or third decade of the twentieth century—to add some type of hospitalization coverage to the original benefit structure.

A forerunner of service-type benefits appeared in 1922 when Grinnell College in Iowa contracted with a local hospital to provide services for students.[3]

---

[2] Franz Goldman, *Voluntary Medical Care in the United States* (New York: Columbia University Press, 1948) , p. 37.

[3] The plan, which originally offered three weeks of hospitalization for a yearly payment of $8, continued in existence until 1943 when the membership became Blue Cross subscribers.

BLUE CROSS BIRTH AND INCUBATION, 1929–1940

The first "family" of individuals to give pronounced impetus to the birth of medical care insurance was a group of teachers in Texas. The superintendent of schools in Dallas, Dr. Justin Ford Kimball, had originated a loss-of-income plan among this group. When Dr. Kimball went to Baylor University as executive vice-president in 1929, he found that unpaid bills of many school teachers were among the heavy accounts receivable at the University's medical facilities. After studying the hospitalization costs of teachers, Dr. Kimball drew up a hospitalization prepayment plan along the lines of the loss-of-income plan he had implemented earlier.

For a monthly payment of fifty cents by 75 per cent of the 1,500 teachers, the use of a semiprivate room and other services for twenty-one days were prepaid in the Baylor Hospital.[4] A one-third discount on the next 344 days was provided. Mental and nervous diseases, venereal diseases, tuberculosis, and certain contagious diseases were excluded from coverage.[5] The plan became effective on December 20, 1929. Business groups in the area subsequently joined the arrangement. For this reason such organizations were initially referred to as "group hospitalization associations."

Dr. Rufus Rorem, then of the Rosenwald Foundation, visited Dallas a few months later and gave nation-wide publicity among the hospitals to the way the plan was working out in Dallas. Dr. E. H. Carrey, at that time President of the American Medical Association . . . by his great professional medical prestige held back medical suspicions until the new experiment could have fair trial. . . .[6]

---

[4] Richard M. Jones, "The Blue Cross Movement," *A Look at Modern Health Insurance* (Washington, D.C.: Chamber of Commerce of the United States, 1948), chap. 10, pp. 1–3.

[5] Louis S. Reed, *Blue Cross and Medical Service Plans* (Washington, D.C.: Federal Security Agency, 1947), p. 10.

[6] Jones, *op. cit.*, p. 4.

In the early 1930's the Baylor Plan was copied in several states. California, New Jersey, and Minnesota were the earliest starters. This was a time when great numbers of individuals were in a financial position similar to that of the Dallas teachers; many had insufficient funds to pay for hospitalization in the event of accidents or illnesses.

The expansion of the group hospitalization idea required decisions as to which hospitals in a community could and would cooperate in the arrangement. The urging by professional groups, who were anxious for individuals to be able to choose both their physicians and the hospitals in which they would be admitted, broadened the original type of organization to include a prepayment of services in *any* licensed hospital which would cooperate in the movement in a particular locality.

By 1933 the American Hospital Association had accepted the importance and desirability of prepayment associations and had established several requirements to be met before an organization would be "acceptable for group hospitalization."[7] These became the stipulations with which an association had to comply in order to use the Blue Cross emblem.

Shortly after these early starts at hospitalization insurance, economic rumblings commenced which became what is now known as the Great Depression. As unemployment increased and incomes sank, businesses observed the precipitous plunge of expenditures for their products and services. Not the least affected was the hospital "business." With high overheads, large funding commitments, and an increasing volume of charity cases, hospitals realized that some method was necessary to increase their paying bed-occupancy rate. Hospital prepayment offered the desired financial assistance.

In the 1930's, politicians, as well as hospital and insurance

---

[7] "Essentials of an Acceptable Plan for Group Hospitalization" required that an organization: (1) stress public welfare; (2) limit its protection to hospital charges; (3) enlist professional and public interests; (4) provide free choice of physician and hospital; (5) maintain itself as a nonprofit organization; (6) maintain itself on a sound economic basis; and (7) promote itself in a cooperative spirit and dignified manner. (*Ibid.*, p. 5.)

groups, were beginning to consider the expenses created by accidents and illnesses as possibly having a social implication, and bills for the solution of sections of this problem began to appear in Congress. Dr. Louis Reed, a highly respected hospital economist, said in 1937 that despite the growth in group hospitalization, "It will not solve the medical care problem. It is incomplete, and there is little prospect, so long as plans are on a voluntary basis, that any large proportion of wage earners will enroll."[8] The next two decades showed this commonly held opinion to be erroneous. States and municipalities gave their support at this time to the prepayment organizations in a desire to have the many medical indigents removed from their rolls.

The social environment which shrouded the movement can be better understood when it is realized that a sizeable percentage of the organizations were started by at least quasi-social institutions. Of thirty-nine hospital service associations studied by Dr. Reed, twenty-two obtained their initial funds from hospitals. Five received capital from both hospitals and civic leaders, while six obtained their start through support of local foundations. None of these organizations started with more than $30,000 of capital. Two commenced with less than $1,000; thirteen began with from $1,000 to $5,000; seven with $5,000 to $10,000; four with $10,000 to $20,000; while eight had from $20,000 to $30,-000.[9]

The medical care protection movement was not without its problems. For some promoters, both in the hospital service associations and in insurance companies, the scheme was looked upon as a funnel flow of easy money. Some backers invaded the till and departed; rates often rose drastically. The need for increased supervision of associations by some governmental body was apparent.

A perplexing problem in the development of medical care

---

[8] Louis S. Reed, *Health Insurance the Next Step in Social Security* (New York: Harper and Bros., 1937) , p. 189.

[9] Reed, *Blue Cross and Medical Service Plans,* pp. 13–14.

protection was presented by the fact that the associated contingencies failed to meet some of the requirements for an insurable hazard. To be eligible for insurance it has been customarily held that a hazard should embody the following features: (1) there should be a large and homogeneous group of risks; (2) the potential loss should be definite and measureable; (3) the loss should be fortuitous, unexpected, and uncontrolled; (4) the loss should be serious in nature; and (5) risks should be widely disbursed and not subject to catastrophic loss. The insurance industry was wary of hospitalization insurance during its early stages because there was a question whether the medical expense hazard could meet the second, third, and fifth principles.

So complete had been the disdain of commercial carriers for medical care coverage that only sketchy historical information can be located about their experiments with it prior to the 1930's. It is known that a few individual policies were available after the turn of the century, although they were sold with little enthusiasm and enjoyed only limited acceptance.

Prior to the success of the group hospitalization associations, most insurance companies had felt they could not satisfactorily insure against medical care contingencies. After insurance companies saw the popularity and favorable results of their own group contracts, individual policies began to be projected with more vigor.

From their early beginnings, and to the present day, Blue Cross plans and insurance companies have taken divergent approaches to the problem of protecting against medical care expenses. As one example, Blue Cross has employed "service-type" benefits while insurance companies have sold "cash-indemnity" policies. The former entitles a subscriber to a certain number of days in a member hospital with a specific type of accommodation, generally semiprivate, including meals and general nursing service. Certain hospital services are also provided, including drugs and medicines while in the hospital, surgical dressings, and use of operating rooms. X rays and laboratory tests are usually available to hospitalized subscribers without charge up to specified dollar limits. The Blue Cross plan to which the patient belongs pays the *hospital* for the above services when rendered, according to a reimbursement contract between the hospital and the association. The major control on benefits in Blue Cross plans is the limit on the number of days of hospitalization that will be provided.

Insurance company contracts agree to pay the *insured* (or more correctly, to *indemnify the insured*) up to specific dollar amounts for services he receives from hospitals. The policy specifies the daily room and board limitations, amounts which will be reimbursed for special services and doctors' visits in the hospital, etc. If the charge for services exceeds the contract limitations, the uncovered amount must be paid by, or for, the insured. The maximum hospital confinement period during which benefits will be provided is generally longer under insurance policies than under Blue Cross certificates. The control on benefits is exercised through dollar limitations and often through such contractual features as deductibles.

Both group and individual coverages are available under the service and indemnity types, although some associations have limitations as to when individual protection may be purchased. Dependents' coverage may be included under either benefit arrangement.

Blue Cross coverage is normally obtained through direct contact between the employer or insured and salaried representatives of the associations. Individual insurance policies are purveyed through salesmen who are compensated by commissions, while group-insurance salesmen are paid either by salary or commission.

Subscribers must use Blue Cross member hospitals to obtain service benefits; otherwise they receive cash-indemnity benefits of a reduced type. (Over 90 per cent of the hospitals in America currently participate in Blue Cross programs.) Insured policyholders may use any accredited hospital.

Blue Cross plans are largely autonomous on a local or state basis and often have a community sponsorship aura. Insurance company policies generally have a national uniformity of benefits within each company.

BLUE SHIELD GENESIS AND GENERATION, 1939–1945

Analogous to the Blue Cross movement to cope with the hospital expense hazard is the Blue Shield evolution for protection against medical-surgical expenses. The latter associations followed in the wake of the former, with the result that the development and current administration of Blue Shield has been closely intertwined with Blue Cross in many areas.

Prior to 1938, several experiments with medical service plans had taken place in the Northwest. The accepted starting point, though, for the acceleration of these organizations was the California Physicians' Service, organized by the California Medical Association in 1939 to counteract proposed state health insurance legislation. The result was a state-wide prepayment plan for physicians' services which was controlled by the medical profession. Under the first arrangement, employed persons earning less than $3,000 annually could obtain one of two contracts: full physicians' service for $1.70 monthly, or a contract with a two-visit deductible for a monthly payment of $1.20.[10] An unexpected volume of service demanded by subscribers made the operation financially unsatisfactory for participating doctors; a considerable modification of premiums and benefits resulted.[11]

During the early stages of the medical service association movement, doctors, as well as medical societies, for the most part maintained a suspicious attitude toward the prepayment idea. Only when doctors controlled an association and

---

[10] Reed, *Blue Cross and Medical Service Plans*, p. 137.

[11] Frank E. Smith, "Blue Shield Develops," *A Look at Modern Health Insurance*, chap. 11, pp. 1–5.

all of the doctors in the locality could participate was support given by the profession. The fear of encroachment on professional prerogatives was widely evidenced, as in the following minority view of the Committee on Costs of Medical Care:

> It is our conviction that the Committee on the Costs of Medical Care would have served its stated purposes and the cause of medical progress and the people's health much better if it had taken a strong stand against all of those methods of caring for the sick which have in them the dangers and evils of "contract practice." By doing so they would have come to the assistance of the medical profession in a battle against forces which threaten to destroy its ideals, disrupt its organization and completely commercialize its practice, and which are at the same time opposed to the public welfare.[12]

The physicians' dissatisfaction was attributed to two causes: first, the contractual prepayment of physicians' services removed many people from the "market" when such individuals would otherwise have gone to doctors who were charging fees-for-service; second, there was the fear that a reduction in the traditional quality of medical care would result if doctors were to work on a mass contractual and commercial basis.[13]

Favorable aspects of the California Physicians' Service were duplicated in other states and counties after 1941. Initial expansion was slow. Problems associated with income limitations for service benefits, excessive utilization by insureds, and abuses by physicians were some of the early obstacles.

In 1942 the American Medical Association gave its approval to the movement. At the same time the Association set forth requirements that plans should meet:

> . . . all features of medical service should be under the control of the medical profession . . . no third party must be permitted to come between patient and physician in any medical rela-

---

[12] *Medical Care for the American People, the Final Report of the Committee on the Costs of Medical Care* (Chicago: University of Chicago Press, 1932), p. 167.

[13] *Ibid.*, pp. 200–204.

tions . . . the patient must have absolute freedom to choose any participating physician . . . the confidential nature of the patient-physician relationship must be preserved . . . medical service should be paid for by the patient in accordance with his income status and in a manner that is mutually satisfactory.[14]

The growing acceptance of Blue Cross was part of the force which added to the launching of Blue Shield plans. The two services—hospital and physicians'—went hand-in-hand; in addition, the two working together were better able to meet the competition from insurance companies whose policies included both hospital and surgical care. This tie-in of benefits, as well as the interdependence in development, accounts for the large number of Blue Cross and Blue Shield plans which are being operated by the same staffs at the present time.

Three Blue Shield organizations started in 1944, ten in 1945, and twelve in 1946.[15] Like Blue Cross, Blue Shield developed as locally autonomous organizations. The early growth pattern of Blue Shield, when contrasted with the far-reaching significance of these associations less than twenty-five years later, presents part of the necessary background for a discussion of regulation in this area. The divergencies in governmental supervision of associations is more easily understood when it is realized that these organizations were initially viewed as small, local groups. It is doubtful whether association executives, let alone regulatory officials, conceived that Blue Cross and Blue Shield would one day be covering such an important portion of the country's entire population.

THE MATURATION, 1940–1955

As Table 2–1 reveals, the phenomenal growth of Blue Cross occurred after 1940. Not until 1937, seven years after their birth, did Blue Cross plans have more than a million participants. In 1940 a total of 12.3 million persons—9 per

---

[14] Smith, *op. cit.*, chap. 11, p. 5.

[15] Reed, *Blue Cross and Medical Service Plans*, p. 145.

cent of the population—had some kind of hospital coverage, approximately one-half of which was provided by associations. Those protected against surgical expenses in the same year totaled 5.3 million—4 per cent of the population—

TABLE 2–1

NUMBER OF PEOPLE WITH HOSPITAL
EXPENSE PROTECTION,
1936–1960 (000 omitted)

End of Year	Grand Total*	Blue Cross, Blue Shield and Medical Society Plans
1936		608 †
1938		2,874
1940	12,312	6,012
1942	19,695	10,215
1944	29,232	15,772
1946	42,112	24,707
1948	60,995	31,246
1950	76,639	38,822
1952	90,965	43,475
1954	101,493	47,484
1955	107,662	50,726
1956	115,949	53,162
1957	121,432	54,923
1958	123,038	55,205
1959	127,896	56,825
1960	131,962	58,050

* Net total of people protected, eliminating duplication among persons protected by more than one kind of insuring organization or more than one insurance company policy providing the same kind of coverage.

† Columbia University School of Public Health, "Hospitals and Blue Cross," Lectures at Columbia University School of Public Health of the Faculty of Medicine, Institute of Administrative Medicine (rev. October, 1957), p. 3.

Source: Health Insurance Council.

while 3 million—2 per cent of the population—had medical expense coverage.[16]

The acceptance of group insurance by management and the pressures of the labor movement were of considerable

---

[16] Odin W. Anderson and Jacob J. Feldman, *Family Medical Costs and Voluntary Health Insurance: A Nationwide Survey* (New York: McGraw-Hill Book Co., Inc., 1956), p. 11.

importance in the upsurgence of medical care insurance during the war period. Management, moved by a combination
of social and mercenary motives, came to view medical care
coverage for workers in much the same light with which they
looked upon the workmen's compensation idea. Labor, often
unable to obtain money increases because of wage freezes,
strove for expansion of fringe benefits. Contractors on governmental cost-plus assignments did not oppose the extension of medical care coverages as they might have under less
advantageous financial contracts. Between 1940 and 1946
the number of individuals with hospital-surgical coverage
quadrupled. The absolute number covered by Blue Cross–
Blue Shield in 1946—24.7 million persons—was close to
double those protected by insurance companies.

Over the 1947–49 period the National Labor Relations
Board declared that employers were required to bargain with
employees regarding group medical care programs; failure
to do so would result in an unfair labor practice. This solidi-
fied the position of hospital, surgical, and medical types of
protection among group fringe benefits and greatly enhanced
their expansion. "Between 1946 and 1950, hospital insurance coverage increased by about 80 per cent, surgical insurance by about 190 per cent, and medical insurance by 230
per cent."[17]

The fantastic acceptance of medical care insurances from
1940 to 1955 brought with it developments which influenced
the regulation of the medical care field:

. . . it is likely that developments in health insurance, as in
almost any other line of human endeavor, are not necessarily the
outcome of well-reasoned choices from many possible alternatives. Rather, the form that health insurance has taken and will
take is a tenuous balance between the many elements that make
up the complexities of personal health services: people, hospitals, physicians, insurance, and finance, interlaced with philoso-

---

[17] Milton Silverman, "Post Reports on Health Insurance," *Saturday Evening
Post*, 230:25–27 (June 7, 1958) , p. 128.

phies of government and private enterprise and with the level of public information and knowledge.[18]

From 1946 to 1956 Blue Cross and Blue Shield plans added an additional 3 million members yearly. The ten-year period saw the total number of persons covered by hospital-expense protection climb from 42 million to 116 million individuals; 53 million of these were in Blue Cross–Blue Shield.

THE PRESENT, 1956–1962

Few economic issues are of more interest to the American people today than the costs of medical care and how best to meet them. Indeed, in recent years, some of our most vigorous (and bitter) national debates have raged around these matters. To many it may seem strange that such concern should develop at a time when clearly more Americans are receiving better medical care and living longer and healthier lives than ever before. The situation, however, becomes much less paradoxical when the amazing strides taken by medical science in the past fifty years are viewed in the light of the social and economic conditions they create and in the total social context of our times.[19]

Personal expenditures on health in the United States totaled $19.6 billion in 1960, which amounted to approximately 6 per cent of total personal consumption expenditures.[20] In addition, about $6 billion was spent by the various governmental levels. The position held by Blue Cross and Blue Shield plans can best be seen and analyzed through a consideration of the individuals covered and the benefit structures for those having medical care protection of this type. An analysis of benefit structures includes a discussion of the types of benefits—hospital, surgical, and medical—and the adequacy of these payments.

---

[18] Anderson and Feldman, *op. cit.*, p. 89.

[19] Franklin D. Murphy, Chancellor of the University of Kansas, in the "Foreword" to Anderson and Feldman, *op. cit.*, p. v.

[20] Health Insurance Institute, *Health Insurance Data, 1961* (New York, 1961), p. 49.

Enrollment

The growth rate in medical care coverage during the late 1950's was less pronounced than it was in the earlier developmental stages. This is natural as the base on which the rate is calculated grows to include an increasing portion of the population. Though more gradual, the persistent increase in the percentage of the population whose medical bills will be at least partially covered continues to make the over-all movement spectacular. Seventy-three per cent of the civilian population was covered by some type of voluntary medical care insurance in 1960, an increase of approximately 4 million persons over 1959.[21] The 1960 figure was comprised of 131,962,000 individuals. Over 92 per cent of these had the combined protection of both hospital and surgical coverages.[22]

The following factors are among those which have influenced the growth of Blue Cross and Blue Shield and, thereby, largely determined the areas in which current expansion would be most rapid: (1) adequacy and organization of voluntary hospitals, (2) nature of urban and industrial environment, and (3) level of local per capita income.[23] Where voluntary hospitals have been important in a

---

[21] The figure of 85 per cent has been mentioned as a possible population coverage goal for medical care insurance. The remainder would include those in various government institutions, military personnel, and those obtaining government assistance. If the 85 per cent is realistic, then about 86 per cent (73 divided by 85) of the *coverage goal* has been reached.

[22] Health Insurance Institute, *op. cit.,* pp. 5, 6, 21. The coverage breakdown at the end of 1960 was:

	Number of Persons Protected (000 omitted)		
Type of Protection	*Primary Coverage*	*Dependents' Coverage*	*Total*
Hospital expense	55,283	76,679	131,962
Surgical expense	49,306	71,739	121,045
Regular medical expense	36,248	51,293	87,541
Major medical expense	10,498	16,950	27,448

[23] Reed, *Blue Cross and Medical Service Plans,* pp. 28–30.

community, there has been more fertile ground for the growth of hospital service associations. This is exemplified by the situation in California:

> Perhaps, largely because the history of the development of hospitals in [California] . . . was generally sprinkled with proprietary institutions, the tradition of hospitals being a part of the community and also being responsible for the care of the sick, irrespective of ability to pay, is largely lacking. As a result, we have a highly developed county hospital system which takes care of the indigent and the medically indigent. . . .
> Because of this situation, the community pressure as well as the pressure from the hospitals for prepayment lacked strength, and the advent of prepayment has not transferred the same significant number of people from "no pay" or "part pay" status, to a "full pay" status. . . .
> The Plans in California, therefore, were started without the benefit of real community backing and have had to secure their enrollment strictly by selling and with very little advantage over the commercial insurance company that is willing to sell this type of insurance at its approximate cost. This may explain . . . to some degree, the lack of spectacular growth as compared with some of the eastern states. . . .[24]

Since the major early growth of associations was through group medical care protection, there has not been as extensive an expansion of Blue Cross and Blue Shield in rural areas. In 1953, one of the latest years for which detailed statistics have been available, hospital coverage in rural nonfarm areas was 131 per cent of what it was in rural farm locales; the urban coverage was 168 per cent of that in the farming areas.[25] Then, too, the higher the income of a family, the more likely it has been that such a family would have coverage against medical care expenses.

A total of 58 million individuals had hospital expense

---

[24] Letter from Mr. J. Philo Nelson, executive director, Hospital Service of California, dated December 22, 1960.

[25] Anderson and Feldman, *op. cit.*, p. 16.

protection under Blue Cross plans at the end of 1960. Blue
Cross–Blue Shield covered 50.3 million persons against surgical expense and 45 million against regular medical expenses.[26]

Benefits

The second aspect of the medical care protection portrait
is the benefit structure. This presents a similarly imposing
picture of growth. Table 2–2 contrasts the medical care expenditures in the United States with the voluntary insurance benefits. The total of hospital, surgical, and medical
benefit payments, including major medical benefits, rose to
$4.8 billion in 1960, an increase of over $500 million from
the previous year.[27] The dollar amount of insurance benefits
paid per year for medical care increased eightfold in the
twelve years after 1948. During the same period, direct payments, that is, payments above those made by insurance, decreased as a proportion of medical care expenditures. The
percentage of the total costs which were covered by insurance benefits tripled during this time.

In 1948 only 8 per cent of the country's medical care expenditures were compensated through insurance benefits.
This increased by about 2 per cent per year, on the average,
until one-fourth of such expenses were paid by insurance
benefits in 1960. The percentage of "medical care expenditures" covered by insurance benefits is considerably higher
when the term is confined to its customary meaning of hospital costs, doctors' fees, drugs, etc., inasmuch as the above
figures were based upon medical care expenses which include
the cost of aspirin and many other relatively minor drugstore
items. Over 51 per cent of the $11.2 billion in private ex-
penditures for hospitalization and physicians' services in 1960
was paid by insurance.

On a per capita basis the benefits picture is similar to that

---

[26] Health Insurance Institute, *op. cit.*, pp. 12, 14, 16.
[27] *Ibid.*, p. 41.

TABLE 2–2

<small>PRIVATE EXPENDITURES FOR MEDICAL CARE
AND FOR VOLUNTARY HEALTH INSURANCE,* 1948–1960</small>

Type of Expenditure	*1948*	*1952*	*1956*	*1959*	*1960*
	Amount (in millions)				
Total	$7,647	$10,098	$14,288	$18,020	$19,566
Direct payments	6,785	8,105	10,644	12,881	13,725
Insurance benefits	606	1,604	3,015	4,399	4,996
Insurance service †	256	389	609	740	845
	Percentage Distribution				
Total	100.0	100.0	100.0	100.0	100.0
Direct payments	88.8	80.3	74.6	71.5	70.1
Insurance benefits	7.9	15.9	21.1	24.4	25.5
Insurance service	3.3	3.9	4.3	4.1	4.4
Hospitalization	24.6	28.1	29.8	29.1	29.9
Direct payments	16.1	15.1	13.2	10.3	10.0
Insurance benefits	6.0	10.6	14.2	16.4	17.2
Physicians' care	31.7	28.3	27.0	27.9	27.7
Direct payments	28.9	21.5	18.2	18.2	17.7
Insurance benefits	2.0	5.2	6.9	8.0	8.4
Medicines and appliances	24.8	26.1	25.8		
Dentists' services	11.8	10.9	11.4	43.0	42.4
All other	7.1	6.6	6.1		
	Percentage of Disposable Personal Income				
Total	4.0	4.2	4.9	5.3	5.6

<small>* Consumer expenditures include employer contributions to health insurance premiums or health benefit costs. Medical care expenditures for the Armed Forces and veterans, those made by public health and other government agencies under workmen's compensation laws, and those of private philanthropic organizations directly to or by hospitals are excluded.

† Represents the difference between expenditures for health insurance premiums (earned income) and amounts returned to consumers as benefits.

Source: *Social Security Bulletin*, Vol. 23, No. 12 (December, 1960), p. 4; and Vol. 24, No. 12 (December, 1961), p. 5.</small>

portrayed by Table 2–2. Table 2–3 shows that insurance benefits in 1959 amounted to slightly over one half of the total expenditures for hospital services. Approximately one-third of the physicians' charges per capita was paid by insurance.

TABLE 2–3

PRIVATE EXPENDITURES FOR MEDICAL CARE AND FOR
VOLUNTARY HEALTH INSURANCE PER CAPITA,
1959 AND 1960

Type of Expenditure	Amount, 1959	Increase of 1959 over 1948 (%)	Amount, 1960
Total	$104.93	99.2	$109.82
Direct payments	75.49	61.5	
Insurance benefits	25.19	504.1	
Expenses for prepayment	4.24	140.9	
Hospital care	31.59	143.8	29.88
Direct payments	12.21	43.6	
Insurance benefits	16.86	438.7	
Expenses for prepayment	2.51	90.2	
Physicians' services	28.57	71.1	28.57
Direct payments	18.52	21.7	
Insurance benefits	8.33	701.0	
Expenses for prepayment	1.73	293.2	
Medicines	20.65	104.5	22.06
Appliances	6.79	128.6	6.84
Dentists' services	11.25	81.5	11.18
All other *	6.08	62.1	11.28 †

* Other professional services and nursing homes with skilled nursing care.

† Also includes the net cost for health insurance.

Source: *Social Security Bulletin*, Vol. 23, No. 12 (December, 1960), p. 6; and Vol. 24, No. 12 (December, 1961), p. 6.

Division of the Market

It is relevant to this study to observe the portion of the medical care protection business held by Blue Cross and Blue Shield. Since 1950, when the insurance companies and the Blues had about equal portions of the coverage in force, the insurance carriers have taken over more of the market. At the end of 1960 insurance companies had 78.9 million policyholders with hospital expense protection, while Blue Cross and Blue Shield covered 58 million persons against the same hazard. Forty-one per cent of those protected against hospital expenses in 1960 were enrolled in Blue Cross plans. Thirty-eight per cent of those with surgical coverage and 48 per cent of those having protection against regular medical expenses were Blue Cross and/or Blue Shield subscribers.[28]

---

[28] Health Insurance Institute, *op. cit.*, pp. 12–16. Over 800 insurance companies wrote medical care policies in 1960.

TABLE 2–4

Income and Expenditures for Medical Care Among Voluntary Health Insurance Plans, 1949–1960

Type of Carrier or Plan	1949	1954	1956	1959	1960
	All Hospital and Physicians' Services				
Income, amount (mil.)	$1,016	$2,756	$3,624	$5,139	$5,841
Total per cent	100.0	100.0	100.0	100.0	100.0
Blue Cross–Blue Shield	44.8	41.1	41.2	42.0	42.5
Insurance companies	45.5	50.5	50.8	51.4	51.8
Group	23.7	31.5	33.6	36.1	36.0
Individual	21.7	18.9	17.2	15.3	15.8
All other	9.8	8.5	8.0	6.7	5.7
Expenditures, amount (mil.)	$ 766	$2,179	$3,015	$4,399	$4,996
Total per cent	100.0	100.0	100.0	100.0	100.0
Blue Cross–Blue Shield	49.9	45.2	44.9	45.4	45.8
Insurance companies	38.5	45.1	46.8	47.3	47.8
Group	23.5	32.9	35.9	38.2	38.0
Individual	15.0	12.2	10.9	9.1	9.8
All other	11.6	9.7	8.3	7.3	6.4
	Hospital Services				
Income, amount (mil.)	$ 706	$1,767	$2,368	$3,384	$3,876
Total per cent	100.0	100.0	100.0	100.0	100.0
Blue Cross–Blue Shield	50.9	45.4	44.0	44.9	45.6
Insurance companies	43.0	47.5	49.7	50.5	51.1
Expenditures, amount (mil.)	$ 539	$1,442	$2,022	$2,945	$3,357.
Total per cent	100.0	100.0	100.0	100.0	100.0
Blue Cross–Blue Shield	56.8	49.9	47.7	48.4	48.9
Insurance companies	35.6	42.2	45.9	46.6	47.2
	Physicians' Services				
Income, amount (mil.)	$ 309	$ 989	$1,256	$1,756	$1,965
Total per cent	100.0	100.0	100.0	100.0	100.0
Blue Cross–Blue Shield	30.7	33.4	36.1	36.4	36.4
Insurance companies	50.8	55.7	52.8	53.0	53.3
Expenditures, amount (mil.)	$ 228	$ 737	$ 993	$1,454	$1,639
Total per cent	100.0	100.0	100.0	100.0	100.0
Blue Cross–Blue Shield	32.9	36.2	39.0	39.3	39.3
Insurance companies	45.2	50.8	48.7	48.8	49.0

Source: *Social Security Bulletin*, Vol. 23, No. 12 (December, 1960), p. 8; and Vol. 24, No. 12 (December, 1961), p. 9.

Table 2–4 contains the income and expenditures breakdowns for insurance companies and Blue Cross–Blue Shield, as well as subdivisions for hospital services and physicians' services. Unfortunately, the figures for Blue Cross and Blue Shield are not categorized by group and individual types of coverage as are the insurance company statistics.[29] On the average, probably about three fourths of those enrolled in Blue Cross and Blue Shield are group members; this figure can thus be used for an approximate allocation of the statistics in Table 2–4 between group and nongroup subscribers.

The fact that the 1949–1961 period saw the Blues lose ground to insurance companies in the over-all income received is attested by Table 2–4. In 1949 each type obtained about the same portion of the total income; in 1960, however, Blue Cross–Blue Shield had 42.5 per cent of the income received by medical expense carriers, while insurance companies obtained 51.8 per cent. The aggregate decline in associations' share of income and expenditures was attributable to the hospital segment of the combined hospital-physicians' services market. Both Blue Cross–Blue Shield and insurance companies gained percentage-wise in the physicians' services section.

Insurance companies held between 47.2 and 53.3 per cent of the market in 1960, depending upon whether income or expenditures, hospital services, physicians' services or the combination of these was being considered. Blue Cross-Blue Shield retained from 36.4 to 48.9 per cent of the market on similar bases.

Direct comparisons between the Blues and insurance

---

[29] The Anderson and Feldman study (*op. cit.*, p. 99, Table A–3) elaborated on the group and individual contract breakdown by percentage of those covered by hospital insurance:

Group		*Individual*	
	73		32
Blue Cross	36	Blue Cross	10
Private	30	Private	21
Independent	10	Independent	1

Since some individuals had contracts of two or more types, the sum of the percentages equals more than 100 per cent.

companies will not be made hereafter on each point to be considered. Before the discussion progresses toward the regulation of only Blue Cross and Blue Shield, however, it is appropriate to record the opinion of one writer among the many who suggest that the similarities between the two systems are quite noteworthy:

Actually, the two approaches have the same basic objective, and there are several fundamental areas where the two approaches are in substantial agreement—for example, the risk-sharing principle, the prepayment principle, and the existence of limitations (even though of different forms) on the benefits provided. Furthermore . . . the two approaches are gradually getting closer together. The two types of plans have both shown great popularity and tremendous growth, so each plan must have features that are attractive to millions of people.[30]

---

[30] Gilbert W. Fitzhugh, "Meeting Hospital Costs," *Accident and Sickness Insurance,* ed. David McCahan (Homewood, Ill.: Richard D. Irwin, Inc., 1954) , p. 60.

chapter III

THE OPERATION OF BLUE CROSS
AND BLUE SHIELD PLANS

The primary research for this study made it apparent that an important part of the regulation of Blue Cross and Blue Shield is instituted and conducted by the associations themselves. It seems appropriate and conducive to easier understanding, therefore, to cover the operations of plans in the historical and descriptive sections of this book. Thus, the following two chapters present information on such features of plans as their benefit structures and internal organization, as well as the mechanics of the composite Blue Cross system and its Blue Shield counterpart. These considerations will be useful when operational aspects of the associations are tied specifically to *regulation* in Part II.

BLUE CROSS PLANS

Membership

National Statistics. Seventy-seven Blue Cross plans are currently operating in the United States.[1] These organizations had a total of 56,489,259 subscribers in 1961; 60 per cent of the members were dependents. The size of Blue Cross plans may be seen in Table 3–1, where it is revealed that almost 57 per cent of the total membership is in the fourteen associations with over a million members. The eighteen Blue

---

[1] Excluding one association in Puerto Rico. Health Service, Inc. is also not included as a "plan." The four Blue Cross plans in Canada will not be considered in most of the subsequent discussions.

Cross plans with less than 200,000 subscribers comprise an insignificant portion of total members. The mean number of enrollees per association was 731,830 in 1961.

Those enrolled in Blue Cross at the end of 1961 comprised 30.74 per cent of the population of the United States, ex-

TABLE 3–1

ENROLLMENT OF BLUE CROSS PLANS IN THE UNITED STATES,
DECEMBER 31, 1961

Size of Plan (Members)	Membership Included	Number of Plans	Percentage of Total Members
Over 1,000,000	32,084,816	14	56.94
500,000–1,000,000	14,475,965	19	25.69
200,000–500,000	8,250,115	26	14.64
100,000–200,000	1,102,744	7 *	1.80
50,000–100,000	400,710	6	.71
Less than 50,000	126,531	5	.22
Total for United States	56,350,881	77	100.00
Total, including Health Service, Inc. †	56,458,452		
Total, including HCMA‡	56,489,259		
Total for United States, Puerto Rico, and Canada	59,812,132	81	

* Excludes the association in Puerto Rico.
† Health Service, Inc. is the national enrollment organization for Blue Cross and is associated with Medical Indemnity of America, a similar organization for Blue Shield.
‡ Medical Care Mutual Association is an affiliate of the Cincinnati Blue Cross plan.
Source: Blue Cross Association.

cluding Puerto Rico. The percentage of enrollment in the forty-eight states served by Blue Cross was as follows:[2]

Over 50 per cent enrollment: District of Columbia (71.88 per cent), Rhode Island (75.17 per cent), Delaware (63.74 per cent), New York (56.82 per cent).

Forty to 50 per cent enrollment: Ohio, Massachusetts, Pennsylvania, Connecticut, Michigan, Colorado.

Thirty to 40 per cent enrollment: New Hampshire, New Jersey, Maine, Maryland, Indiana, Missouri, Utah.

Twenty to 30 per cent enrollment: North Dakota, Kansas,

[2] Blue Cross Association, *Enrollment Reports of Blue Cross Plans, Year of 1961*, pp. 14–18.

Tennessee, Minnesota, Illinois, Kentucky, Iowa, Alabama, Wisconsin, North Carolina, Wyoming, Oklahoma.

Ten to 20 per cent enrollment: Virginia, Arizona, Florida, Nebraska, Mississippi, West Virginia, Arkansas, Oregon, Texas, California, Georgia, Louisiana, South Carolina, Idaho.

Less than 10 per cent enrollment: New Mexico (9.36 per cent), Washington (8.54 per cent), Alaska (6.11 per cent), South Dakota (5.90 per cent), Montana (3.46 per cent), (Puerto Rico).

States not served by Blue Cross: Hawaii, Nevada.

TABLE 3–2

GROWTH RATE OF BLUE CROSS PLANS IN THE UNITED STATES, 1961

Size of Plan (Members)	Range of Growth Rates High (%)	Low (%)	Mean Rate (%) 1961	1960	Median Rate (%) 1961	1960
Over 1,000,000	6.92	−4.36	.34	.95	.99	.82
500,000–1,000,000	17.23*	−5.41	1.52	3.47	2.48	2.53
200,000–500,000	21.39	−4.41	2.21	2.75	1.10	2.76
100,000–200,000	18.99	−12.31	0.19	3.49	1.75	.04
50,000–100,000	20.17	−5.68	3.63	12.12	0.70	7.65
Less than 50,000	16.85	−10.50	−3.62	4.53	−5.84	−2.99
Total for United States			0.92	1.91		

* This unusually high figure is accounted for by the inclusion of approximately 90,000 members enrolled through self-insured groups not previously reported by the North Carolina plan by order of the Insurance Department. The next highest growth rate was 5.81 per cent.

Source: Statistics for individual plans from the Blue Cross Association.

Of the 6-million persons aged sixty-five and over who had hospitalization coverage in 1958, approximately 3.5 million were Blue Cross members.[3]

Blue Cross had an overall growth rate in membership of 0.99 per cent in 1961, as compared with 1.96 per cent in 1960 and 2.66 per cent in 1959. There was little consistency in rates of growth among associations of similar size, as may be seen in Table 3–2. Plans experienced less relative growth, on the average, in 1961 than they enjoyed in 1960. Four of

---

[3] Agnes W. Brewster and Ruth Bloodgood, *Blue Cross Provisions for Persons Aged 65 and Over, Late 1958*, U.S. Department of Health, Education, and Welfare, Research and Statistics Note No. 5, 1959, p. 1.

the Blue Cross plans with over 1 million subscribers had a net loss of members in 1961. Twenty-seven associations had negative growth rates during the year, while twenty-six of the organizations lost members in 1960.

Types of Enrollment. The hospital service association movement started by enrolling groups rather than individuals, and up to the present time Blue Cross has had a much larger percentage of group subscribers than nongroup members. It has been estimated that approximately one fourth of the Blue Cross subscribers are nongroup enrollees.

Blue Cross members may be classified by their method of enrollment as follows: group members, individual members (also called nongroup or direct-pay members), and group conversion members (sometimes referred to as left-group members). Group conversion subscribers are those who exercised conversion privileges when they retired or terminated their employment with a firm which had Blue Cross group coverage. In many plans those who convert are put in the individual subscribers' class, and there is then no differentiation between the two categories.

Enrollment Eligibility. Group Subscribers. Almost all Blue Cross plans accept group members regardless of their age, and health statements are not generally required of potential group members. Dependents of eligible subscribers are allowed as members under both group and nongroup arrangements of most associations.

Nongroup Subscribers. Seventy-four Blue Cross plans permitted nongroup enrollment during 1959. Forty-seven of these allowed nongroup members to join at any time while the remainder had periodic enrollment campaigns.[4] Nineteen of the organizations currently (1962) have no age limit for initial enrollment under standard certificates while four associations periodically lift their age limitations for nongroup membership. Special benefit certificates are available to those over age sixty-five who enroll in thirty-three addi-

---

[4] *Ibid.*

tional associations. It is anticipated that all Blue Cross plans will offer initial enrollment to the elderly by early 1963. All of the associations allow members to retain their coverage after becoming age sixty-five.

The most usual eligibility limits for children to be included in family contracts is from birth to nineteen years, although in 1957 almost 50 per cent of the Blue Cross plans had minimum age limits of from one to three months after birth.[5]

Sixty-one of the seventy-four associations which allow non-group enrollment require a health statement from prospective subscribers.[6]

Benefits

National Statistics.   Statistics available for December 31, 1961, indicate that Blue Cross plans in the United States paid benefits in excess of $1.8 billion during that year. Claim payments amounted to 92.6 per cent of total subscription income during 1961, while operating expenses were 4.9 per cent of the subscription receipts. The latter figure was an all-time low for average Blue cross operating expense ratios, which have gradually declined from levels of 12 to 13 per cent in the early 1940's. Operating expenses amounted to $0.34 per contract per month, a figure which has increased from $0.23 in 1953. Fourteen associations paid out more in benefits and expenses during 1961 than they received from subscription and investment income. Seventeen other Blue Cross plans had benefit ratios of 95 per cent or higher in 1961.[7] (Organizations with very high benefit ratios present some of the most urgent regulatory problems. In addition to the concern for rate adequacy, they raise such issues as the need for contingency reserves, changes in benefit provisions, and greater supervision and control over claim payments.)

---

[5] U.S. Department of Health, Education, and Welfare, *Health Insurance Benefits Provided for Children in Blue Shield and Blue Cross Plans, 1957,* Research and Statistics Note No. 5, 1957, p. 5.

[6] Brewster and Bloodgood, *op. cit.,* p. 2.

[7] Blue Cross Association, *Financial Reports of Blue Cross Plans, Year of 1961,* pp. 1, 4–6.

Sixty-three per cent of the Blue Cross *group* subscribers who required hospitalization in 1957–58 had 90 per cent or more of their hospital bill paid. Eighty-five per cent of the group subscriber-patients had 70 per cent or more of their bills covered. Blue Cross paid 90 per cent or over of the bill for 46 per cent of hospitalized subscribers who were *nongroup* members, and 70 per cent or more was paid for 73 per cent of such patients.[8]

Benefit Structures. The individual, group, and group conversion membership classifications are further divided by most Blue Cross plans as to single members, members with one dependent, and families. Thus it is common for associations to have at least nine types of certificates. Many organizations also have optional, higher benefit contracts.

Since Blue Cross plans provide room and board *services* in member hospitals, one of the most important benefit considerations is how long the association will continue to pay for a member's hospitalization. An indication of the nature of hospitalization limits may be observed in Table 3–3, which was taken from the results of a 1958 survey. While the research for that study concerned only the benefit days available under group conversion certificates, it was noted that: "The benefits under nongroup contracts are generally quite similar to those available under left-employ [group conversion] contracts though a few plans restrict the benefits."[9] The most usual limit was seventy to seventy-five days of hospitalization. Thirteen Blue Cross plans were found to allow only twenty-one days, although some of these granted partial benefits for additional days. Limits of from thirty to thirty-five days were maintained by twenty-three associations. Ten organizations permitted hospitalization for ninety days or more.

In 1958–59, forty-two Blue Cross plans paid full service

---

[8] Odin W. Anderson, Patricia Collette, and Jacob J. Feldman, *Health Insurance Benefits for Personal Health Services* (New York: Health Information Foundation, 1960), p. 18.

[9] Brewster and Bloodgood, *op. cit.,* p. 2.

benefits for those hospitalized in contracting hospitals;[10] thirty of these associations provided for semiprivate accommodations and twelve offered ward care.[11] The remaining thirty-seven organizations had specified dollar limits which

TABLE 3–3

BENEFIT DAYS AVAILABLE UNDER GROUP CONVERSION CONTRACTS
OF 79 BLUE CROSS PLANS LATE IN 1958

Number of Days of Basic Benefits*	Total Plans	None	Days Covered by Additional Partial Benefits†				
			30, 35, or 40 days	60 or 70 days	80, 90, or 100 days	180 days	245 or 295 days
Total	79	56	6	2	9	4	2
21 days	13‡	4	3		3	3	
30, 31, 35 days	23	15	2	1	4	1	
45 days	1	1					
60 days	4	2	1	1			
70 or 75 days	28	25			2		1
90 days	3	3					
120 days	6	5					1
365 days	1	1					

* The benefit may apply "per certificate year" or "per period of hospital confinement" and in a few instances may include a deductible amount such as $25 paid by the patient or a cooperative payment by the patient of $2.50 per hospital day.

† In the twenty-three plans providing additional days of partial benefits, the plan pays 50 per cent of the daily room and board charge in eleven plans; 25 per cent in two; and daily rates of $3, $5, $6, or $10 in ten plans.

‡ In five of these plans, the basic days of benefit increase in each year of membership up to three, f our, five, or six years.

Source: Agnes W. Brewster and Ruth Bloodgood, *Blue Cross Provisions for Persons Aged 65 and Over, Late 1958*, U.S. Department of Health, Education, and Welfare, Research and Statistics Note No. 5, 1959, p. 6.

they would credit toward room cost.[12] Fifty-one per cent of the patients in 1958 who had Blue Cross coverage occupied rooms costing $15 a day or more.[13]

In addition to room and board benefits, associations provide general nursing care and the use of operating rooms and equipment. A hospitalized subscriber's expenses for dressings, routine laboratory examinations, drugs and medications

---

[10] Blue Cross plans have contractual arrangements with hospitals which contain over 90 per cent of the general hospital beds in the United States.

[11] "Semiprivate" usually refers to a two-, three- or four-bed room.

[12] Brewster and Bloodgood, *op. cit.*, p. 3.

[13] Anderson, Collette, and Feldman, *op. cit.*, p. 20.

(except blood and blood plasma) are covered in most certificates. It is also common for an association to pay for anesthesia and its administration if administered by a hospital employee.

Maternity benefits, including care for the mother and infant, customarily have a specified maximum, stated either in days of care or in dollar limits. Nongroup members and most group subscribers must be enrolled with a family certificate for ten months before maternity benefits will be allowed.

The following list indicates the number of Blue Cross plans which provided for special services, in whole or in part, in 1958.[14] Canadian Blue Cross plans are included in the figures.

Type of Special Service	*Number of Associations Offering the Service:*
Special diets	83
Emergency room (in accidents)	81
Anesthesia	73
Basal metabolism tests	71
Oxygen therapy	68
X-ray	61
Electrocardiogram	54
Physical therapy	49
Pathology	46

Rules and Conditions. Exclusions. Blue Cross certificates usually exclude: those eligible for workmen's compensation coverage or hospital benefits under municipal, state, or federal agencies; diagnostic hospitalization; rest cures; and minor communicable diseases. A few associations allow limited benefits for the treatment of mental disorders, although most organizations have not done so as yet. "Hospital service" is defined so as not to cover the use of an ambulance or the care of a physician, surgeon, or private nurse. It is not customary to grant benefits for outpatient treatment. Neither is nursing home care generally covered. The rise in hospital

---

[14] Paul R. Hawley, "Blue Cross and Blue Shield," *Readings in Medical Care,* edited by the Committee on Medical Care Teaching of the Association of Teachers of Preventive Medicine (Chapel Hill: The University of North Carolina Press, 1958) , p. 565.

costs has focused new interest on the part of Blue Cross organizations in nursing home benefits, however, inasmuch as care in such institutions is less expensive than hospitalization. One of the most noteworthy inclusions of nursing home benefits has been in the recently proposed nationwide Blue Cross program for those over age sixty-five (under which financial support is being sought from the government). The suggested plan bases the allowable days on the number of days of hospital confinement, subject to a maximum.

Pre-existing Conditions. If a nongroup subscriber has some pre-existing condition or affliction when his Blue Cross coverage becomes effective, forty-seven associations (in 1959) would provide benefits for such an ailment if it reoccurs after he has been enrolled for a specified period prior to being hospitalized. This is a particularly liberal feature in insurance-type hospital coverages. Group members are customarily covered against pre-existing conditions.

Private Room Credit. Subscribers with full service benefits for semiprivate accommodations who occupy a private room generally receive a credit on their bill. Most associations grant a specific dollar credit, which is normally less than the semiprivate room rate. There is a growing tendency, though, to allow the normal semiprivate room charge.

Hospitalization in Nonmember Institutions. A specified dollar amount per day is paid to members who are hospitalized in institutions which have not contracted with a Blue Cross plan. This amount is usually below the semiprivate room rate.

Conversion. A group subscriber is customarily allowed to convert his coverage to a nongroup certificate when the employer terminates a contract with a Blue Cross plan; when the subscriber is no longer a member of a group; or when the group enrollment percentage requirements are no longer met. The subscriber must make a request for transfer within fifteen days after the expiration of the group contract, or within thirty days if he ceases to be a member of a group.

The converted contract is the direct-pay (nongroup) certificate with benefits closest to those under the former group coverage. "In fifty-seven of the seventy-nine plans there would be no reduction in benefits under the 'left-employ' contracts except where the member had formerly been enrolled in one of the more comprehensive or special group contracts rather than in the standard or 'most-widely-held-group contract.'"[15] The premiums for converted contracts may be higher, however, than for the group coverage.

Some associations may require a recipient of services under a converted certificate to prove that he is not covered by another hospital or medical contract. If the individual has other coverage, at least a few Blue Cross plans stipulate that their certificates will be excess protection. In such a case an association will pay only the difference, if any, between the cost of eligible services and the amount of benefits received under the other coverage. "Other insurance" or "excess insurance" provisions of this nature are generally not included in individual and group certificates.

A subscriber covered under a family group who becomes ineligible, because he has reached his nineteenth birthday or has married, may normally convert to his own coverage (including a family-type contract). Pre-existing conditions which were excluded for the subscriber under the old contract can be eliminated from the converted certificate. (Pre-existing exclusions of most associations are satisfied after a subscriber has been a member for from six months to a year.)

If an applicant (head of the family) dies, the conversion privilege is extended to the remaining members of the family group.

Finances

Premiums. The premiums for nongroup certificates and group conversion certificates are similar in most Blue Cross

---

15 Brewster and Bloodgood, *op. cit.*, p. 4.

plans. Group subscriber premiums, however, are considerably less than for the other two types in almost all associations. The general nature of premiums for the various types of membership may be seen in Table 3–4.

TABLE 3–4

DISTRIBUTION OF 79 BLUE CROSS PLANS BY THE MEDIAN AND RANGE OF THEIR ONE-PERSON AND FAMILY PREMIUMS UNDER GROUP, GROUP CONVERSION, AND NONGROUP CONTRACTS, 1958

Type of Contract	Number of Plans	Annual Premium	
		Median	Range
Group contract	79		
One person		$30.00	$16.20–$ 70.80
Family		73.20	43.80– 162.60
Group conversion contract	79		
One person		42.20	19.20– 87.00
Family		84.70	51.00– 202.80
Nongroup contract	74		
One person		42.00	22.08– 87.80
Family		84.00	51.60– 202.80

Source: Agnes W. Brewster and Ruth Bloodgood, *Blue Cross Provisions for Persons Aged 65 and Over, Late 1958*, U.S. Department of Health, Education, and Welfare, Research and Statistics Note No. 5, 1959, p. 8.

Financial Position. On December 31, 1961, the Blue Cross plans in the United States had total assets of $974 million. Investments other than real estate accounted for 70 per cent of the assets, while 10.6 per cent was in cash, 6.3 per cent in subscription income receivable, 3.4 per cent in real estate, and 9.7 per cent in other assets. The assets offset $410 million in reserves. Reserves averaged 42.2 per cent of total liabilities, and this was equivalent to 2.5 months of average hospitalization and operating expenses for the associations.[16] Chapter XII will discuss the reserve position of plans in detail.

Administrative Organization

Board of Directors. Hospital service associations are governed by boards of directors. These boards elect the officers of plans; they have over-all policy-making authority; and

[16] Blue Cross Association, *Financial Reports, op. cit.,* pp. 1–2.

they control such appointments as those of the organization's executive director and major committees.

Individuals who serve on the governing boards are chosen by a variety of procedures. The most common manner seems to be election by the members of the "corporation." The "corporation" is generally a large group of individuals from various professions and businesses. In many Blue Cross plans all contracting hospitals have one member in the corporation. In addition, local medical societies often are allowed to appoint one or more physicians to the corporation membership. The exact composition of the corporation is set forth in the bylaws of associations which have this body. Where hospitals appoint a major portion of the members of the corporation, it is obvious that the board of directors is likely to be controlled by hospital representatives.

Some Blue Cross plans do not have a "corporation," in which case it is common to have a self-perpetuating board of directors. Boards are "self-perpetuating" when board members have the authority to fill the majority of vacancies which occur.

The bylaws of a plan specify the size of the board of directors and the length of terms for members. Many bylaws indicate the proportions which must be maintained by representatives of hospitals, the medical profession, and the public. Then, too, national organizations to which plans belong have requirements which influence board composition.

Executive Director. The board of directors appoints a managing executive who is subordinate to the executive committee, and generally to the president, as well as to the board. The title used by most (thirty-nine) Blue Cross plans for this position is "executive director." The name of "executive vice-president" has been adopted by twelve other organizations, while in fifteen the operating executive is the "president." The latter title is assuming more prominence for the position. The remaining associations use such titles as "director" or "managing director."

The executive director is assisted by an extensive staff. He sits with the board of directors but is not a voting member. Since he is a full-time employee who is closely associated with the operation of the organization it is common for the governing board to accept his judgment in many situations. In some associations the board gives almost perfunctory approval for operational changes desired by the executive director.

CHART 3–1

ORGANIZATION CHART OF A TYPICAL HOSPITAL SERVICE ASSOCIATION

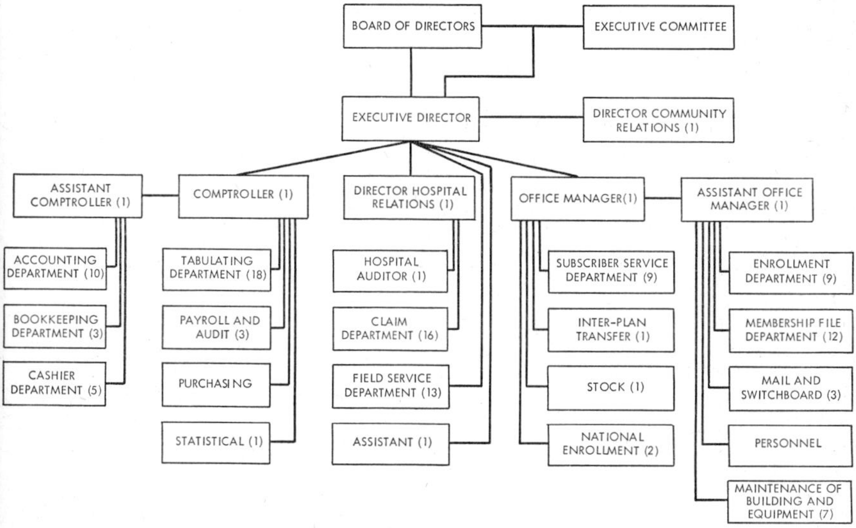

Parentheses indicate the number of personnel in each section.

Departments and Functions. The administrative functions of a Blue Cross plan can be segregated into six categories: enrollment, rate making and underwriting, accounting and general record-keeping, service to subscribers, hospital relations, and public relations. Chart 3–1 indicates how these functions are delegated within the organizational structure of a "typical" association. Enrollment and related operations are under the authority of the office manager, while the comptroller is responsible for the accounting and general record-keeping functions. Hospital relations is a separate department, as is community relations. Rate making and underwriting take place through the cooperation of the comptroller's department and the operations (office manager's) department. Services required by subscribers are provided through all but the community relations department.

Enrollment. The procedure by which individuals become members of a Blue Cross plan is referred to as "enrollment" and it is analogous to the sales function of an insurance company. Those who "enroll" in a Blue Cross plan are termed "members" or "subscribers," as contrasted to "policyholders" in insurance companies. Blue Cross enrollment has traditionally taken place through salaried employees called "enrollment representatives."

Enrollment was formerly thought to concern only the inclusion of group and nongroup members in the locale served by an association. National enrollment has now come to assume considerable magnitude as a responsibility and a problem. This will be discussed in Chapter V.

Rate Making and Underwriting. The financial needs of an association, other than for operational expenses, are established by the benefit structures, the degree to which benefits are utilized by subscribers, and the reimbursement contracts with member hospitals. Recent years have seen increases in each of these three elements. (Administrative expenses of hospital service associations have always been a minor part of their expenditures.) The problem has been how to keep rates within the financial reach of subscribers in an era when benefits are being utilized more widely and hospital costs are mounting. Then, too, there is the consideration that rates must be competitive with those of insurance companies, as well as being adequate. The community nature of Blue Cross plans dictates that all segments of the population be allowed to become members. If a rate is obtained by averaging all elements in the community, however, low-loss groups may be lost to insurance companies which use experience-rating techniques. All of these issues will be considered in Chapter XI, and certain aspects of the rate-making problem will affect the discussions in other chapters.

Services to Subscribers. The needs of subscribers vary from claim service to adding a baby to a family's coverage. The operations department handles the addition of new members and transfers of subscribers between the organization and other approved hospital service associations. When a member is confined to a hospital, his eligibility is determined by the hospital through the comptroller's department in most Blue Cross plans.

Hospital Relations. The hospital relations department often handles the claims functions because of the close association of claims with the fees charged by hospitals. This department is in the best position to scrutinize all claims for errors and excessive charges. Some associations have a separate claims division.

In addition to handling the processing of claims, the hospital relations department negotiates reimbursement schedules and related details with hospitals.

An important innovation in Blue Cross administration has taken place in a few associations through what is called a "Hospital Review Committee." This group is generally composed of doctors who review the length of stay of hospitalized subscribers. At the same time, "Physicians' Review Boards" are used by some Blue Cross plans to examine the admission of Blue Cross members to hospitals. The purpose of these bodies is to reduce unnecessary utilization and to determine those responsible for the abuses. Regulatory action by state officials seems destined to cause the use of similar committees in many associations.

Community Relations. The public relations function, most of which concerns advertising, publicity, and enrollment, is handled by a separate department in many associations. In larger organizations these responsibilities are of greater dimensions and can even extend to lobbying activities. It is of considerable importance to all Blue Cross plans to disseminate information about the nature of hospitalization costs.

By this method it is hoped to overcome adverse attitudes prompted by rising subscriber rates. Community relations activities have been expanded in many Blue Cross plans to cope with the problem.

Interrelation with Blue Shield Plans

Most Blue Cross and Blue Shield plans either have a single executive director for the two types of organizations or they have two directors but with administrative coordination of their activities. In twenty-nine areas Blue Cross and Blue Shield plans are operating under two corporations and two boards but with a single executive director and staff. In a similar number of areas the two types of associations are operating under two corporations, two boards, and with two executive directors, but with their operations coordinated. The Blue Cross and Blue Shield plans in seven areas have been established as single corporations with one board and one staff.[17]

Cooperative arrangements through one executive director and staff eliminate duplication of administrative functions, particularly in enrollment and billing. It also facilitates a more coordinated benefit structure. State regulatory authorities in many areas are coming to think this is desirable, since the problem of medical care and medical care coverages includes both hospital and medical-surgical expenses. The merger of Blue Cross and Blue Shield plans has been said to be hampered by: " (1) fear on the part both of doctors and of the hospital people that the other group wants to control such a plan; (2) the fact that in most areas the Blue Cross Plan was there first, and the medical plan is often not yet sufficiently well developed to command an equal share of public acceptance; (3) the fact that a number of states require by law that medical and hospital prepayment must be provided by separate corporations."[18]

---

[17] Unpublished materials of the Blue Cross Commission and the Blue Shield Medical Care Plans.

[18] Hawley, *op. cit.*, p. 571.

Not all associations have exclusive areas. Several Blue Cross plans compete for subscribers with other hospital and/or medical service organizations, and the same is true for a few Blue Shield plans. Situations of this sort exist in such states as California, Illinois, Montana, North Carolina, Oregon, Washington, and Wisconsin.[19]

BLUE SHIELD PLANS

Membership

National Statistics. There were 46,325,554 subscribers enrolled in the sixty-nine Blue Shield plans in the United States on December 31, 1961. Approximately 60 per cent of those enrolled were dependents. Sixty per cent of the subscribers were members of associations having more than one million enrollees, as Table 3–5 reveals. The forty-seven Blue Shield plans with 200,000 members or more had 96 per cent of the total enrollment. The mean was 669,459 subscribers per association.

In 1961, twelve of the Blue Shield plans had 40 per cent or more of the population in their operating area enrolled. The total membership amounted to 25.53 per cent of the nation's population.[20] The following list reveals the percentages of enrollment in the various states on December 31, 1961.[21]

Over 50 per cent enrollment: District of Columbia (81.29 per cent), Rhode Island (67.86 per cent), Delaware (61.46 per cent).

Forty to 50 per cent enrollment: Connecticut, Massachusetts, Hawaii, New York, Michigan, Colorado.

Thirty to 40 per cent enrollment: New Hampshire and Vermont, Pennsylvania, Ohio, New Jersey, Indiana, Utah, Kansas.

---

[19] Unpublished material of the Blue Cross Commission and the Blue Shield Medical Care Plans.

[20] National Association of Blue Shield Plans, *Enrollment Reports*, December 31, 1961, p. 3.

[21] *Ibid.*, pp. 2–4.

Twenty to 30 per cent enrollment: Maine, Tennessee, North Dakota, Alabama, Kentucky, Iowa, Missouri, Washington, Illinois, Wisconsin, Maryland, Idaho, Oklahoma, Wyoming.

Ten to 20 per cent enrollment: Virginia, Florida, Arizona, Nebraska, Mississippi, Minnesota, West Virginia, Arkansas, Texas, North Carolina, Montana, Georgia.

Less than 10 per cent enrollment: Oregon (9.54 per cent), New Mexico (8.65 per cent), South Carolina (8.53 per cent), South Dakota (6.75 per cent), California (6.41 per cent).

States not serviced by Blue Shield: Alaska, Louisiana, Nevada.

The total growth in Blue Shield subscribers, including those in Canadian associations, during 1961 was at a rate of

TABLE 3–5

ENROLLMENT OF BLUE SHIELD PLANS, DECEMBER 31, 1961

Size of Plan (Members)	Number of Plans	Membership Included	Percentage of Total Membership	Average Number of Subscribers Per Contract*
Over 1,000,000	12	28,107,761	60.67	2.45 (1)
500,000–1,000,000	16	11,010,442	23.74	2.63
200,000–500,000	19	5,635,096	12.16	2.64 (4)
100,000–200,000	4	665,802	1.44	2.73
50,000–100,000	6	438,790	.95	2.84 (1)
Less than 50,000	12‡	334,869	.72	2.62
Total—United States	69‡	46,192,760	99.71	
HSI—MIA†		132,794	.29	
Grand Total		46,325,554	100.00	

* Includes Canadian Blue Shield plans, the numbers of which are indicated in parenthesis.
† Health Service, Inc., and Medical Indemnity of America, the national enrollment companies of Blue Cross and Blue Shield, respectively.
‡ The merger of the Fairmont and Wheeling, W. Va. plans will reduce this figure by 1.
Source: National Association of Blue Shield Plans.

5.5 per cent. This was almost five times the rate of growth for Blue Cross members. The Blue Shield growth rate rose from 5.12 in 1960, while the rate for Blue Cross declined from 1.96 in 1960 to 0.99 in 1961. The difference is generally explained by the fact that Blue Shield has had a smaller proportion of the population enrolled. Thus, not only is it easier to obtain subscribers but, also, identical increases in absolute membership would be a higher growth rate for

Blue Shield. Table 3–6 indicates the variations in rates of growth by associations in various size groupings.

Types of Enrollment. Like Blue Cross, most Blue Shield plans have two or three major categories of enrollment: group subscribers, nongroup members, and group conversion members. It is not uncommon for those in the latter classification to be considered as regular nongroup members. Within these categories most medical service associations have the subclassifications of single members, members with one dependent, and families (or members with more than one dependent).

Enrollment Eligibility. Generally, there are no age limits for group members. Fifty-one Blue Shield plans will enroll individuals over age sixty-five on a nongroup basis. Twenty-seven of these have special contracts for the aged, while twenty-four associations cover such individuals under their regular certificates.

Most Blue Shield plans allow dependents to be covered under both group and nongroup certificates. Children were

TABLE 3–6

GROWTH RATE OF BLUE SHIELD PLANS IN THE UNITED STATES, 1961 *

Size of Plan (Members)	Range of Growth Rates High	Low	Median
Over 1,000,000	5.71 *	−4.01	3.64
500,000–1,000,000	17.23	−20.15	3.27
200,000–500,000	19.91	−5.88	3.53
100,000–200,000	6.53	−13.34	1.37
50,000–100,000	2.96	−51.55	−1.20
Less than 50,000	29.11 *	−24.19	2.32

* Other than plans which became Blue Shield members during the year.

Source: Statistics for individual plans from the National Association of Blue Shield Plans.

eligible from birth until age nineteen in twenty-four medical service associations in 1957. The remainder of the organizations allowed children to be covered at varying times up to three months of age.[22]

---

[22] U.S. Department of Health, Education, and Welfare, *Health Insurance Benefits Provided for Children in Blue Shield and Blue Cross Plans, 1957,* p. 4.

Benefits

National Statistics.   Blue Shield plans paid benefits total-
ing $816 million in 1961. These payments were equivalent
to 88.75 per cent of earned subscription income.[23] During
1961, fourteen Blue Shield plans paid out more for claims
and operating expenses than they took in as income. Four of
the twelve Blue Shield plans with more than a million members had negative operating incomes during this period.[24]

In 1958 Blue Shield paid for 80 per cent, or more, of the
surgical charges for 61 per cent of their hospitalized subscribers.[25]

Benefit Structures.   Blue Shield plans offer two principal
types of benefits: surgical and medical. Surgical benefits concern specified surgical procedures, while medical benefits
refer to nonsurgical consultations or treatments by a physician. Medical benefits customarily include only doctors' visits
to hospitalized subscribers. Some associations provide medical benefits when a subscriber visits a doctor in his office, and
still fewer organizations provide coverage when a doctor visits
a patient's home. Medical benefits are limited to a specific
number of visits. Fifty Blue Shield plans in the United States
provide both surgical and in-hospital medical benefits. Seventeen other associations have surgical and in-hospital, home,
and office medical benefits.

The coverages available from Blue Shield may be classified
according to whether "service" or "indemnity" benefits are
provided. A pure service contract allows subscribers to receive specified surgical treatments without charge from doc-

---

[23] National Association of Blue Shield Plans, *Financial Reports of Blue
Shield Plans, Year of 1961,* p. 1. Operating expenses of Blue Shield plans in
1961 averaged 9.5 per cent of earned subscription income. Expense ratios are
traditionally higher for Blue Shield than for Blue Cross. Blue Shield has more
dealings with many more physicians than Blue Cross plans have with hospitals. Thus the former has to write a larger number of checks, conduct more
correspondence, etc. Operational costs averaged $.144 per member per
month during 1961.

[24] *Ibid.,* pp. 11–14.

[25] Anderson, Collette, and Feldman, *op. cit.,* p. 20.

tors who have contracted with an association. In such instances, the contracting doctors agree to accept the fees paid by the Blue Shield plan as full payment for services rendered. Under indemnity contracts a doctor charges a patient for the difference between his normal fee for the treatment rendered and the amount he receives from the association therefor. Actually, most service contracts can become indemnity contracts if a subscriber's income is above specified amounts. Blue Shield service certificates usually have "income limits" and full service benefits are provided for only those subscribers whose incomes are below these limits. Those with incomes in excess of the limits receive indemnity benefits.

Indemnity-type provisions may apply to either surgical or medical benefits. An indemnity medical benefit, for example, allows up to a certain dollar amount, such as $3 or $5, for each of a specified number of doctors' visits.

Fifty-five Blue Shield plans in the United States offered service benefits on June 30, 1961, to those subscribers whose incomes did not exceed prescribed limits. Six others would provide full service benefits regardless of a member's income. The remaining associations offered only indemnity benefits.

Associations have at least two income limits; one applies to single subscribers while a higher limit is applicable to families. Some organizations also have an income limit for subscribers with one dependent. In addition, most Blue Shield plans have a higher, optional set of limits which are available to subscribers who are willing to pay an added premium.

The lower set of income limits for single subscribers in the United States ranged from $1,500 to $4,500 on June 30, 1961. The range of such limits for families in various associations was from $2,400 to $6,000, with $4,000 the mode. The optional higher income limits (at a higher premium) ranged from $2,400 to $9,000 for single subscribers and from $4,200 to $9,000 for families. While statistics are available regarding the percentage of enrollment under the various income levels, there are no composite figures as to the proportion of subscriber-*patients* whose incomes were under the limits. An indication of this may be obtained, however, from the previously stated fact that 6 per cent of the subscribers had 80 per cent or more of their *surgical* bills paid by Blue Shield.

A $6,000 limit is considered by some officers of the National Association of Blue Shield Plans to be about the appropriate level for benefit adequacy at the present time. Only five associations are known to be using this level for families with lower limit certificates. When the most widely-held certificates of plans are considered, eighteen use a limit of $6,000 or more.

Whether a subscriber meets the income restrictions is generally left to the discretion of the doctor. If there is a controversy, however, the association usually has final authority to classify the individual's income position.

Obstetrical services and care of the newborn are often included among the benefits of both group and nongroup certificates; a waiting period of from nine to twelve months after initial enrollment is customary for entitlement to these benefits. Administration of anesthesia by a physician anesthesiologist is usually included in the coverage if the individual providing the service is not employed by a hospital.

Rules and Conditions. Exclusions. Hospitalization, X-ray examination, laboratory services, and plastic operations (other than those resulting from accidents) are not included in most Blue Shield coverage. Also excluded are conditions eligible for workmen's compensation benefits, and services provided or paid by any governmental body or institution. Recurrent services for the same affliction are allowed only if the maximum benefit applicable in the fee schedule has not been reached. If a doctor receives compensation for his services from a hospital, Blue Shield associations will not reimburse him.

Pre-existing Conditions. Pre-existing conditions are usually covered for subscribers who belong to groups which are above a minimum size. Many nongroup certificates will provide benefits for pre-existing conditions if they do not occur during a specified waiting period after initial enrollment—generally six months to one year.

Nonparticipating Doctors. Nonparticipating doctors are usually paid their normal fee or the applicable amount from the fee schedule for contracting physicians, whichever is lower. The payment is often made to the subscriber and not to the doctor, thereby constituting an indemnity-type benefit.

Conversion. Group members who become ineligible for such protection are allowed to become nongroup subscribers and pay the necessary fees directly to Blue Shield. Conversion rights are similar to those of Blue Cross.

Financial Position

On December 31, 1961, the total assets of all Blue Shield plans amounted to $481 million (including $38 million held by the six Canadian organizations) . Seventy-four per cent of the assets were in investments (other than real estate) . Cash accounted for 12 per cent of total assets; subscription income receivable, 7 per cent; real estate, 4 per cent; and other assets, 3 per cent. Reserves, not including those for losses and claims outstanding, were equal to 53.05 per cent of total assets. On the average, the associations held reserves equivalent to 3.3 months of average monthly claims and operating expenses.[26] The reserve figure was 3.47 at the end of 1960 and 3.72 at the end of 1959.

Blue Shield plans usually have higher reserve positions than do Blue Cross plans. This can be largely attributed to the fact that indemnity benefits are a larger part of Blue Shield coverage than they are of Blue Cross protection. When the costs of subscriber services are rising, as they have been over the past two decades, organizations with service benefits are affected more disadvantageously than those offering indemnity provisions. Service-type arrangements agree to pro-

---

[26] National Association of Blue Shield Plans, *Financial Reports of Blue Shield Plans, Year of 1961,* pp. 2–7.

vide the specified services regardless of what they cost; an association with service benefits therefore pays more to provide the same service if doctors' fees (or hospital reimbursements) increase. If subscriber rate increases are delayed, or not permitted, a plan's financial position is undermined. Where indemnity benefits are provided, subscribers bear the major burden of increased costs since associations' indemnity limits are not changed unless an additional premium is paid.

Administrative Organization

Boards of Directors. The methods of selection for Blue Shield boards of directors are very similar to those used to choose Blue Cross governing boards. It is common in Blue Shield to have doctors appointed directly to the board by the state or county medical societies. (In Blue Cross it is cus-

CHART 3–2

ORGANIZATION CHART OF A TYPICAL MEDICAL SERVICE ASSOCIATION

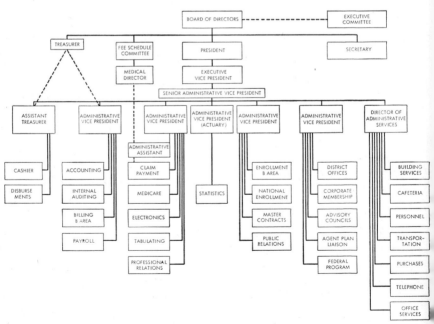

tomary for member hospitals to appoint representatives to the "corporation" and members of the corporation elect the board of directors.) It is also more prevalent to have doctors dominate Blue Shield boards than it is to have hospital representatives in the majority on Blue Cross boards. The particulars of these relationships will be explored in Chapter VIII.

Executive Director. The functions of executive directors of Blue Shield plans are similar to those of related positions in Blue Cross organizations.

Departments and Functions. The departmental organization of Blue Shield plans is broadly analogous to that of Blue Cross plans. "Professional" (or "medical") relations activities take the place of hospital relations functions. It is not difficult in most instances to coordinate or integrate the administrative activities of hospital service associations and medical service associations. This usually involves only such considerations as leaving those areas of authority which concern doctors solely to departments controlled by physicians. The similarity between the organization of the two types of associations may be seen by comparing Charts 3–1 and 3–2.[27]

Even where Blue Cross and Blue Shield plans are not otherwise administratively coordinated, it is customary for Blue Cross to handle the enrollment functions for Blue Shield organizations in their area. A few Blue Shield executives feel, though, that the enrollment goals of the two types of associations differ. Some of those so disposed state that Blue Cross is for enrollment, i.e., for a volume of subscribers, at any cost. Blue Shield, on the other hand, they say, is more concerned with providing a good benefit structure. If a potential account is not satisfied with the benefit structures offered, these Blue Shield officials feel they should forget such business rather than try to tailor a benefit pattern which could reduce the quality of benefits as well as increase over-all ad-

---

[27] See page 41 for Chart 3–1.

ministrative costs. Some Blue Cross personnel counter the arguments of this sort by saying that Blue Cross attempts to serve broadly those in a plan area and this accounts for the concentration on volume. These observers feel that Blue Shield is more concerned with "benefits" because such affect the payments to doctors—who often control the organizations. Apparently these divergencies in attitudes are not too great, however, as there is no trend among Blue Shield plans toward taking over enrollment functions for themselves.

Boards of Review. A new development in some Blue Shield operations is to establish an internal committee or board to review the claims paid by an association in an attempt to locate abuses of benefits. When abuses, or "over-utilization," occur, they generally involve physicians. Doctors largely determine those who will be hospitalized as well as the medical and surgical treatment to be received by patients. Review boards, therefore, in most instances are composed only of doctors. When a board of review ascertains that a particular doctor is responsible for abuses of association benefits, it is the usual procedure to work through local medical societies to discipline the doctor concerned. Payment of the claim is also denied. Although not currently widespread, public and regulatory interest, in addition to the concern of Blue Shield plans, will undoubtedly encourage the use of review boards. This parallels a similar development in Blue Cross organizations.

chapter IV

THE COMPOSITE BLUE CROSS
AND BLUE SHIELD SYSTEM

One important aspect of the Blue Cross–Blue Shield
method for medical care protection is the *local autonomy*
of each organization. The regional independence of associations was part of the reason for the enabling legislation
which set hospital and medical service associations apart
from insurance companies; it is also the crux of many internal problems facing Blue Cross and Blue Shield; finally,
and of principal importance for this section, local autonomy
is the characteristic which has most strongly influenced the
mechanics of the Blue Cross and Blue Shield system.

Mobility has become a pronounced feature of American
social and business life. This created several difficulties for
hospital and medical service associations. The temporary or
permanent movement of individuals protected by a Blue
Cross or Blue Shield plan into an area in which hospitals
had not agreed to provide service for members of that association meant that subscribers had but very limited hospital and medical service availability area-wise. The extension of travel as a means of recreation has been a part of the
rising American standard of living, and improved transportation media have facilitated an immeasurable expansion
of journeying for business purposes. Both of these developments called attention to the growing inadequacy of a protection program which limited the number of hospitals and
doctors whose services would be covered. Partial solutions
evolved when Blue Cross and Blue Shield plans cooperated
in caring for members of other associations who were tem-

porarily out of their area or who were moving permanently
from their home-plan locale. In addition, indemnity-type
benefits, that is, payments up to a certain dollar limit upon
the incurrence of specific expenses, were granted to those
confined in hospitals which had not agreed to provide services to subscribers.

Another problem was created by the need to offer medical
care coverage to large corporations and organizations whose
operations were on a national scale and thereby encompassed
several, if not scores of, Blue Cross and Blue Shield plans.
A number of philosophical and procedural difficulties have
been posed by the desire to offer some uniformity as to coverage, benefits, and contributions. The various subdivisions of
the Blue Cross and Blue Shield national organizations attempt to handle these problems.

One would assume that Blue Cross (and Blue Shield)
plans would wholeheartedly cooperate with each other to
solve the developmental, political, and competitive dilemnas
which have faced the composite system that is the "Blues."
This has not been the case in many instances. The associations are not as close brothers-in-the-bond as some proponents
of the movement would like to make believe. One national
Blue Cross executive stated in connection with this study,
"It is difficult to get agreement between the Pittsburgh and
Philadelphia organizations, let alone getting uniformity between associations on two different coasts." Nevertheless,
maturity in age and experience is breeding greater concord
within the system, and the mechanics to be discussed strive
for this unanimity and uniformity.

BLUE CROSS INTERRELATIONS[1]

Conference of Blue Cross Plans

Each Blue Cross plan is represented at plan conferences
which occur at least annually. This is an outgrowth of meet-

---

[1] Much of the information for this section was obtained through interviews
with executives of the Blue Cross Association and certain Blue Cross plans.

ings commenced in 1937 by the predecessor organization of the Blue Cross Commission. Voting at the conferences is based upon the number of members in each association, with one vote given for each 20,000 subscribers, or portion thereof, up to a maximum of ten votes. It is in these conferences that policies are dictated to the Blue Cross Association or the suggestions of the Association are ratified or rejected.

Recent Developments Concerning Blue Cross Coordinating Agencies

The year 1960 was an historic one for Blue Cross as it saw plans laid for joining and solidifying the functions of the two national agencies which were the coordinating bodies for the Blue Cross system. The first formal steps in this direction were taken at the annual conference of Blue Cross Plans in April, 1960, when member associations voted to consolidate the activities of the Blue Cross Commission and the Blue Cross Association. The remaining action necessary to effect this transition from two organizations into one occurred in September, 1960, when the American Hospital Association's House of Delegates ratified the earlier expressed desire of the organizations. It is still important to discuss the heretofore separate functions of the Blue Cross Commission and the Blue Cross Association because such an understanding will indicate what responsibilities the Blue Cross Association and the American Hospital Association divided when the Blue Cross Commission was disbanded.

Blue Cross Commission

Since their inception, Blue Cross plans have been inextricably associated with their member hospitals. It has been mentioned that even the stimulus for the birth and growth of hospital service associations came from the hospitals themselves or sources close to them. It is natural, then, for a coordinating agency of the Blue Cross plans to have been at least an indirect vehicle of the American Hospital Association.

The early coordinating organization of the over-all Blue Cross system was the Commission on Hospital Service, established in 1936 as a part of the American Hospital Association. Dr. C. Rufus Rorem was the first director of the commission, and financial support for the agency during the first five years was provided by the Julius Rosenwald Fund. Dr. Rorem had been acting in a consultant capacity to the AHA since 1932, when he drafted the "Essentials of an Acceptable Plan for Group Hospitalization"—the forerunning principles of the approval program subsequently administered by the Blue Cross Commission and the AHA.[2]

The initial purposes of the Commission on Hospital Service were:

1. To provide information and advice to hospitals or communities contemplating the establishment of voluntary hospital care insurance plans.

2. To serve as a clearing house of information for the executives of existing hospital service associations.

3. To study other related problems of hospital administration and finance.[3]

The name "Commission on Hospital Service" was subsequently changed to "Hospital Service Plan Commission" and, finally, to "Blue Cross Commission" in 1946. Legally, the Blue Cross Commission was a subordinate trust of the American Hospital Association. The Board of Trustees of AHA could disapprove any course of action of the commission. Thus, the Blue Cross Commission was in a literal sense an arm or "commission" of the American Hospital Association.

There were fifteen commissioners on the Blue Cross Commission, twelve of whom were elected by member associations. The administrative regulations of the commission required that these "district" commissioners be members of a

---

[2] Louis S. Reed, *Blue Cross and Medical Service Plans* (Washington, D.C.: Federal Security Agency, 1947).

[3] *Ibid.*

Blue Cross governing board, its chief salaried executive or one of its senior officers. The other three commissioners were appointed by the president of the American Hospital Association.

The purposes of the Blue Cross Commission included: administration of the approval program whereby associations were considered for membership in the Blue Cross system; encouragement of cooperation among the organizations; and maintenance of the machinery through which the national aspects of Blue Cross functioned.

The commission's method of operation was not dictatorial. On major issues it functioned through the ratification of member associations and the American Hospital Association. Changes in the commission's activities were instituted in one of two ways: the annual plan conference could specify actions that the commission should take, or the commission could suggest that changes be instituted and submit such recommendations to the annual conference for confirmation.

The tools available to the commission for carrying out its objectives were limited. It could recommend disapproval of an association's use of the Blue Cross symbol if specified conditions were not met. It could require compliance with any program which had been approved by 75 per cent of the organizations. There were no additional powers, other than publicity and information, to force specific Blue Cross plans to work toward particular goals.

Blue Cross Association

The second coordinating division of the composite Blue Cross system prior to 1960 was the Blue Cross Association, a nonprofit corporation formed in Illinois in 1949. The initial purpose of the Association was to start an insurance company which would provide uniform group benefits on a national basis. This company was named Health Service, Inc., and it will be discussed subsequently.

In addition to its responsibilities regarding Health Service, Inc., the Association was given jurisdiction over the Local

Benefit Agreement for National Accounts.[4] Then, too, it administered the protection program available through the federal government for servicemen's dependents and federal employees.

Among its collateral functions, the Association established group life insurance and retirement programs for the employees of associations desiring such benefits. The telegraphic communications between Blue Cross organizations (Blue Cross Private Wire Communications System) have always been operated by the Association.

The consolidation of activities of the Blue Cross Commission and the Blue Cross Association into a single organization, which retained the latter name, took place in late 1960 and early 1961. Seventy-six plans in the United States are now members of the Blue Cross Association.

Plans which join the Association must agree to: (1) offer all benefits approved by the board of governors for national accounts; (2) cooperate in the Local Benefit Agreement for National Accounts, the Interplan Transfer Agreement, and the Interplan Service Benefit Bank; and (3) join in the coverage of national accounts larger than 1,000 members, as well as cooperate in the use of mutualization or equalization arrangements[5] decided upon by the board of governors.

The Association's twenty-five-man board of governors includes one member elected from each of the eleven Blue Cross districts in the United States. An additional eleven directors are elected at large by a weighted voting process based upon the number of subscribers in member associations. The other three board members are nominated by the AHA (just as two individuals from Blue Cross, nominated by the Blue Cross Association, sit on the AHA Board of Trustees). Under the new arrangement, half of the AHA Council on Prepayment is composed of Blue Cross personnel.

---

[4] See page 64.

[5] These arrangements are used when an association covers only a small number of employees of a national group. Equalization levels out the risk of loss when the Law of Large Numbers is inoperative.

The concentration of power in one national body now gives greater leverage for obtaining uniformity in benefits and premiums among the Blue Cross plans. When the Blue Cross Commission was disbanded, three of its former activities were transferred to the American Hospital Association: administration of protection for the service marks, including license agreements, registration and infringement matters; responsibility for development and administration of the approval program; responsibility for relations between hospitals and Blue Cross plans, i.e., the "hospital relations" area which includes reimbursement, education, and the like.

Other than the above three areas, all functions of the commission were assumed by the Blue Cross Association, whose headquarters are in Chicago. Administration of the Inter-Plan Service Benefit Bank and the Inter-Plan Transfer Agreement[6] are among the functions assumed by the Association, in addition to retaining all of its former responsibilities.

Public relations, national advertising, research and lobbying activities at both state and federal levels are within the scope of the Association's functions. These aspects are of mounting importance as governmental and competitive forces buffet Blue Cross with increasing intensity.

It is of considerable importance to note that the American Hospital Association now administers the approval program by which hospital service organizations become members of, or retain their membership in, the Blue Cross system. The AHA does its own policing of this program with no participation by the Blue Cross Association. This is very different from the Blue Shield situation, as will be seen, where the National Association of Blue Shield Plans controls the approval program for medical service plans without any participation by the American Medical Association.

Inter-Plan Service Benefit Bank

The problem created when a Blue Cross subscriber receives hospital services in an institution outside of his home-

---

[6] See below and page 63.

plan area is largely solved through the Inter-Plan Service Benefit Bank. The Blue Cross Association now oversees the affairs of this body, and the Advisory Board which supervises the bank's business is appointed by the Association. The importance of a formal arrangement of this nature is obvious when the extensive use of hospitals in medical centers and large cities is contemplated. It is self-evident that many of the users of such facilities come from distant areas—locales served by a different Blue Cross plan than that in operation where the hospitalization is received.

When a subscriber is hospitalized in a Blue Cross member hospital away from the jurisdiction of his home association, at least three parties in the Blue Cross system become involved: the host plan, that is, the Blue Cross organization in whose area and in whose member hospital the afflicted is hospitalized; the home plan, that is, the association in which the patient is a subscriber; and the Inter-Plan Service Benefit Bank, often called "the bank." In certain cases Health Service, Inc., is also a party.

The notification procedure for determining those qualified for benefits, when a supposed Blue Cross member is hospitalized in a member hospital outside of his home-plan area, is an amplification of the reporting method used when a subscriber is confined in a home-plan institution. The home plan notifies the host plan of the patient's eligibility and the number of days of care allowed by his certificate.

The patient receives the Blue Cross benefits of the host plan. The normal type of bank account with a prescribed minimum amount is maintained by each association in the bank. Debits and credits are made in the individual accounts as transactions occur between the various associations. The host plan pays the hospital for the services rendered, then the bank reimburses (or more correctly "credits") the host plan for this payment plus additional amounts for special situations.

In essence the home plan pays approximately what it costs the host plan to provide the care. In addition to the cost-of-care arrangement, there is a possibility that an association will receive a credit if there is a substantially higher cost in the host plan than in the home plan. The home plan pays $3 to the host plan for overhead expense in handling the case and 25 cents to the bank to cover its operational expense and to pay for the credits some associations receive.

The bank now has accounts for all Blue Cross plans. In 1959, the bank cleared 368,524 cases which covered almost 2.7 million days of hospital care. The cost per case for the bank was 23 cents. The benefits paid through the bank amounted to $73.8 million.

Health Service, Inc., uses the facilities of the Bank when one of its direct-pay subscribers is hospitalized or when a group subscriber receives covered hospital benefits which have not been provided by one of the associations.

Inter-Plan Transfer Agreement

All Blue Cross plans cooperate in the transfer and acceptance of subscribers who make a permanent move into an area serviced by a different association.[7] This arrangement takes place through a voluntary Inter-Plan Transfer Agreement which is administered by a transfer board appointed yearly by the Blue Cross Association.

The current agreement is a compilation of revisions to extend the transfer method to Blue Shield as well as to Blue Cross members (1953) ; to cover maternity if the waiting period has been met during the combined membership in the previous and present organizations (1954) ; to provide membership in an association to subscribers of Health Service, Inc., and Medical Indemnity of America, Inc. (the national group enrollment organization for Blue Shield) who become ineligible for coverage under these organizations (1955) ; and, finally (1956), to transfer a group member to another group when he moves to a different area. Direct-pay

---

[7] Two Canadian *affiliate* plans do not participate in the agreement. They are located in provinces which have governmental medical care coverage and they offer benefits only above those provided by the government.

members were included in the transfer arrangement of the
original agreement.

The procedure for transfer specifies that one quarterly
payment will be accepted from a new plan-area address.
Thereupon the home plan notifies the subscriber of the
location of the Blue Cross plan in his new area, the type of
membership he holds (group, nongroup, etc.), his membership status, maternity benefits available, and the fact that no
further payments can be accepted by the home plan. Protection is continued until the paid-to date. The association in
the area to which the subscriber has moved is sent a copy of
the notification. If the member applies to the new association
for membership before his paid-to date, he must be accepted
as a subscriber under the type of membership certificate he
originally held with no additional exclusions. When application for membership is received by the new association
within thirty days after the paid-to date, membership must
also be granted. Then, however, a different type of certificate and other exclusions may be provided.

A substantial problem is evolving over the transfer of
members who are age sixty-five, or older, since certain areas
of the country are becoming havens for those in their de-
clining years. This means that the Blue Cross plans which
service such states and locales will have more than their share
of the elderly transferred to them, and a concomitant increase in their hospitalization rate among the members, as
well as a rise in the length of hospital stay, will ensue. No
solution for this situation has been developed at this writing.

Local Benefit Agreement for National Accounts

The need to furnish medical care protection to a corporation's employees when they are located throughout the
country presents a quandary for Blue Cross inasmuch as
as more than one association becomes involved. Two paths
have been paved by the Blue Cross system as means for
handling this problem: the Local Benefit Agreement for National Accounts and Health Service, Inc. Syndicates are a

third and independent method for solving the difficulties involved in national enrollment. Blue Cross plans, however, have not accepted these methods to a sufficient extent for the dilemma to be completely solved. Insurance companies have engulfed an increasing share of the group-protection market because of their ability to offer a unified type of coverage on a national basis. Meanwhile, Blue Cross has not been able to overcome some of the undesirable features associated with territorial independence, when more than local coverage is necessary. The Local Benefit Agreement for National Accounts is a conciliatory arrangement whereby each association's local control is not compromised, although it is possible to tie the organizations together to protect interarea groups. (Health Service, Inc., is a more mature extension of the national approach in that *uniform benefits* are available on an interassociation basis, as well as interassociation coverage of individuals in national groups.)

The Local Benefit Agreement has been under the jurisdiction of the Blue Cross Association since 1958. Only one Blue Cross plan fails to participate in the arrangement and that association is legally prohibited from doing so. As has been mentioned, cooperation in the agreement is one of the requirements for membership in the Association.

The purpose of the Local Benefit Agreement is to provide a uniform method for enrolling and handling those groups spread over many Blue Cross plan areas while retaining the group benefits peculiar to the association in each area. Thus, employees covered under the arrangement receive medical care protection benefits which vary according to their location.

One advantage credited to this approach is that each Blue Cross plan supposedly has a benefit structure which best meets the protection needs in its locality; thus, the agreement is said to provide adaptability as well as universality. The advantage seen in local adaptability is being reduced as rising standards of living and improved means of transportation decrease the variances in local conditions.

The originating Blue Cross plan for a national group is referred to as the "control plan," while the cooperating associations are called "participating plans." Participating plans determine what group contracts they will make available for use with national organizations. A Blue Cross plan must notify the Blue Cross Association and the control plan ninety days in advance of any rate or benefit change.

The Local Benefit Agreement provides a common set of enrollment, underwriting, billing and servicing requirements. Any Control Plan may know in advance exactly what it may commit a Participating Plan to do, without having to inquire on each separate occasion. . . .

To qualify as a "Local Benefit Account" under the terms of this Agreement, a group must be established on the basis of payroll deduction or employer participation, and must include at least 50 employees (a smaller number may be considered if at least three Plans are involved). A minimum enrollment of 75% of the total eligible employees is required, and enrollment by marital status is required unless waived by the Participating Plan.[8]

Health Service, Inc.

The second method developed to handle groups on a national basis was the organization of Health Service, Inc. In 1949, certain associations voluntarily contributed funds to the Blue Cross Association so it could organize a stock insurance company. This company was incorporated in Illinois under the name "Health Service, Inc." The initial capital was $200,000 with $282,000 surplus. The latter accounted for the excess funds over the required capital which were considered necessary for stable operation of the new organization. HSI is licensed to operate in all but the following states: Alabama, Colorado, Connecticut, Hawaii, Kansas, Massachusetts, Missouri, New Jersey, North Carolina, and South Dakota.

Ten of the fifteen directors of Health Service, Inc., are selected by the associations which contributed money to form

---

[8] *Blue Cross Guide—1962* (Chicago: Blue Cross Commission, 1962) , p. 8.

the organization. This selection privilege will continue until the funds have been repaid, and up to this time no contributions have been returned to the sponsoring plans. For the purposes of repayment, all earnings of the corporation (HSI) are given to the Blue Cross Association. The Association chooses the other five directors.

HSI offers a uniform contract and standard variations for groups whose employees and activities are located in areas served by more than one association. Plans which cooperate in offering this standard coverage at the prescribed rates for single-person, two-person, and family contracts are assigned the subscribers located in their respective areas. HSI provides all the benefits in those instances where a Blue Cross plan is unwilling or unable to do so; or the corporation handles the protection that is necessary, in addition to that offered by an association, to bring coverage up to the uniform benefit structure. When an organization cooperates to provide the basic coverage it accepts what is called a National Account Agreement.[9] There is a separate agreement for writing "standard variations."

Participating associations generally pay hospitals directly for services provided for members assigned to them. When Health Service, Inc., is responsible for part or all of the protection and resulting charges, the facilities of the Inter-Plan Service Benefit Bank are employed. HSI in such a case is considered a home plan.

The basic contract provides thirty days of semiprivate hospital room services, as well as laboratory examinations, electrocardiograms, anesthetics (including their administration), and X-rays. There is a $6 per day allowance if private accommodations are desired. The maternity benefit has an $80 maximum. The standard variations include 70 or 120 days of coverage and $8 to $15 allowances toward private facilities. There is also a supplemental major medical expense contract under which $5,000 is the maximum reim-

---

[9] Not to be confused with the Local Benefit Agreement for National Accounts.

bursement during a twelve-month benefit period. The contract has a $100 deductible and a 75 per cent coinsurance provision.

H.S.I., however, has not done as well as Blue Cross Officials once hoped. Only 49 of the 79 local plans have bought stock in the firm. Last year, after 10 years of operation, H.S.I. premium income totaled about $6 million. Premium income of the local Blue Cross and Blue Shield plans in 1958 . . . totaled more than $2 billion. . . .

Employers, it has been found, have been reluctant to take on the heavy paper work of dealing not only with several local Blue Cross plans but with H.S.I. as well. Moreover, the plans themselves have not shown much willingness to cooperate with H.S.I.[10]

The success or failure of HSI cannot be determined, however, merely by observing its premium statistics, as this quotation would seem to imply. For example, if HSI were completely successful, *all* associations would cooperate by assuming *all* of the national coverage placed in their respective areas by HSI. In such a case, HSI premium income would by zero, since funds would accrue as income to the individual organizations.

Among the deficiencies in Health Service, Inc., is the fact that it is virtually impossible to tailor a benefit structure to the desires of a specific employer or group. The basic contract and its variations are the only benefit and financial alternatives available under the HSI approach. Thus, the attempt at national uniformity in benefit structures has not had built-in versatility, and it is at this Achilles' heel that other insurers have directed their group hospitalization efforts. Insurance companies can make changes—large or small, important or trivial—in the coverage with consequent premium alterations. These features have an important influence on employers, who are major participants in group insurance financing, and labor unions, which are also interested parties in many arrangements concerning medical care coverage. Thus, it has been potent competitive am-

---

[10] *The Wall Street Journal,* February 17, 1960. p. 20.

munition when insurance companies advance the concept that they build the contract to the needs of the group and the cost to the requirements of those financing the benefits.

Syndicates

Forty-eight Blue Cross plans cooperate in syndicate arrangements whereby a benefit structure can be constructed or tailored to the needs of a potential group. Syndicates attempt to fill gaps or undesirable aspects in the current national program run through Health Service, Inc. Blue Shield is also tied into this benefit and sales device. Syndicates primarily handle major occupational groups; thus, there is a "coal syndicate" and a "steel syndicate," to name two of the most important. Plans in areas which do not have such industries are not members of the syndicates.

Under the syndicate method, and contrary to the procedure of HSI, the organization originating the business has complete administrative control of the coverage. In this manner associations in a syndicate subordinate some of their activities to other Blue Cross plans. This does not agree with the philosophy of associations which want local control in all situations and it is the reason some refuse to cooperate.

Complete cooperation by all associations in pursuing the HSI goals would reduce the need for syndicates. An incentive for the utilization of syndicates, however, is that they circumvent the taxes which would have to be paid if the business were placed in HSI. This factor is discussed more fully in the subsequent section on the syndicate arrangements of Blue Shield.

BLUE SHIELD INTERRELATIONS[11]

Early Relations with the American Medical Association

In the early stages of the Blue Shield movement member associations conducted most of the required coordinating ac-

---

[11] A considerable portion of the information for this section was obtained in interviews with executives of the National Association of Blue Shield Plans and specific Blue Shield plans.

tivities through an American Medical Association subdivision called the Council on Medical Service, established in 1943. The purpose of this body was "to serve as a clearing house for information about the Plans, to study and suggest means for distribution of medical care to the public consistent with the principles adopted by the AMA, and to assist the state and county associations in their medical service activities. A set of 'Standards for Acceptance' were drawn up, compliance with which entitled a Plan to use the Council's 'Seal of Acceptance' in its printed matter."[12]

In 1946, Associated Medical Care Plans, Inc. (AMCP) was started by the American Medical Association as a nonprofit association in the State of Illinois.[13] The functions of this organization were to coordinate the affairs of approved plans, including the stimulation of reciprocal benefits between associations and the transfer of members; collection and dissemination of statistics; and assistance in the birth and development of new Blue Shield plans.

The commissioners of Associated Medical Care Plans included three members from the AMA Council on Medical Service, and AMCP was directly responsible to this council. In addition, in 1946, the American Medical Association developed "Standards of Acceptance for Medical Care Plans." At that time the standards provided that a medical care plan could be underwritten by either an insurance company or a voluntary medical prepayment association.

The first attempt to join the medical service associations under a common name came in 1947 when the AMCP proposed use of the name "Blue Shield" by all accepted organizations. This did not meet with AMA sanction initially, as may be seen in a quotation from a letter from that organization to the AMCP in September, 1947:

It is inconceivable to us that any group of state medical society plans should band together to exclude other state medical so-

---

[12] Unprinted material from the National Association of Blue Shield Plans.

[13] Actually, AMCP was conceived by AMA's Council on Medical Service and nine representatives of medical care associations.

ciety programs by patenting a term, name, symbol, or product. It is questionable whether it would be a defensible policy for a group of plans sponsored and/or approved by a segment of the medical profession to patent any symbol or shield, the use of which would be denied other plans enjoying equal sponsorship or approval. May we suggest, then, that the question of patenting the term "Blue Shield" be given serious study before the adoption is even considered.

Nevertheless, AMCP did adopt and patent the Blue Shield name and symbol in December, 1947. Up to this juncture at least indirect control of the coordination of medical service associations was in the hands of the American Medical Association. At the same time it was apparent that the AMA wanted to avoid any conflict with the insurance industry by openly supporting the medical service association movement.

The widening chasm between the AMA and AMCP became obvious in July, 1949, when the AMA House of Delegates approved a recommendation by the Council on Medical Service that there be absolute separation of the AMCP from its former parent—the AMA. A summary of this action may be seen in a report of the Council on Medical Service to the then Blue Shield Commission:

The American Medical Association is not engaged in the insurance business and has no intention of giving a preferential standing to any one type of voluntary plan. The American Medical Association does believe, however, that it has a definite function to perform, that of evaluating any insurance plan presented to the people, thus protecting them as far as possible against unscrupulous or unsound plans. The American Medical Association further believes that the people should be free to purchase the type of health security they desire. To this end the Council on Medical Service has for the past four years critically examined various plans and has given its approval to numerous plans operating on a local or state basis. The Council has felt the need for a national organization which would act as a trade and coordinating agency for all medically sponsored plans.

We (the AMA Council on Medical Service) therefore recommend:

(1) The formation of a national coordinating agency representing all qualified voluntary prepayment plans. . . .

(2) That there shall be no official connection between the American Medical Association and the Associated Medical Care Plans. However, the American Medical Association will continue to approve or disapprove all voluntary medical care plans.

(3) The recognition of AMCP as a trade organization of member plans and Blue Cross as occupying a similar position for voluntary prepayment hospital care plans.

(4) The recognition of the responsibility of the American Medical Association to (a) Promote the principle of voluntary insurance by educating the people as to their need for such coverage and by obtaining full cooperation from state and county medical organizations in the local field; (b) Inform the American people of the availability of approved plans that propose to supply on a prepayment basis security against the economic hazards of serious illness.[14]

Blue Shield executives still refer to 1949 as the year in which AMA "kicked them out."

In 1950, the name Blue Shield Medical Care Plans was adopted in preference to that of Associated Medical Care Plans. The former was a more appropriate title inasmuch as the accepted associations were called "Blue Shield plans." The new coordinating agency was supervised by a body similar to a board of directors, called the "Blue Shield Commission." Included in the membership were six commissioners elected at large, two elected in each of the eleven Blue Shield districts by the member organizations, and three appointed by the AMA.

National Association of Blue Shield Plans

"Blue Shield Medical Care Plans" was a name not descriptive of the scope of Blue Shield's national organization, so the new title "National Association of Blue Shield Plans" was adopted in 1960. Similarly, the name of the governing

---

[14] Minutes of the Blue Shield Commission meeting, Hollywood, Florida, April 15, 1949.

board was changed from the "Blue Shield Commission" to the "board of directors."

All Blue Shield plans are members of the national Association. Each member organization has one delegate at the association's annual meeting. A weighted voting arrangement on other than election of directors is employed whereby each association has one vote plus an additional vote for each 10,000 subscribers, or portion thereof, subject to a minimum of two votes and a maximum of twenty-five votes. The Association has a normal complement of officers, along with the requirement that the president, president-elect, chairman, and vice-chairman of the board must be medical doctors. The reference-committee system is used.

The national Association is a self-governing body which reports to no other organization. Its board of directors is composed of district directors, directors-at-large, the president, and the president-elect of the corporation. Each district elects two directors annually to one-year terms, on the basis of one vote per member association. One of the district directors from each region must be a medical doctor, while the other must be either an employee of a Blue Shield plan or on its governing board. There are nine directors-at-large, at least two thirds of whom must be doctors of medicine. The American Medical Association appoints three of these directors, each of whom serves a three-year term. The board of directors or member associations submit nominations for the other positions if the board feels that vacancies should be filled.

The purpose of the association as stated in its bylaws is:

. . . to promote the establishment and operation of such nonprofit, voluntary, medical society approved medical care plans throughout the United States, its territories and possessions, and to assist in the development of similar nonprofit medical care plans outside the United States, as will adequately meet the health needs of the public and maintain high quality of medical care. . . .

Inherent in this purpose is the recognition that state and local

Plans are and should be autonomous in their control and operation, in order that the needs, facilities and practices of their respective areas can be given due consideration.

The national association administers the approval program without any requirement to report to the AMA.[15] The Blue Shield symbol is registered by the national association, as well. If the standards are not met, an association has one year to correct the situation after which further inability to comply with approval requirements would result in loss of permission for the organization to use the Blue Shield symbol and name.

Member plans support the national association by paying dues as determined at annual meetings. In 1961, the monthly rate of contribution by Blue Shield plans was 5.5 mills for each subscriber up to 500,000, then 1.5 mills per subscriber. There are no minimum nor maximum contribution limits. An amendment is being proposed which would raise the contribution rate to 6.5 mills per subscriber up to 500,000, then 1.5 mills for each member. Assessments require the approval of both a majority of the member associations present at the meeting and more than two thirds of the weighted votes.

Actions of the National Association of Blue Shield Plans have been described by one of its executives as "guiding" rather than "governing" member organizations; it watches the activities of each Blue Shield plan and will give advice and send technicians, such as actuaries, to assist when necessary.

The national association does not have the requirement used by the Blue Cross system, whereby if 75 per cent of the Blue Cross plans join in a certain program, all other member organizations must participate in order to retain approval.

The efforts of the national association to obtain emphatic support for the Blue Shield movement from the AMA, even

---

[15] One of the requirements for approval, however, is that an association be endorsed by the medical societies in the areas in which it operates.

though the two groups had been divorced, attained some success in 1960. Blue Shield officers felt the AMA was being skittish in this respect because it desired to appease insurance companies. (Officials of insurance companies interpreted the AMA attitude as impartiality.) The national association did not want AMA interference or control but it did feel entitled to AMA's positive endorsement, it was reported, since Blue Shield was considered the doctors' answer to the medical care problem. The AMA House of Delegates in 1960 listed principles which should be included in the term "Blue Shield concept" and, at the same time, indicated somewhat weakly its support of Blue Shield. The resolution stated that Blue Shield should encompass:

(1) Acceptance of leadership by the medical profession in sponsoring or approving mechanisms for assisting the public in meeting medical care costs.

(2) The use of the prepayment mechanism in spreading the cost of medical care on a rating basis to make it possible for plans to assist people to meet the costs of health care.

(3) Physician participation to make it feasible for plans to provide continued leadership in experimentation in the improvement and expansion of benefits to subscribers.

(4) Medical society representation in determination of policy to prevent interference with the right of the physician in exercising professional judgment in rendering medical care and to assure that the scope of benefits and benefit allowances of the plan are fair to both patient and physician.

(5) Medical society cooperation in preventing abuses of the patient, physician, or plan.

(6) Freedom of choice of physician for each patient.

AMA's endorsement of Blue Shield was phrased in the following terms:

Blue Shield plans organized and operated to implement these principles are a proper economic arm of the medical profession and, under medical direction, have become a major component of the nation's voluntary health insurance system. To serve the public best, Blue Shield plans need and deserve the support of physicians and medical societies. Therefore, the Council on Medical Service proposes the following recommendation in reference to the American Medical Association-Blue Shield plan relationships:

(1) The American Medical Association urges physician participation in Blue Shield plans.

(2) Liaison between the American Medical Association and the Blue Shield plans should be strengthened: (a) By the Board of Directors of the National Association of Blue Shield Plans accepting two members from the Council on Medical Service in an ex-officio capacity. This would be in addition to the three already appointed by the American Medical Association Board of Trustees; (b) Through at least one formal conference annually between the Council on Medical Service and the Board of the National Association of Blue Shield Plans; . . .

(3) The American Medical Association encourages direct liaison between medical societies and the Blue Shield plans serving their areas to maintain the best possible physician-plan relationship. . . .

The American Medical Association is a foundation of state medical associations each of which makes its own determinations on approval or sponsorship of medical care plans. . . . They (Blue Shield plans) have been an important factor in making the voluntary system a bulwark against compulsory Federal encroachment. The goal of physicians, medical societies, Blue Shield plans, and the American Medical Association is to provide continuing proof that the voluntary system is the better system.[16]

The relationship between the National Association of Blue Shield Plans and the American Medical Association facilitates no control of one body by the other. Although there is reciprocal representation on the two governing boards, this is to encourage liaison, cooperation, and information. Voting control would be impossible when, for instance, the AMA appoints only three directors of more than thirty possible members on the national association's board.

---

[16] Report of the Council on Medical Service, American Medical Association House of Delegates, 1960.

Out-of-Area Benefits

There is no formal arrangement among Blue Shield plans to provide surgical or medical benefits for a member who requires such services when away from his home-plan area. Normally the subscriber receives indemnity-type benefits. The out-of-area doctor who provides the services is paid personally by the subscriber who then sends the receipt to his Blue Shield plan. The association pays him the amount they would have remunerated a doctor in the home area for providing such services.

Transfer Arrangements

The transfer of a Blue Shield subscriber from one association to another, if he relocates permanently, has been facilitated since a transfer agreement was put into effect by the Blue Shield plans in 1953. This agreement is identical to the Blue Cross Inter-Plan Transfer Agreement.[17]

Medical Indemnity of America, Inc.

The necessity of providing a uniform national contract of benefits was a problem which befell Blue Shield plans as it had Blue Cross organizations. Medical service associations never had a Local Benefit Agreement, such as existed in the Blue Cross system. Since Blue Shield national coverage is largely on an indemnity basis, a Local Benefit Agreement would be inapplicable.

There was considerable urging for Blue Shield to join in the original organization of Health Service, Inc. This action was prevented primarily by concern over the possible subjection of the practice of medicine to nondoctor authority. Instead, Medical Indemnity of America, Inc. (MIA) was conceived as the solution to Blue Shield's problem of enrolling national accounts. MIA was organized as a stock insurance company in the State of Ohio; its charter was granted on December 5, 1950. Blue Shield plans contributed

---

[17] Discussed on page 63.

$200,000 capital and $183,719 surplus to Blue Shield Medical Care Plans (now the National Association of Blue Shield Plans) for the formation of MIA. Eight of MIA's fifteen-man board of directors must be medical doctors. Ten of the directors are elected by the associations which contributed funds to establish the corporation. The national association selects the other five directors.

Uniform surgical, medical, and maternity benefits are offered to national corporations by MIA. Coverage is passed on to member associations which will accept national group members located within their area. The functions of Medical Indemnity of America are both similar to, and closely connected with, those of Health Service, Inc. This is probably the area of most intensive cooperation between coordinating agencies of Blue Cross and Blue Shield. The inclusion of both hospital and surgical-medical benefits in a single contract by the two types of associations has been fostered by the competition of insurance companies which do combine such benefit structures.

One man in the highest echelon of the National Association of Blue Shield Plans feels that the problem of national group enrollment is the major challenge facing Blue Shield, even ahead of such issues as coverage for the aged, low-income groups, and persons in rural areas. Medical Indemnity of America has not realized all of its goals in this respect. One difficulty is that many Blue Shield plans are limited to service benefits and are precluded from taking indemnity-type contracts. The National Account Agreement meshes indemnity and service benefits, but the agreement needs reworking before all associations can participate.

Syndicates

Blue Shield syndicates operate in a manner similar to syndicates in Blue Cross. Actually, a syndicate is often a combination of Blue Shield and Blue Cross plans. In essence, certain associations cooperate to offer coverage to national groups. In Blue Shield the association which originates the business is known as the "contracting plan." This association receives all of the premiums from the corporation or group being covered, and the funds are then distributed among the participating organizations. Claims are paid by each cooperating association for the group subscribers located in its area.

It would seem that syndicates duplicate the function that Medical Indemnity of America, Inc. (and Health Service, Inc.) was intended to perform. Syndicates currently exist because they tailor contracts to the desires of particular groups; they present a means of avoiding taxes, such as the premium tax in many areas; and they were used prior to the incorporation of MIA and HSI and some plans feel it is administratively easier to use the older arrangements (particularly when large and specialized industries are being covered). Since MIA-HSI are stock insurance companies they are subject to the taxes normally imposed on insurance companies, even though they were originated and controlled by Blue Cross and Blue Shield plans. Syndicates can offer more competitive rates by circumventing these taxes.

So close is the cooperation among associations in syndicate arrangements that occasionally a plan in one state actually insures group employees in another state. This extra-legal event occurs when a corporation demands certain benefits which some organizations cannot offer. Associations which can provide the desired coverage sometimes assume that portion of the out-of-state risks which cannot be covered by organizations in the area. This is occasionally necessary in order to obtain the business of a national group.

As in Blue Cross, some Blue Shield plans refuse to cooperate in a syndicate because they feel they are subordinating themselves, and their local control, to other organizations. Generally, the smaller associations are those which harbor this attitude. About thirty-five Blue Shield plans now take part in syndicates.

chapter V

CHARACTERISTICS AND
DIFFERENCES[1]

Foregoing chapters have described the major components of Blue Cross and Blue Shield, and it is now possible to consider those characteristics said to be the philosophical fiber of the hospital and medical service association movement. Highly emotional disagreements have developed both inside and outside the Blue Cross and Blue Shield systems over the existence and importance of these features. This chapter therefore seeks to attain conceptual clarity, since many of the characteristics have a bearing on the legislative enactments and supervisory procedures applicable to the associations.

NONPROFIT STATUS

When applied to a hospital or medical service association, "nonprofit" obviously means that no profit ensues from their operation. The distinction, though, is not quite as definitive, nor as simple, as the adjective might imply. First, it was observed in Chapter I that nonprofit status is not a feature distinctive with the Blues; mutual insurance companies may be considered technically "nonprofit" in that "excess" earnings are returned to policyholders or retained as surplus for their benefit. The only "owners" in a mutual insurance company are the policyholders.

---

[1] Many of the aspects covered in this chapter are treated in detail by the author in "The Fundamental Nature of Blue Cross and Blue Shield," *The Journal of Insurance* (Fall, 1962), pp. 385–402.

The requirement of nonprofitability, as specified in the national approval programs and as intended by state laws, does not mean that an association's income must not exceed its expenditures, at least in the short run. The requirement is generally interpreted to mean, however, that no individual may receive any part of the net earnings of a Blue Cross or Blue Shield plan. Even the latter statement allows some leeway in interpretation. No dividend arrangements (to those who provided capital) nor profit-sharing programs are permitted. Full-time executives may nevertheless receive salaries, as is appropriate if such amounts are proper remuneration. (It is possible for personnel of both associations and insurance companies to "profit" in the personal sense by high salaries.) Blue Cross stipulations do prevent members of boards of directors from being paid for their services, other than for expenses. The approval standards of Blue Shield are worded broadly enough to permit "loss-of-time" payments to board members, in addition to expense allowances. Loss-of-time payments compensate an individual for the time he has taken from his usual work or profession in order to participate in board activities.

As a general statement the nonprofit status of Blue Cross and Blue Shield may be said to mean that any *net* earnings, i.e., the excess of plan income over claim payments and increases in reserves, will eventually be returned to subscribers in the form of increased benefits or reduced subscription payments. The determination of "net" earnings permits salaries to executives, as well as other employees, and, in the case of Blue Shield organizations, payments to board members.

Hospitals and doctors contract with associations to provide subscriber services. In addition, many hospitals (in the case of Blue Cross) and doctors (in the case of Blue Shield) agree to provide these services even if there are insufficient funds to pay for them. The ultimate insurer, therefore, can often be either the member hospitals or the contracting doctors.

The confusing situation which occurs in associations is that those who actually control the organizations can be, and often are, those whose fees the Blue Cross and Blue Shield plans were organized to pay. The question in this circuitous relationship is whether an organization can be *truly* nonprofit under these circumstances. If the vendors of services to subscribers control a governing board, there is a possibility that reimbursement or fee schedules, or salary payments to executives, could be increased unduly without violating the current interpretation of "nonprofitability."

It is interesting to observe that the nonprofit status does not have a favorable connotation for all individuals. Association of the term "nonprofit" with "cooperatives" and "socialization" has led some observers to view nonprofitability as opposed to the American principle of private enterprise and the profit motive. This attitude has been noted even on the part of a few regulatory authorities. Others state that protection against medical care expenses should not be considered in exactly the same light as other businesses. As long as there is competition and/or governmental supervision, they say, Blue Cross and Blue Shield are not violating any principles of the country's political and economic system.

Associations ardently defend their nonprofit position since they feel this characteristic is one justification for their exclusion from most, or all, taxes. Historically, this is an incorrect conclusion; insurance companies which have a nonprofit type of operation are subjected to taxation nevertheless. The actual reason for the original exemption from taxation was that Blue Cross and Blue Shield were offering hospital and medical-surgical coverage to *individuals for whom commercial insurance was largely unavailable,* at least at "reasonable" premiums. In most cases these were low-income groups, including the aged and individuals in rural areas. Major executives in both Blue Cross and Blue Shield are coming to agree that this is the major *current* reason for their preferred tax status. Statements from regulatory authorities also support this opinion. In fact, the enabling legislation in a few jurisdictions specifically states that hospital and medical service associations are excluded from certain regulatory requirements, including tax payment, because they are intended to be a social type of organization.

Obviously, associations are granted tax exemption only if they are nonprofit; additional criteria are required, however. It is desirable to remove the attitude that Blue Cross and Blue Shield plans are different largely because they are nonprofit. Actual differences between plans and insurance companies are often clouded or not recognized because so much emphasis has been placed on the associations' nonprofit status.

COMMUNITY SPONSORSHIP

Community sponsorship implies that the supporting force for the organization and development of Blue Cross and Blue Shield comes from the community in general. In the case of a statewide association this would mean that a significant portion of the citizens of the state was behind the organization. The community sponsorship idea originated because hospitals endorsed many Blue Cross plans. Since hospitals were considered humanitarian and community-interest institutions, the attitude prevailed that associations supported by the hospitals were in the community interest and, thereby, had community sponsorship. Current weight is added to this opinion by the fact that in some areas more than 50 per cent of the local population is covered by Blue Cross or Blue Shield.[2]

The significance of community sponsorship goes beyond its publicity value. Any insurance-type institution or organi-

[2] Ten hospital service associations covered more than 50 per cent of the population in their areas on December 31, 1961: Washington, D.C. (81.88%), Allentown, Pa. (79.17%), Providence, R.I. (75.17%), Rochester, N.Y. (71.39%), Wilmington (63.74%), New York City (62.91%), Cincinnati (60.30%), Cleveland (57.99%), Philadelphia (57.98%), and Toledo (53.80%). (Blue Cross Association, *Enrollment Reports of Blue Cross Plans, Year of 1961*, pp. 11–12.) See pages 30 and 45 for additional enrollment percentages.

zation which currently enrolls a large segment of the citizenry, especially on a national basis, may have particular importance if a federal program of medical expense protection is instituted. Already several proposals have utilized existing organizations as the insurance mechanism in a federal plan for the aged.

Even with a high population coverage in particular locales, it must be remembered that the governing boards of Blue Cross associations require only one third of their memberships to be representatives of the public. The remaining members represent hospitals (one third of the board), doctors, and possibly the public. While hospital and medical representatives are certainly public spirited, they nevertheless represent institutions and professions which have special interests.

At the end of 1961, 30.74 per cent of the population in the United States[3] were members of Blue Cross. Ten Blue Cross plans had less than 10 per cent of the citizens in their areas enrolled.[4] It thus becomes clear that only some of the associations are truly community sponsored, if it is considered necessary for a sizeable part of the citizens in the locale to be subscribers before such sponsorship exists.

Approximately the same situation exists in the Blue Shield system. It was previously observed that the local medical societies must support a medical service association before it will be approved. For this reason, it would certainly be proper to say that Blue Shield is "physician sponsored"; physician control makes it difficult to determine whether a Blue Shield plan is community sponsored, however. Most regulatory officials seem to feel there is less community sponsorship, in general, for a Blue Shield plan than there is for a Blue Cross organization.

---

[3] Including Puerto Rico.

[4] Montana (3.46%), Portland, Ore. (4.52%), South Dakota (5.90%), Baton Rouge, La. (5.80%), Alaska (6.11%), Seattle (8.67%), Durham, N.C. (8.68%), Bluefield, W. Va. (8.88%), Columbus, Ga. (9.15%), and Albuquerque, N.M. (9.36%). (Blue Cross Association, *Enrollment Reports of Blue Cross Plans, Year of 1961*, pp. 16 and 17.)

At the end of 1961, five Blue Shield plans had participation of more than 50 per cent of the population in the locales they serve,[5] and ten of the associations had less than 10 per cent enrolled.[6] An average of 25.53 per cent of the population in the United States was covered by Blue Shield on December 31, 1961.

It is surely correct to say that Blue Cross and Blue Shield plans are in the "community interest." The broadest statement regarding their sponsorship would be that they are hospital sponsored (Blue Cross) and doctor sponsored (Blue Shield). While their purposes and principles are often social in nature, the presence of "community sponsorship" can be determined only by reference to specific areas.[7]

SERVICE APPROACH

The service approach is best understood when it is contrasted with the indemnity approach which has long been used in many types of insurance company coverage. Indemnity contracts agree to pay an insured up to specified dollar amounts to indemnify (or reimburse) him for an economic loss he has incurred. Pure service-type benefits do not refer to dollar amounts of coverage. Rather, they specify that

---

[5] Washington, D.C. (81.29%), Providence, R.I. (67.86%), Rochester, N.Y. (65.89%), Wilmington (61.46%), and Cleveland (52.64%). (National Association of Blue Shield Plans, *Enrollment Reports, Blue Shield Plans, December 31, 1961,* pp. 2–3.)

[6] Rockford, Ill. (1.58%), Fairmont, W. Va. (6.17%), California (6.41%), Bluefield, W. Va. (6.44%), South Dakota (6.75%), Columbus, Ga. (7.72%), Madison, Wisc. (8.38%) (this association competes with the Milwaukee Blue Shield plan; 22.28% of the state's population is enrolled), South Carolina (8.53%), New Mexico (8.65%), and Oregon (9.54%). (National Association of Blue Shield Plans, *Enrollment Reports, Blue Shield Plans, December 31, 1961,* pp. 2–3.)

[7] Probably the most sophisticated manner to ascertain the presence or absence of community sponsorship for a particular association would be first to determine the number of eligible subscribers in the area served and then figure the percentage of this base with the actual members. By comparing this figure with the percentage considered necessary for community sponsorship—50 per cent is a defensible percentage—the true relationship may be observed.

certain types of service will be given the person covered, when he encounters stipulated contingencies. In the case of Blue Cross the latter approach often means a subscriber is guaranteed the services of a semiprivate room for a specified number of days. Service benefits in a Blue Shield plan provide for the services of a participating doctor, under specific conditions, for surgical operations and possibly for a certain number of doctors' visits.

In times of an upward secular price trend the value of service benefits increases for a subscriber. If his contributions to an association remain unchanged, he has *more* dollar protection for the same dollar contribution. If he has indemnity benefits under identical economic conditions, he receives the *same* dollar protection for the same dollar contribution, as the price of hospitalization increases. This is the reason that Blue Cross plans, and to a lesser extent the Blue Shield organizations, have encountered financial difficulties in recent years. Regulatory restrictions have prevented plans from increasing their rates as rapidly as costs have mounted for the services they have agreed to provide.

The service approach applies only to certain hospital services and not to all of the services patients may require while in a hospital. The majority of Blue Cross members have indemnity-type modifications in their certificates (such as the private room credit and the dollar amounts paid to those hospitalized in nonmember institutions. Service benefits are seldom paid for maternity cases) . One factor which supports the service approach is the American Hospital Association's requirement that a Blue Cross plan cover, on the average, not less than 75 per cent of the total bill for the usual hospital services received by subscribers having the most widely-held certificate.

The indemnity approach is more significant in Blue Shield than it is in Blue Cross. Under *service* benefit contracts issued by medical service associations, subscribers with incomes below certain limits receive medical services without additional charge. When a member has an income above the limit, a physician may charge whatever fee he pleases. Subscribers, in such instances, pay the doctor the difference between his "normal" charges and the amount he will receive from an association. Blue Shield approval standards stipulate that where service benefits are offered the plan will "attempt" to set an income limit that will include 75 per cent of the population in the area.

In 1958, 21 per cent of the Blue Shield plans were indemnity-type, 26 per cent gave full-payment service benefits, and 53 per cent combined these approaches. In terms of total number of subscribers covered by the various types in the same period, 29.7 per cent had indemnity benefits, 2.3 per cent had service coverage, and 68 per cent were in associations with combination benefits.[8]

There is a minimal difference between indemnity benefits offered by an association and protection against similar contingencies by insurance companies. The major variance is that associations pay the hospital or in-area physician directly while the policyholder *might* have to pay the bill himself, then be reimbursed by his insurer in accordance with the policy contract. It is now common, however, for a policyholder to be able to assign his benefits to the hospital or doctor and the insurer send a check to the assignee.

Service benefits have often been termed the "first-dollar" approach. The implication is that associations pay for the first dollars of medical care expense incurred by subscribers. Since many insurance companies also pay on a first-dollar basis, the term is not distinctively appropriate for associations. Where the daily limits of hospital insurance policies are adequate to cover the actual charges, for instance, there can be no question but that such contracts offer first-dollar benefits when there is no deductible provision.

The first-dollar appellation has wrought considerable misunderstanding in Blue Cross and Blue Shield. It has given the impression that subscribers will not have to pay any

[8] American Medical Association, *Voluntary Prepayment Medical Benefit Plans—1958* (Chicago: 1958) , Charts and Graphs Supplement, pp. 6, 14.

amount for their hospitalization or medical-surgical treatment, other than for excluded services and procedures, unless they are confined beyond the number of days for which benefits are provided. Thus, associations which have used deductible or coinsurance features have been chastised as violators of the service approach. This is an overly harsh attitude, particularly since, in reality, service benefits are not necessarily synonymous with first-dollar benefits. Benefits can be provided in terms of hospital or medical service, even if members pay the first few dollars of a daily hospital rate, for example, during initial days of confinement.

The service approach is unique historically and currently with hospital and medical service associations and the independent group health clinics. Then, too, Blue Cross and Blue Shield plans are under continuous pressure from their national organizations to expand the use of service-type contracts. It seems appropriate, therefore, in light of the foregoing discussion to consider the service characteristics as a proper generalization for Blue Cross plans, and in specific instances for Blue Shield associations.

CONTRACTUAL RELATIONSHIP WITH HOSPITALS AND DOCTORS

One of the most obvious, as well as least debatable, characteristics of Blue Cross and Blue Shield is the contractual relationship these organizations have with hospitals and doctors. Over 6,000 institutions, which account for approximately 90 per cent of the hospitals in America, have contracts with Blue Cross plans. About the same percentage of doctors cooperate in Blue Shield arrangements. Insurance companies generally have no prearranged commitments from hospitals (or doctors) to provide services for policyholders, nor are there any widespread financial arrangements between hospitals (or doctors) and insurance companies as to amounts of reimbursement if services are rendered to policyholders.[9] Some of the most important pioneers in the Blue Cross and Blue Shield movements feel this contractual relationship is the most important distinguishing feature of the associations.

The association between Blue Cross–Blue Shield and the hospitals and doctors is closely aligned with service benefit contracts. Service benefits could not be made available without prior commitments from those who provide medical care.

COMMUNITY RATING PROCEDURES[10]

Dr. Kulp's definition for insurance, which was employed earlier (p. 8), revealed that a pooling or averaging of exposure was a prerequisite. The debate in most lines of insurance, not the least of which is the hospital and medical area, is how broad an exposure classification must be in order to meet the pooling or averaging requirement. It is self-evident to those familiar with the mathematics of insurance that as exposure limits are narrowed in the desire for greater homogeneity and sophistication, the number of exposure units contained within the category is reduced. The ultimate in this type of refinement is an individual exposure unit. When the rate paid for the coverage of a particular exposure unit is affected to some extent by the loss experience, and possibly the expense experience, of such a unit, the procedure is called "experience rating."

Originally, Blue Cross and Blue Shield plans used broad class-rating procedures exclusively. That is, the experience of covered groups was combined to determine a "community" rate. This rate was paid by each member of a class of subscribers, and no modifications were made on a particular group's rate if its experience differed from the average of

---

[9] Physicians have cooperated in a few "state surgical plans" under which prearranged fees are paid for certain services rendered to individuals who have approved insurance coverage and whose incomes are below a specified limit.

[10] Chapter XI is devoted to the subject of rates and rate regulation.

the entire class. Actually, a class rate was determined for single group members, group subscribers with one dependent, and family group members. Similar classifications were used for nongroup subscribers and often for group conversion members.

The philosophy behind a community rate was in keeping with the social aura which surrounded the "Blues." If this was a social technique to meet a social problem, then it was felt that all groups cooperating in the system should share the cost of operating the scheme without individual consideration. An "average" rate for an entire class of subscribers carried out this principle. If deviations from the average rate were allowed for groups with good loss experience, the result would be that those groups with poor experience would be paying higher rates for their protection, and a basic tenet behind the social insurance-type system would be broken.

As insurance company encroachments into the hospital and medical coverage field increased, many Blue Cross and Blue Shield plans were forced to compromise with their philosophic principles and adopt some of the methods of their competitors. This was particularly true for the rating of "blue-chip" corporations who, understandably, would otherwise procure their coverage from insurance companies which would provide similar benefits at lower cost to the insured.

In relation to nongroup coverage the community-rate idea has been more zealously defended. Some would say that a *true* community rate for those not having group coverage would charge the same amount for each "spending unit." In this manner single wage-earners would contribute the same amount as those spending units with several dependents. Most Blue Cross and Blue Shield plans, however, have three broad classifications: single-person units, two-person units, and family units. Thus, all single subscribers pay the same rate, although it is less than that charged a two-person unit.

The community-rate principle is particularly evident in the family coverages. In most associations a family with ten children pays the same rate as one with two children.

PREPAYMENT PRINCIPLE

Among the other characteristics attributed to Blue Cross and Blue Shield as bases for differentiation from insurance companies is the idea that associations are "prepayment programs."

Blue Cross is a prepayment program for the purchase of hospital service. It is not insurance, but it operates on the basis of insurance principles. This distinction is frequently challenged as being meaningless. There is a technical difference between prepayment and insurance . . . which gives validity to the distinction, leaving aside the social concept of Blue Cross, which separates it from the insurance industry as such. Insurance is a device whereby a numerous group of individuals through a system of equitable contributions may reduce or eliminate any measurable risk of economic loss common to all. Each element of this definition has some significance. The first element is that the group must be large; it is not a phenomenon in which a single person or two or three persons may participate. Second, contributions are necessary and these contributions must be equitable. Third, the risk must be measurable, it must have to do with an economic loss.

The distinction between Blue Cross and insurance comes on this third aspect of the definition. Insurance, notably casualty insurance of which commercial hospital insurance is a part, measures a risk in terms of dollars of protection. Blue Cross measures the risk in terms of needed care. Although there are obvious deviations, Blue Cross is basically a vehicle for providing hospital service when needed without concern to dollar value of the care required by any individual participant in the risk. This is the concept of "service benefits."[11]

---

[11] Columbia University School of Public Health, Institute of Administrative Medicine, *Lectures: Hospitals and Blue Cross* (rev. October, 1957), pp. 21–22.

It is difficult to perceive how a scheme could utilize "insurance principles" yet not be "insurance." It is true that the means of measuring the potential loss experience is more difficult under Blue Cross (and Blue Shield) where service benefits are offered; nevertheless, Blue Cross and Blue Shield actuaries obviously use mathematical techniques to convert "needed care" into dollars of expected claims. In addition, they use pooling or averaging methods, which was all Dr. Kulp required to constitute "insurance."

The word "prepayment" in itself is confusing, because insurance policyholders could be considered to "prepay" for the protection they receive. As used by Blue Cross personnel, however, the term is meant to imply "prepayment of all the services required." It has been previously noted that full service benefits are not offered by all associations, so this also reduces the value of the distinction.

Finally, those associations which utilize retrospective rating do not technically have a prepayment of benefits for contracts so rated inasmuch as payments are determined after the protection period is completed.

HOSPITAL ADMISSION PROCEDURES

Blue Cross plans emphasize the advantage their subscribers have when hospitalization becomes necessary. Upon entry to a hospital a member merely shows his Blue Cross card and no deposit of money is needed. In the past those protected under insurance company policies often had to make such a deposit. The hospitals justified this treatment by saying that there were so many insurance companies and so many types of benefits offered by each company that a hospital could not possibly know whether a patient had sufficient coverage to pay a major portion of the hospital bill, even if he was insured.

Some of this difference regarding hospital admissions has been manufactured by certain Blue Cross plans and hospitals, as may be seen in the following quotation:

Concerted action by hospital groups have [*sic*] stymied efforts of insurance companies to force hospitals to grant them the same rights that Blue Cross had in the matter of admissions, billings, etc. It is this type of public relations efforts that Blue Cross needs from hospitals.[12]

It *is* simpler for a hospital to determine the nature and extent of benefits to which a patient is entitled under Blue-Cross than under the policies of insurance companies. When a subscriber is admitted to a member hospital in his home area, the hospital contacts the association's headquarters under a routine arrangement to determine the patient's eligibility for benefits. Even when an out-of-area member is hospitalized, the use of the Blue Cross Private Wire Communications System will provide the necessary eligibility information.

Insurance companies have countered this disadvantage through a procedure developed by the Health Insurance Council. This body established a standard qualification procedure for hospitals to use regarding hospital insurance policyholders. Under this arrangement, most insureds do not have to make a cash deposit upon entry into the hospital. Thus, the difference in hospital admission procedures between Blue Cross–Blue Shield and insurance companies is being reduced. Where this difference does exist, it is much less important to insurance commissioners than it is to hospital patients.

Another possible variance in Blue Cross and insurance company procedures concerns the billing of a patient upon his discharge from a hospital. A Blue Cross member pays only the difference between his total bill and the amount of his Blue Cross benefits, if he has been in a cooperating hospital. The Blue Cross plan pays the hospital according to predetermined rates for the facilities and services included in the subscriber's coverage. A policyholder can now usually authorize his insurance company to pay the amount

---

[12] *Ibid.,* p. 45.

he would receive directly to the hospital; he then remits to the hospital only the difference between his total bill and the insurance benefits to which he is entitled. Formerly, all patients with insurance company protection had to pay the entire bill. Then, after completion of claim papers and their approval by the insurance company involved, policyholders would be indemnified for the payment of the expenses against which they had protection.

In order to appease those who vehemently uphold these differences between the Blues and insurance companies, and in order to maintain some of the established terminology, this book has used such terms as "insurance carriers" and "policyholders" to apply only to insurance companies. "Hospital and medical service associations," "insurance-type organizations," "associations," "plans," and sometimes "organizations," as well as "subscribers," "members," and "enrollees" are terms which here refer to Blue Cross and Blue Shield.

SUMMARY REGARDING CHARACTERISTICS AND DIFFERENCES

The foregoing discussion indicated that at least some of the characteristics formerly attributed to Blue Cross and Blue Shield are still appropriate on an individual plan basis and in several instances on a national scale. The purpose of the evaluation was to focus attention on those aspects which appear to be truly distinctive for associations at the present time. Subsequent chapters will elaborate on, and in some cases document, the attitudes which have been presented; the "Conclusions" set forth in Chapter XV will specifically build upon these features.

Part Two

REGULATION

chapter VI

DEVELOPMENT OF REGULATION
FOR MEDICAL CARE COVERAGES

The need for regulation of insurance and insurance institutions is not widely questioned. The unique features of an insurance contract and the requirements for the existence of an insurance system provide considerable justification for governmental supervision. The insured generally has no part in drawing up the terms of the agreement; even if he had, few individuals possess the technical knowledge to evaluate the contractual provisions. Under these circumstances, it is quite possible that all parties to the scheme will not always be on the same footing.—Particularly when the large number of participants required is considered. Then, too, the contract can mature at a distant time when the interested parties may not have the physical, mental, nor legal powers to substantiate their original position in the agreement. Finally, regulation is encouraged, if not necessitated, by the fact that such a great proportion of the citizenry is involved in insurance transactions.

When negotiations and operations are supervised by some disinterested body or authority there is greater assurance that citizens are being treated fairly. Governmental regulation, however, is not in complete harmony with the economic and political fiber of a nation built upon the pillars of private enterprise and the profit motive. It is here that deliberations arise concerning how much regulation is necessary, as well as over the manner, and by what authority, it should be exercised.

HISTORY OF INSURANCE REGULATION

The first insurance companies in the United States were granted individual permission to conduct business by the state legislatures in areas where they desired to operate. As insurance expanded in the 1800's, it became impracticable to go through a special legislative enactment each time a jurisdiction wanted to give an organization authority to conduct insurance activities. Laws were passed by the various states to set basic requirements with which insurance companies had to comply, and personnel were designated to exercise authority over the organization and operation of such companies. Discretionary powers, which varied in extent by areas, were granted these officials to interpret the statutes. Eventually all states found it necessary to establish a special governmental section whose function was to regulate the business of insurance conducted within its boundaries.

The basic feature of insurance regulation is the presence of state governments as the direct supervisory level. The *Paul* v. *Virginia* decision[1] of 1869 declared that insurance was not commerce and, thus, was not subject to federal jurisdiction. The states' domain over this area was preserved through subsequent years by a series of court conflicts known as the "insurance cases," most notable of which was the Deer Lodge Case.[2] The issue was not seriously questioned again until the momentous SEUA verdict was rendered in 1944.[3] The Supreme Court declared in the latter case that *insurance was commerce*. To the extent, then, that the insurance business constituted interstate commerce, such activities would be subject to federal regulation. This confusing situation was somewhat clarified by Public Law 15, approved by Congress

---

[1] *Paul* v. *Virginia,* 8 Wall. 168 (1869).

[2] *New York Life Insurance Company* v. *Deer Lodge County* (Montana), 231 U.S. 495 (1913).

[3] *United States* v. *South-Eastern Underwriters Association, et al.,* 64 Sup. Ct. 1162 (1944).

on March 9, 1945. The enactment granted states the *conditional* right to supervise the business of insurance.

The events which surrounded Public Law 15, more properly known as the McCarran Act, are well documented. The act incorporated to a great extent the proposals of the National Association of Insurance Commissioners. The resulting law subjects the insurance business, and individuals engaged in it, to supervision and taxation by state governments. It specifies, in addition, that no Congressional Act "shall be construed to invalidate, impair, or supersede any law enacted by any State for the purpose of regulating the business of insurance, or which imposes a fee or tax upon such business, unless such Act specifically relates to the business of insurance"; neither should Congressional silence be construed as erecting any barrier to state supervision. The law does provide, however, that the Sherman Act, the Clayton Act, and the Federal Trade Commission Act are applicable to the business of insurance "to the extent that such business is not regulated by State Law."

After the passage of Public Law 15, an All-Industry Committee was organized to develop model state statutes and procedures which would comply with the new federal mandate. The committee included representatives from all phases of the insurance business, and the proposals of this group were the basis of new enactments in many states. Some areas had previously adopted laws of a similar nature.

LEGISLATIVE HISTORY CONCERNING BLUE CROSS AND BLUE SHIELD PLANS

Blue Cross and Blue Shield plans cannot be considered immune to federal control just because most of them operate within state boundaries. The Inter-Plan Service Benefit Bank, Health Service, Inc., Medical Indemnity of America, Inc., and syndicates are examples of interstate operations of the associations. Since the composite Blue Cross and Blue Shield systems in which associations cooperate are involved in interstate commerce, Public Law 15 has importance for these organizations as well as for insurance companies.

The current importance of state supervision is accompanied in the case of Blue Cross and Blue Shield by another common feature of regulation; this is the use of special enabling acts. These statutes set forth the regulatory agency and procedures to which the associations are subject. Enabling legislation in a state exempts Blue Cross and Blue Shield plans in the area from the provisions of the insurance code, except where sections are specifically declared to apply. Most plans have been founded under enabling acts.

States which have not developed enabling statutes allow associations to incorporate either under the general nonprofit statutes or according to the provisions for insurance companies. Where the general laws have been utilized, only the nonprofit position of the associations has been considered and the fact that insurance-type activities are to be conducted has been ignored. Those associations which have had to meet the requirements for insurance companies have been organized under the regulatory attitude that there are no significant differences between the purposes or operations of health insurance companies and Blue Cross or Blue Shield plans. The formation procedure which is used depends upon how the state in which the plan is to be domiciled views the nature of hospital and medical service organizations.

The concept of enabling legislation was conceived a decade prior to the time that insurance was declared to be commerce. The first enabling act resulted when a group in New York attempted to organize a hospital service plan in 1933. They were advised by state authorities that the proposed association would have to meet the normal capital and reserve requirements if organized as a stock company, or subscribers would have assessment liability if the group was established as a mutual company. The plan would have been subject to taxation as well. This prompted leaders of hospital, medical, and lay groups to foster passage of an enabling act by the New York legislature in May, 1934. In general, the resulting legislation exempted hospital service associations from the provisions of the state's insurance laws. They were also excused from the payment of state and local taxes, other than those on real estate and office equipment. Such associations were required to organize with the approval of both the Insurance and Welfare Departments of the state. Members of the boards of directors had to be representatives of contracting hospitals. Any plans organized under the law had to meet the rate approval, reporting, and examination requirements to which insurance companies were subjected. In addition, the rates of reimbursement to contracting hospitals had to be passed upon by the Superintendent of Insurance.

California, Illinois, and Pennsylvania were among the states which adopted enabling statutes for hospital plans within a short span of years after New York broke the legislative ground—California and Illinois in 1935, and Pennsylvania in 1937. Insurance commissioners and courts were of almost universal opinion by the late 1930's that these associations were involved in insurance-type transactions. The only way to prevent them from being subject to insurance laws was to pass enabling acts. Many states patterned such statutes after a model law which was developed by the Blue Cross Commission in 1939. (Appendix B is a copy of this suggested law.) Its provisions were not altered in subsequent years. The year 1939 saw the largest number of states—fourteen— enact enabling statutes. Thirty-two states and the District of Columbia had passed enabling acts by the time of the SEUA decision, ten years after New York utilized the first statute of this kind.[4]

Early enabling acts provided regulations only for hospital service corporations. Medical service organizations were not included in the provisions. This is understandable when it is recalled that the latter had their start about a decade after the former. If the medical service associations were not to be supervised and taxed as insurance companies in most

---

[4] Odin W. Anderson, *State Enabling Legislation for Non-Profit Hospital and Medical Plans* (Ann Arbor: University of Michigan, 1944) , p. 39.

states, they also had to come under enabling statutes. New York had another "first" with such an act in 1939. Provisions for medical plans under separate legislation have provoked some confusion in the operation of associations, inasmuch as the organizations have had difficulties combining coverages into one contract. Problems arise, for example, when enabling acts for hospital service associations prohibit including any medical-surgical benefits. A similar situation exists when medical service associations are prevented from including hospital coverages.[5] The situation was circumvented in states which were late in passing enabling acts, in that they allowed for the organization and regulation of both hospital and medical service organizations under the provisions of one statute. Some states which originally had separate laws have since revised them, so that current legislation provides either a combination act or separate acts which are compatible with the cooperative needs of plans.

Enabling enactments resolved several disputes which had attended the development of the associations: what should be the requirements before a hospital service plan could commence operation; were these organizations engaging in the corporate practice of medicine; what state department, if any, should supervise the plans' activities; what taxes should be levied against the organizations?

It should be noted that the enabling legislation and differential regulatory treatment applicable to Blue Cross and Blue Shield plans do not imply that the supervision of the plans and the requirements they must meet are any less exacting than those pertaining to insurance companies. While this *was* true in the early regulation of associations, it would

---

[5] The practice in California is unique in this respect. The Blue Shield plan (California Physicians' Service) and the Blue Cross plans (Hospital Service of California and Hospital Service of Southern California) originally cooperated with each other to offer combination benefit structures. In the early 1940's dissension between the Blue Cross and Blue Shield organizations caused severance of their relations. The result has been that the hospital service associations offer a full package of medical care benefits, including a surgical schedule, and the medical service association offers hospitalization benefits among its coverages.

be a most unfortunate, as well as incorrect, generalization at this point.

Among the state authorities who responded to questions for this study, eleven indicated that they have no statutes which can be considered as enabling legislation for Blue Cross plans. Four states—Indiana, Louisiana,[6] Nebraska, and Nevada—stated that the plans would come under the laws for "commercial" insurance companies.[7] Alaska, Colorado, Delaware, Hawaii, Missouri, and Washington classify the plans under special-type statutes—generally those which cover nonprofit corporations. The statutory situation in Wyoming is one of considerable confusion: "In Wyoming the exemption (from state control) was accomplished by tacit approval, the legislature at no time providing for control or governance of the plans. Conversely it must be noted that the legislature at no time has acknowledged the existence of the 'nonprofit' plan." [8]

Blue Cross plans are regulated to some extent in forty-four states.[9] No plans are domiciled in two additional states—Hawaii and Nevada, and there is no supervision of the associations in Colorado, Delaware, Missouri, and Wyoming.[10] In forty-one states, plus Puerto Rico, regulation is by the insurance department. In four of these states the insurance department shares some supervisory authority with another

---

[6] Louisiana gives tax exemption to the plans except for $250 annually, but all other statutes applicable to accident and health insurers apply to the associations.

[7] There are no Blue Cross plans in Hawaii and Nevada. Alaska and Vermont have no plans with headquarters within their boundaries; they are, however, served by plans in Washington and New Hampshire, respectively. Vermont presents a particularly unusual regulatory situation where in the New Hampshire-Vermont Hospitalization Service is domiciled in Concord, New Hampshire, and is licensed in Vermont as well.

[8] Letter from the Deputy Insurance Commissioner, State of Wyoming, dated December 15, 1960.

[9] Regulatory control in the State of Washington has been extremely limited heretofore. Senate Bill 259, passed by the 1961 session of the state legislature, provides for much more extensive supervision.

[10] Apparently there would be regulation in Hawaii if plans were located there.

state division.[11] The regulatory authority in Montana is the Attorney General,[12] and in Virginia it is the Bureau of Insurance of the State Corporation Commission.

Thirty-five states, including New York, Pennsylvania, and Illinois, had enacted special legislation applicable to Blue Shield plans by 1960.[13] Three[14] of the remaining states have no Blue Shield plans. Two others—Indiana and Nebraska—regulate the associations under regular insurance statutes, while Wyoming has not officially determined which laws are appropriate for these organizations. The remaining nine states have Blue Shield plans organized under statutes for nonprofit corporations. These states are Arkansas, California, Colorado, Delaware, Hawaii, Missouri, Montana, Utah, and Washington.

The vast majority of all Blue Shield plans, like their Blue Cross counterparts, are under the regulatory purview of state insurance commissioners. A notable exception is the California Physicians' Service (Blue Shield for California) which is under the sole jurisdiction of the State Attorney General. The association was able to secure a ruling that declared it to be a nonprofit organization outside the scope of the insurance laws,[15] and it has what amounts to a nonregulated status.

NATURE OF ENABLING ACTS

Purposes of Enabling Statutes

A few of the special laws for hospital and medical service associations state the reasons organizations are granted dif-

---

[11] The other state divisions involved are Kentucky, State Board of Health; Massachusetts, Division of Hospital Costs and Accounts; New York, Department of Social Welfare; and Pennsylvania, Department of Welfare.

[12] The Attorney General's function with reference to the associations in Montana is restricted solely to the investigation of complaints.

[13] Of these, Idaho has no Blue Shield plan and Vermont is served by the plan located in Concord, New Hampshire.

[14] Alaska, Louisiana, and Nevada. If plans were organized in Louisiana and Nevada they would come under the regular insurance company laws, while in Alaska a plan would be under the Health Care Services Act (for nonprofit corporations).

[15] *California Physicians' Service* v. *Garrison,* Sup. Ct. of Calif. 46–28C-2nd 790.

ferential treatment. Where such considerations are included, they may provide the basis for conflicts in the triangle of associations, insurance departments, and vendors of services provided by the plans. Pennsylvania's enabling act explains its existence as follows:

An Act providing for the regulation and supervision of nonprofit medical and osteopathic and dental service corporations organized to provide medical or osteopathic or dental services to subscribers of *low income*. . . .

Constitutional Construction. It is hereby declared to be the purpose and intent of this act and the policy of the legislature to authorize qualified persons to provide adequate medical or osteopathic or dental services for residents of this State who are *unable to provide* such services for themselves or their dependents at their own cost without depriving themselves or their dependents of such necessaries of life as food, clothing and shelter, and provide persons of over-income with the limited medical or osteopathic or dental service benefits hereinbefore set forth. (At the same time it is the purpose and intent of this act and the policy of the Legislature to maintain the standing and promote the progress of the science and art of medicine in this State.) The courts of this State are hereby directed to construe this act liberally, in order to accomplish those ends.[16]

The laws are very specific about the financial purpose and approach which must be pursued by associations. For example, Article 1 of the California act states:

This chapter shall not apply to nor govern any corporation which is organized for profit, which contemplates any pecuniary gain to its shareholders or members, or which conducts or is authorized by its articles of incorporation to conduct any business whatsoever on a profit basis. . . . No corporation subject to the provisions of this chapter shall own or operate any hospital nor engage in any business other than that of establishing, maintaining and operating a nonprofit hospital service plan.

Statutes in other areas have similar statements.

A pronounced feature of the laws is the requirement that subscribers have a free choice of hospital or physician. This

---

[16] Italics added; parenthesis in the original.

provision is one means of assuring that plans do not engage in the corporate practice of medicine.

Applicability of the Insurance Code

Enabling acts stipulate in definite terms that hospital and medical service corporations which meet the requirements of the statutes will be generally exempt from the provisions of the state laws applicable for insurance companies. This, of course, is the reason for having an enabling act.

The acts prescribe in certain sections that associations will be subject to *specific* provisions of the insurance statutes. One almost universal example is that of investments, whereby the investment limitations for associations are the same as those appropriate for life insurance companies as stated in the insurance code. Reporting and examination requirements are also identical for both types of organizations in most states.

Formation and Organization of Plans

Enabling acts delineate the method by which associations may legally commence their activities. A typical provision is that the articles of incorporation be approved by the department of insurance. About half of the states have some type of capital or surplus requirement which must be met before an association will be approved.

It is common to stipulate that all public hospitals and/or licensed physicians in the state or plan area be *eligible* to participate in the plans. Final *approval* of hospitals eligible to cooperate is sometimes left up to a state agency, such as a department of public welfare.

Specifications as to representation on the boards of directors are included in some acts. This is particularly true for medical service corporations, where it is a common requirement that the majority of board members be medical doctors.

Plan Operation

Most enabling acts require prior approval of rates (and contract forms) by the insurance commissioner. The bases on which he is supposed to evaluate these rates are prescribed in only a few of the laws. Some statutes mention "adequacy" of the rate; a lesser number include "reasonableness" as a requirement. Income levels for service benefits under medical-surgical plans are seldom included.

Approximately one half of the laws require the commissioner approve the rate of reimbursement to hospitals. The basis on which a hospital will be paid by a plan is defined only infrequently. A similar number of states also require approval of fee schedules for physicians participating in a Blue Shield plan. The model law contains the approval feature for both reimbursement and fee schedules.

Enabling acts in about twenty states specify limitations and requirements for reserves. Administrative and acquisition expense limits are usually given as a stipulated percentage of premium income.

A certain number of the acts specify qualifications and forbidden practices for enrollment representatives along lines similar to those for insurance agents. These are in the minority, however.

The requirement of annual reports, as well as granting the insurance commissioner the power of plan visitation and triennial examination, is a normal inclusion. Procedures for the dissolution of a plan are also specified.

Services Covered

Most enabling acts for hospital service associations provide that services may be covered if received in any hospital licensed or approved by an appropriate state agency. Many statutes do not allow the Blue Cross plans to cover services received in rest homes.

A considerable number of states have modified their original medical service association laws to include dental and/or osteopathic services. Legislation in seven states specifically limits participation in medical service associations to medical doctors. The laws covering fifty-three Blue Shield plans in the United States allow dentists to cooperate in the arrangement. Forty-three plans have governing statutes which facilitate participation by osteopaths.

The provisions of the laws applicable to medical service organizations, whether in a separate or combination act, are generally more extensive than those which provide for hospital service plans. This stems from the less definitive nature of "medical services" as opposed to "hospital services"; the fact that medical service plans lean more toward indemnity-type provisions than do hospital service plans; and, finally, the insistence of the medical profession in demanding that relationships between plans, physicians, and subscribers be specific. The acts include a section for "definitions" to clarify and establish what is included under various terms and services.

Taxation

The final, and all-important, provision in the majority of enabling statutes is classification of the plans as charitable and benevolent institutions and, thereby, exempt from taxation on either plan income or assets.

ENABLING LEGISLATION SUMMARY

The obvious feature inherent in enabling acts is that hospital and medical service associations are not considered the same type of entity as insurance companies offering protection against similar hazards. The very nature of the enactments suggests that there is a social aura about these plans which does not exist in the milieu in which so-called "commercial" coverages are purveyed. If this is true, the acts are a very important element in the expansion of a social system. If it is incorrect, the acts provide an unfair competitive bulwark which should be removed if the principles of a private-enterprise economy are to be supported. The fact that associations are often supervised more closely than are insurance companies indicates that "special" regulatory treatment may be a disadvantage for Blue Cross or Blue Shield. It is strange, therefore, that so little is written or discussed about the justification for these noteworthy statutes. The environment in which they were conceived may have changed considerably in the subsequent thirty years, or the characteristics of the plans may have undergone modification during that period. These characteristics were explored in Chapter V in order to shed light on such possible changes.

Enabling acts are the most extensive and influential set of legislation affecting health insurance in the United States. It is likely that pressures for a governmental health system, as well as competitive forces in the health insurance field, will focus renewed interest in the pros and cons of these unusual laws. If so, the supervisory procedures they foster will also be scrutinized.

chapter VII

SOURCES OF REGULATION[1]

Supervisory controls over Blue Cross and Blue Shield plans emanate from five sources: regulatory statutes, insurance commissioners, the National Association of Insurance Commissioners, courts, and personnel associated with the plans who are in a position to exercise "self-regulation." Laws and individual state commissioners are generally thought to be the most important of these sources. The National Association of Insurance Commissioners is customarily considered in conjunction with commissioners and laws, while the influence wielded by the nation's courts is seldom given much weight. Courts, however, can subordinate all other regulatory elements. Self-regulation, a less formal source—or method—of supervision, implies self-restraint and public mindedness on the part of those associated with Blue Cross and Blue Shield organizations.

STATUTES

The limits imposed upon legislatures regarding the passage of laws concerning insurance and insurance-type activities are set forth in the particular state constitution and the Federal Constitution. These documents contain only general

---

[1] It is difficult to find a one-word description which includes all "types" of regulation for Blue Cross and Blue Shield. "Sources" is probably the most appropriate in that it implies "origins." "Methods" is an alternative term which means "procedures" or "practices." Since some readers may not consider laws or commissioners to be procedures, the word "source" has been used. For the purposes of this study, however, "sources" and "methods" will be interchangeable.

provisions with no reference to insurance; thus, the sections which could be considered applicable are those relating to the protection and service of citizens and their rights.

The history and general features of special laws applicable to hospital and medical service plans were given attention in the previous chapter. The position these legislative decrees occupy in a coordinated system of regulation is self-evident. Laws are the backbone of the organization and operation of Blue Cross and Blue Shield plans. They set the requirements and limits, while insurance commissioners assure compliance with the appropriate statutes. Enabling acts indicate, in concept, the broad manner in which citizens of a state feel associations should be controlled. When old laws are not changed it implies, again in principle, that the citizens endorse existing statutory provisions.

REGULATORY OFFICIALS

Even though enabling acts render insurance codes partially inoperative with regard to Blue Cross and Blue Shield plans, the insurance commissioner and his departmental staff are of extraordinary importance to these associations. The majority of states places the associations under the jurisdiction of the insurance department, and it is the commissioner who adapts and carries out the edicts of enabling statutes.

In most areas the insurance department is on a level with other state divisions. In twelve states, however, the department is a subordinate part of another agency, e.g., the banking or finance divisions.[2] The commissioners in twenty states have responsibilities which include activities other than insurance.[3]

The head of the insurance department may be appointed

---

[2] Dickerson, *Health Insurance* (Homewood, Ill.: Richard D. Irwin, Inc., 1962), p. 437.

[3] Dan M. McGill, *Life Insurance* (Homewood, Ill.: Richard D. Irwin, Inc., 1959), p. 751.

by the governor with confirmation by the state legislature or elected by the populace. He has various titles, depending upon the state; "insurance commissioner" is the most widely utilized. "Superintendent of insurance" is the official name in six states and "director of insurance" in four others.

Regulations of Insurance Commissioners

A commissioner's position is more than that of a perfunctory overseer of Blue Cross and Blue Shield plans. The broad wordings of enabling statutes require interpretation in addition to adaptation. An example of discretionary powers granted a commissioner may be observed in California's enabling act for hospital service organizations:

The commissioner may after notice and hearing promulgate such reasonable rules and regulations, not inconsistent with the provisions of this chapter, relating to the substance, form and issuance of any contract covering the furnishing of hospital services as defined. . . .

Formal acts of a commissioner are set down in either "adjudications" or "rulings" (also called "regulations"). The former relate to individual actions such as the denial of a rate-change request by a Blue Cross plan or the approval of a fee schedule for a Blue Shield plan.[4] Rulings of a commissioner are widespread in nature and, when promulgated, apply to all the activities supervised by the insurance department unless otherwise excluded.[5]

---

[4] " 'Adjudication' means any final order, decree, decision, determination or ruling by an agency affecting personal or property rights, privileges, immunities or obligations of any or all of the parties to the proceeding in which the adjudication is made, but shall not mean any final order, decree, decision, determination or ruling based upon a proceeding before a court, or which involves the seizure or forfeit of property, or which involves paroles or pardons." (Administrative Agency Laws [New] of Pennsylvania: PL 1388 Sec. 2 of June 4, 1945 as amended Sept. 28, 1951, PL 1561, Sec. 1.)

[5] " 'Regulation' means any rule, regulation or order in the nature of a rule or regulation, of general application and future effect, promulgated by an agency under state authority in the administration of any statute administered by or relating to the agency, or prescribing the practice or procedure before the agency." (*Ibid.*)

A commissioner can give "opinions" for unofficial purposes. These amount to statements as to how he views a particular activity or procedure, or how he intends to handle a certain situation if it should arise. Opinions often stand as warnings. The only way to test their validity would be for an association (or a company) to conduct an activity in conflict with the opinion. Then, after the commissioner followed through with his stated action, a court interpretation of the validity of such treatment could be sought.

All these regulatory techniques by a commissioner are, in effect, an extension or interpretation of the state insurance statutes in accordance with his discretionary powers. In this regard, the following quotation is applicable to enabling acts as well as to insurance codes:

> . . . the courts interpret them [statutes] liberally because they regard the strict regulation of insurance companies as socially desirable. Hence, they tend to overturn the commissioner's rulings only in a clear case of action in excess of power or abuse in discretion. Moreover, the commissioner sometimes obtains obedience to decisions or rulings which could be upset if the companies would resort to litigation. Insurers often do not deem it good policy to litigate, because litigation will bring the kind of publicity that injures business. The commissioner's decisions are litigated with decreasing frequency.[6]

The commissioner, unlike a court of law, is not bound by precedents. He is free to disregard the rulings previously made by himself or his predecessors.[7]

Attitudes and Relations of Commissioners and Blue Cross–Blue Shield Plans

Discussions with state supervisory officials, as well as with Blue Cross and Blue Shield officers, indicate an uncertainty on the part of many commissioners as to the exact position of

---

[6] Edwin W. Patterson, *Essentials of Insurance Law* (New York: McGraw-Hill Book Co., Inc., 1957), p. 12.

[7] *Ibid.*, p. 14.

associations in the regulatory framework. Some commissioners consider the hospital and medical service organizations
as just another type of insurance company, and in such case
the regulatory attitudes and procedures are identical to those
applicable to commercial companies, except where legal provisions specifically stipulate to the contrary. Over half of the
commissioners who would commit themselves with a "yes"
or "no" replied in the affirmative to the question, "Do you
feel that Blue Cross and Blue Shield plans are sufficiently
similar to health insurance companies for both types of organizations to be treated alike by regulatory authorities?"

Some of the aspects of this attitude were exemplified in a
speech by the president of the National Association of Insurance Commissioners in 1952 at the Annual Blue Cross
Conference: ". . . You are a quasi-public service unit. You
owe the public an accounting in a systematic manner . . .
your contracts, obligations, and practices should meet the
tests of law which are met by the various insurance companies
performing a similar service." [8]

Other commissioners view plans as social organizations
with philosophies and features entirely distinct from health
insurance carriers. The actual regulatory posture varies
within these two poles, although there is more magnetization
currently from the former.

Blue Cross and Blue Shield plan executives are of almost
unanimous opinion that insurance commissioners apply
stringent, rather than liberal, interpretations to the statutes.
There are also accusations by association officials that the
supervisory attitude, particularly in less prosperous states, is
one of confusion. The commissioner in such jurisdictions is
said to possess neither the staff nor the desire to clarify the
position of associations. Such authorities are characterized as
wanting merely to retain the status quo with as few changes
as possible; thus, a definitive regulatory structure never

---

[8] Mr. Frank Sullivan, commissioner of insurance, State of Kansas.

evolves. The law is usually adequate in such areas, it is reported, but the commissioners often do not foster concrete interpretations of the statutes. Blue Cross and Blue Shield plans in such locales charge that there is no consistency of action within one administration, much less between administrations. Benefit experimentation is one aspect which undoubtedly has suffered at the hands of confused or obstinate regulatory officials.

Insurance commissioners are, in turn, voicing increased concern about the amount of time they and their staffs are required to spend supervising Blue Cross and Blue Shield affairs. The commissioner of one of the largest states told the writer that more than 30 per cent of his time is occupied with activities of these associations. Several state regulatory authorities are considering the implementation of a special division headed by a deputy commissioner whose responsibilities will deal only with the associations.

The Insurance Commissioner . . . is the more important for the mass and complexity and bad drafting of this endless stream of law: he puts meat on the legal skeleton, gives content to general, vague, or even impossible legislative grants of power; because these laws are often silent on his rights and duties he has largely made his office as he has gone along.[9]

The functions of both insurance laws and insurance commissioners are fused, and a segregation of their individual values is highly subjective. If either the laws or the supervisory official and his staff in a particular state are weak, it is likely that the regulation of Blue Cross and Blue Shield will be hampered. If the enabling statute or appropriate laws are inadequate, the commissioner may find himself without sufficient powers. Conversely, as one commissioner remarked, "Laws must be enforced to have value. Even good laws lose effect when weakly enforced."

---

[9] C. A. Kulp, *Casualty Insurance* (3rd ed.; New York: The Ronald Press Co., 1956) , p. 557.

THE NATIONAL ASSOCIATION OF INSURANCE COMMISSIONERS

Unlike many insurance companies, Blue Cross and Blue Shield operations were largely confined within state borders until after World War II. It was not vital up to that time, therefore, that the associations be treated consistently among the states. With the advent of group coverage for national organizations, and the desire of the Blues to provide benefits across state lines, comparability of regulatory treatment for the associations became more necessary. It was natural to expect some guidance along these lines from the National Association of Insurance Commissioners (NAIC), since this group had been a major force in the attempt to synthesize insurance regulation throughout the country.

NAIC membership is composed of the insurance commissioners or the ranking supervisory official for insurance of each state. In addition, senior members of the appropriate agency in each state participate in the activities of the organization.

The Association provides a forum for discussion and solution of problems inherent in our system of regulation. . . . Its service to the system as a bond and balancing influence is of inestimable value. As a result of its activities the policies and practices of the insurance business pass through the purifying cauldron of public scrutiny on a nation-wide basis.[10]

The techniques used by the NAIC, once it has agreed upon the desirability of certain statutes, interpretations, or procedures, are pacific and persuasive. In the case of recommended statutes, each commissioner can take the recommended law to his legislature if he is so inclined. Since many legislatures accept the commissioner's recommendations almost without question, there is a good chance that the state

---

[10] Joseph A. Navarre, "The System of Insurance Regulation in the Several States in the United States," *The Review* (London) (April 18, 1958), pp. 356–57.

will accept the NAIC recommendation if the regulatory official is in favor of it. If he is not, the legislature may not be made aware of the association's suggested action or, if it is, will receive an unfavorable opinion of it.

Group hospitalization associations started to receive active attention from the NAIC in 1938. One of the early actions of the group with reference to nonprofit hospital and medical service associations was to develop the model bill for enabling legislation.[11] As the quotation below reveals, the NAIC was aware of the goals and problems of the associations almost two decades ago.

> The objectives and scope of the non-profit Hospital Service Plans are broad as the hopes and aspirations of the American people. The non-profit Hospital Service Plans exemplify the American spirit of individual initiative in the provisions of an essential service to the entire public. They lend a public service without public compulsion. They combine private leadership with public responsibility. As such, they characterize an aspect in our American way of life seriously needed in these times, and place an opportunity in the hands of regulatory bodies to bring Health Service to the largest possible number of the American people in an economical manner consistent with the American tradition.
>
> There is, however, a need for national uniformity in the regulation of Hospital and Medical Service Plans if they are to serve the greatest public need and if the necessity for Federal control and Legislation is to be avoided.[12]

In 1950 it was recommended that a permanent Subcommittee on Blue Cross–Blue Shield Problems be appointed. By 1956 the increased importance of the Blues, and the problems they encountered and generated, caused the NAIC to replace the subcommittee with the current Nonprofit Hospital and Medical Service Associations Committee. This committee is presently divided into a Subcommittee to Study

---

[11] See Appendix B.

[12] *Proceedings of the National Association of Insurance Commissioners,* 1944, p. 225.

Greater Standardization of Blue Cross and Blue Shield Regulations and a Subcommittee to Study the Problems of Reimbursement Formulae between Hospitals and Service Associations. There are now thirteen standing committees in the NAIC.

As regulatory problems disappear, are solved, or are proven unsolvable, the subcommittees are discharged. An expeditious procedure for disbanding a subcommittee, e.g., when seemingly hopeless conflicts are encountered on the issue for which the group was organized, is to "decide" that the solution is more properly determined by the commissioners and their staffs at the state level. This was the manner of finally handling the maternity benefits and maternity reserves problem which had been the subject of consideration by one of the first subcommittees of the Nonprofit Associations Committee. It is undoubtedly proper and desirable for many issues to find their final resolution at the state level after being thoroughly discussed at the sounding board of the NAIC.[13] This does not foster uniformity, however. The inability, or refusal, of the NAIC to thresh out with greater perseverance the labyrinth of Blue Cross–Blue Shield regulation has relegated the association to a more minor position than is necessary in the minds of many plan executives. Even some regulatory authorities share this attitude. One official remarked, "The NAIC is not very important as far as Blue Cross is concerned because all states do not have the same feeling toward the Blues. Therefore, the NAIC just does not tackle their problems."

The very fact that important issues are often discussed in the NAIC for years before being resolved is considered to foster stability and soundness in insurance and insurance-type legislation. Extensive deliberations are a guard against impulsive action. For example, the major studies of hospital and medical costs and of the associations, themselves, are be-

---

[13] The final determination always takes place technically at the state level, inasmuch as the NAIC has no powers other than persuasion over regulatory authorities or state legislatures.

ing closely watched by the NAIC in such states as Maryland, Massachusetts, Michigan, New Jersey, New York, Ohio, and Pennsylvania. After certain studies are completed, the NAIC committee will probably discuss and consider with more intensity such issues as contingency reserves and experience rating. The deliberations will then be backed by statistics the NAIC has neither staff nor funds to procure for itself.

Numerous state regulatory officials have indicated to the writer that they "wait for the NAIC" to establish a suggested course of action on pertinent issues. This is a cogent reason for the most expeditious action commensurate with regulatory soundness on the part of the NAIC. It also requires suggested policy, or a *statement that the organization does not intend to establish a policy at the particular time,* on all important regulatory situations of Blue Cross and Blue Shield as they arise. Otherwise, some states will wait for the millennium before acting on their own.

In spite of these discordant notes, at least a few regulatory officials feel that the NAIC can emerge as an effective body in the regulation of the associations. The organization certainly will have an opportunity to show its capabilities after the widely publicized state studies are completed.

COURTS

Courts serve more as a potential source of regulation than as a present element of control. They have appeared as a force in the regulation of Blue Cross and Blue Shield in but few instances. As a result, the ability of these judicial bodies to make alterations in regulatory procedures is seldom considered.

Courts can become involved in the regulation of associations in several respects. First, a subscriber, or subscriber group, can take a plan and its management to court over contract provisions. Second, a nonsubscriber group could sue an association, and a court decision might be required. An example of this would be litigation over Blue Cross' reimbursement schedules for hospitals and Blue Shield's fee schedules for physicians. In all legal determinations of this type the regulatory authority is not directly involved. Third, a plan, or party concerned with plan operation, could seek court action against a supervisory official. In most such cases the dispute relates to an enabling act provision or an insurance commissioner's interpretation of powers granted under the law. Fourth, the regulatory official may take a plan into court to seek compliance with legislative provisions or administrative decrees.[14] (It is not uncommon to find stipulations in enabling acts which outline the penalties to be assessed by a court in case the statute is violated.)

Courts now serve mainly as a place for appeal from directives of regulatory authorities. The burden of proof rests with the nongovernmental litigant and only a severe breach of implied authority on the part of a commissioner would cause a court to set aside his actions. One court decision with reference to the Administrative Agency Laws of Pennsylvania stipulated: "Where an administrative agency has acted upon a matter properly before it, the courts will not reverse, except where there is a manifest and flagrant abuse of discretion."[15] A perusal of enabling acts in Pennsylvania indicates that the broad powers granted thereunder limit the opportunities for holding a matter not to be "properly before" the commissioner. This typifies the situation in a majority of the other states. Thus, court "law" has been largely subordinated to statutory and administrative law for Blue Cross and Blue Shield plans.

The opportunity for recourse to the courts should not be completely disregarded, however. Most enabling statutes provide specifically for a court review of the commissioner's decisions. The enabling act in New York specifies, for example, that ". . . all official orders of the superintendent of insurance and all final orders or decisions of the commissioner of

---

[14] The attorney general of a state may be the plaintiff, rather than the insurance commissioner.

[15] *Sanitary Water Bd.* v. *Eckert,* 71 Dauph. 288, 1959.

social welfare made under the provision shall be subject to judicial review. . . .''

In this manner the laws give assurance that the powers of supervisory officials will not become dictatorial.

SELF-REGULATION

The components of self-regulation are more difficult to isolate than those of other sources of regulation. This informal, nongovernmental type of supervision can be imposed by any one of several parties associated with Blue Cross and Blue Shield. Self-regulation can take place through activities of the operating heads and managements of plans, their boards of directors, national organizations of the plans—the Blue Cross Association and the National Association of Blue Shield Plans—and such other bodies as might have controls over the plans, as for example the American Hospital Association and the American Medical Association.

The principles embodied in self-regulation are somewhat foreign to the business attitudes which prevail in the United States.[16] Competition and the desire for bigness on the part of organizations have, on occasion, clashed with business ethics. At times the maturity and acumen to exercise self-control have been lacking. This has fostered the attitude that if there is to be regulation it will be through a government agency, and a business organization has only to keep out of the bad graces of the supervisory body. Such a situation has not encouraged the use or support of self-regulatory methods, inasmuch as *knowledge* of what is in the public's best interest and a *desire* to serve this interest are imperative prerequisities for true self-regulation.

Anti-trust laws have also served as a detriment to self-regulation in the United States. The possible intervention of

---

[16] In Europe self-regulation is a tool utilized extensively and effectively. There, as in this country, business survival and prosperity are paramount. Yet there is a recognition within the insurance business abroad that individual company restraint and governing by a business association are necessary adjuncts to the success of each insurance organization.

the federal government in insurance regulation has contributed to the hesitancy of insurers to become involved in cooperative activities which do not have governmental supervision. Governmental action has been successful, for instance, in attempts to dissolve the nonregulated efforts of insurers in cooperative rate determination and acquisition cost controls.

Self-regulation is often of particular importance when the social insurance field is encountered. The broad area of health insurance is often considered as a *social-type* insurance, while Blue Cross and Blue Shield have been looked upon by some insurance commissioners as being purely *social* insurance groups. As a matter of fact, even insurance companies did not offer stiff opposition to enabling legislation when it was first developed because plans were not operating in what was then considered an insurance area. Hospital insurance was not offered by insurance companies nor was hospitalization widely considered an insurable hazard. In this social milieu self-regulation was an important aspect in the supervisory treatment of the associations. These organizations, it was said, were not motivated by the competitive drives which stimulated insurance companies. Blue Cross (and Blue Shield) were serving the broad community interest; thus, they were capable of regulating at least some of their own activities without the ever-watchful eye of an insurance commissioner.

Self-Regulation Through Plan Executives[17]

All plan executives are presumed to possess integrity. Nevertheless, the objectivity necessary for self-regulation goes beyond this virtue. Even if association managers could set aside personal and professional interests and work only for the community interest, it is doubtful if many would want to shoulder alone the responsibilities associated with self-

---

[17] This category considers only those executives who are full-time employees of an association. The unqualified terms "executive," "plan manager," or "association executive" refer to operating heads of Blue Cross and Blue Shield plans.

regulation. Furthermore, citizens would seldom be willing to cede to one individual, or management team, the sole power to determine what was proper regarding hospital and medical care coverages in the plan area.

Certainly the operating head of a Blue Cross or Blue Shield plan can be an important factor in supervising the association along community-interest lines. His position places him in touch with the community and the needs of its citizens. The executive meets the knowledge requisite in most cases more closely than does any individual board member. The executive's objectivity is less certain, but it need not be questioned if he is working with a "qualified" board. Thus, while it is not probable that an executive director can achieve self-regulation alone, he can assist most importantly therein.

Self-Regulation Through Boards of Directors

As has been mentioned, the requirements for self-regulation rest upon *knowledge* and *desire*. It has been more difficult than might be expected to obtain board members who possess these characteristics. "Ability" implies that a director will take the time to be familiar with association problems and that he can use such knowledge in guiding the organization. By the mere fact that board members of corporations organized for profit generally accept compensation for serving, they are encouraged to bring a certain amount of knowledge to meetings and to take the time prior thereto to become informed. Blue Cross board members do not receive compensation for their services, and the same is generally true for Blue Shield. This has always been a principle by which Blue Cross has abided since its inception and it is incorporated into the approval program. The membership standards for Blue Shield allow board members to be compensated on a "loss-of-time" basis. Usually, however, no compensation is granted. Thus, nonfinancial considerations are the primary motivators for Blue Cross and Blue Shield directors. The major pressures of this sort are moral; if a man agrees to serve as a director, he indirectly commits himself to keep current with organizational matters. It requires unusual dedication, however, for an individual in any business or profession to take time from his ordinary endeavors to remain informed about Blue Cross and Blue Shield affairs. Then, too, self-regulation at the board level is impossible if members acquiesce to the opinions of a plan executive without true board deliberation.

If it is assumed that all board members are dedicated, the further question arises as to what backgrounds are necessary to serve the policy-making function of a director. It is obvious that many of those on a board need to be well-grounded in business principles and procedures, with particular emphasis on financial operations. Others must be familiar with the medical care field. At least one or more doctors should be on Blue Cross governing boards and certainly a greater number and proportion on Blue Shield boards.

The *desire* [18] requirement for self-regulation may be phrased as a question. Are any of those serving on the board in such a position that they cannot divorce self-concern from public interest? In other words, are all members capable of complete objectivity without being influenced by personal or associational interests?

The ability of members to be objective is questionable when they stand to benefit personally from actions taken by the board. The question also exists if an organization they represent could gain by board decisions. Both doctors and hospital representatives are in these positions. Hospital trustees, unlike hospital administrators, generally do not have any personal considerations at stake in board actions. Some observers doubt, however, whether trustees can avoid being influenced by what is best for the hospital when several choices are faced by a board.

---

[18] "Desire" may be an unfortunate word choice. Some readers may infer that a lack of desire means a negative attitude by those who do not possess this "desire." Lack of desire can mean something quite different. Absence of motivation can signify *no affirmative* attitude. Here a position of apathy or nondecision would characterize a lack of desire to serve the public interest, without such lack being negative or *against* the public interest.

Even if some directors have biases, this does not preclude self-regulation on the part of a board as long as majority rules apply and a majority present do have the ability and objectivity discussed above. The situation is altered, though, if doctors dominate Blue Shield boards and hospital administrators (and possibly hospital trustees) are in the majority on Blue Cross boards. The self-interests of these individuals could place, at least subconsciously, a haze over their conception of what is in the public interest. The board's ability to self-regulate would be impaired thereby. This is not to say, at this stage, that the vendors of plans' services should not control the boards of directors. The point is that if they do have such a position effective self-regulation by the board of directors cannot be anticipated.

Self-Regulation Through Associations

Control can be exercised by organizations to which plans belong or to which they must account. Self-regulation of this type is at the national level. Such supervision for Blue Cross plans could come from the Blue Cross Association and the American Hospital Association. Potential controls over Blue Shield organizations could be exercised by the National Association of Blue Shield Plans and, to a lesser extent, the American Medical Association. Regulation by national associations still amounts to self-regulation because the plans themselves make up the Blue Cross Association and the National Association of Blue Shield Plans. Blue Cross plans are Regular Type IV members of the American Hospital Association and there is reciprocal membership on the boards of directors of AHA and BCA.[19] There is also reciprocal representation on the governing boards of AMA and NABSP (National Association of Blue Shield Plans) .[20]

The most powerful controls currently exercised over Blue Cross and Blue Shield plans by national associations regard the approval programs. The American Hospital Associa-

[19] See page 59.
[20] See page 72.

tion now supervises the Blue Cross approval program,[21] while satisfaction of similar standards by Blue Shield organizations must be established with the National Association of Blue Shield Plans.[22] These organizations are more important presently as elements of self-regulation than either the Blue Cross Association or the American Medical Association.

It is through approval programs that associations become entitled to use the Blue Cross or Blue Shield emblems. Utilization of such signs of recognition is very important inasmuch as it ties a plan in with the publicity, reputation, and social attitudes which attend the Blues. A detached association has much more selling to do than one which belongs.

The approval programs represent a source of supervision and control which, in some respects, is more stringent than the regulation imposed by state agencies. The element of reserves provides major support for this statement. Less than half of the states mention reserves in their enabling acts. Only nineteen statutes are known to have definite reserve requirements for Blue Cross, while twenty do so for Blue Shield. No more than a handful of state regulatory officials have indicated what the extent of these finalcial stabilizers should be. Even then, the requirements are not as exacting, generally, as are those established by AHA and NABSP. Approval programs stipulate that before a plan may use either the Blue Cross or Blue Shield emblem its reserves must be at a specific level, or contributions to reserves must be made at a prescribed rate. Organizations which do not qualify under either of these requirements must prove to those conducting the approval programs that their financial policies are sound.[23]

The AHA requirement that one third of the governing boards for Blue Cross plans be composed of public representatives is also a more definite stipulation than those imposed by most state laws or authorities. In addition, Blue

Cross plans must cover, on behalf of afflicted subscribers who have the most widely held certificate, "an average of not less than 75 per cent of the total amount billed for usual and customary hospital services." The claim expenses of a Blue Shield plan may not be less than 75 per cent of earned subscription income. No state statutes are known to have benefit requirements of this type.

Regarding such elements as rates and specific benefits, the national associations are relatively unimportant sources of regulation.

The ability requirement as set forth for the existence of self-regulation can possibly be presumed to exist in these national organizations, although many question it on the part of AMA and AHA. Political entanglements and slowness of action could impair the ability of these two important and honorable national associations to do a *complete* job of supervising Blue Cross and Blue Shield plans, if such authority were granted to them. Here, too, it is dubious if either body would want to have sole authority over plans. Their judgment would always be subject to question, if only because of the nature of their memberships. It is difficult to evaluate the objectivity of these national associations. The American Medical Association and the American Hospital Association are the most vulnerable on this point, simply because they are the dominant national bodies representing the purveyors of services covered by Blue Cross and Blue Shield plans. Many of those queried in connection with this book doubt whether these groups can act in the best interest of the public without being influenced by what is best for doctors or hospitals. The two "bests"—for the public and for doctors or hospitals—may, of course, be identical in some instances.

Compared to other national organizations, the capacity and desire of the Blue Cross Association and the National Association of Blue Shield Plans to serve the public interest objectively are less subject to question. There would be even less suspicion as to whether objectivity could exist if the BCA was not as closely associated with the AHA. It is apparent on the Blue Shield side that the NABSP does not serve the AMA.

Summary of Self-Regulation

As might be expected, more than half of the plan operating heads who were visited in connection with the research for this study felt that self-regulation should and could be the major source of regulation. Only three insurance commissioners supported this opinion. One regulatory authority observed that, "Self-regulation is where regulation starts. Public officials can supervise insurance activities only so far." Among other comments from officials were the statements that, "Self-regulation is the best method for handling problems peculiar to plans, but which do not greatly affect the public interest," and, "When a plan is of high caliber, self-regulation can be of help, although it is not the final answer." An attitude which probably most typifies that of supervisory officials is that all aspects of control over the associations cannot be left to self-regulation. There must be underlying laws and an enlightened administration of them as well.

A small number of executives think that self-regulation cannot operate through national associations because they are governed by too much politics. Comments were also made that, "Who you are and the size of your association determine the treatment to be received from the national organizations." The dearth of such statements on the part of small associations seems to indicate that this situation is not of major importance at the present time. It is true that the national bodies have discretionary powers in their treatment of Blue Cross and Blue Shield plans, such as in the approval requirements. The approval programs appear to be administered, however, with very little prejudice and with a sincere desire to assist any plan experiencing difficulties.

The assertion was made by a limited number of executive directors that the Blue Cross Association and the American Hospital Association have undertaken more self-supervising activities than has the Blue Shield system. One alleged reason for this was that fewer parties are at interest in Blue Cross, i.e., fewer hospitals than doctors, so control is not as difficult. Also, the negative attitude which doctors in general have toward any regulation which could affect their profession is said to hamper self-supervision in Blue Shield. These influencing factors have undoubtedly been the reasons that more regulatory-type supervision has come from Blue Cross boards than from Blue Shield boards.

The lack of appropriations and personnel for state insurance departments may give future support to self-regulatory procedures in some, if not many, states. At the same time, the general trend of opinion has been that the national associations will assume the most prominence among the possible sources of self-regulation, unless board representations are changed so that vendors of plans' services are not in control. The need for uniformity in some aspects of regulation is also likely to give increased importance to national associations, particularly if state laws and regulatory officials do not foster comparable supervision of Blue Cross and Blue Shield.

chapter VIII

FORMATION AND OPERATIONS

FORMATION AND ORGANIZATION OF PLANS

Nonprofit hospital and medical service association laws are so worded that many of the requirements apply at the formation stage of the organizations and on a continuing basis thereafter. This section is concerned with some of the broad requisites which must be met before an association may be admitted to operation in individual states. Formation requirements of a continuing nature and of particular importance also will be treated in parts of this and subsequent chapters. Among those so included are: composition of boards of directors, requirements for enrollment representatives, certificate provisions and filings, financial and reporting obligations, and rates.

Hospital Participation in Blue Cross Plans

The regulatory stipulations for Blue Cross plans usually indicate which classes of hospitals are eligible to contract with associations; some laws specify the percentage of hospitals (with a certain proportion of hospital beds in the area) which must agree to provide services for an organization before it may commence operation. Among the types of hospitals whose eligibility must be ascertained are state institutions, county and municipal hospitals, and proprietary organizations which offer hospital care. Proprietary hospitals are subject to the most searching inquiry. In earlier years the lack of hospitals maintained by governments encouraged the growth of these as profit enterprises. As medical

130

care became more and more of a social issue, disapproving glances were cast upon any institution which profited from the physical misfortunes of individuals. The quality of medical care available from proprietary hospitals has also been a subject of some concern.

Hospital service is defined in the New York enabling act to include hospitalization in:

> . . . a hospital which is maintained by the state or any of its political subdivisions, or maintained by a corporation organized for hospital purposes under the law of this state, or such other hospitals as shall be designated by the state department of social welfare, and hospitals of other states subject to the supervision of such other state, or convalescent care provided by any convalescent institution. A hospital service corporation may also provide reimbursement for expenses incurred outside of the hospital for continued care and treatment following the subscriber's discharge from the hospital, for nursing service . . . drugs, medicines, supplies, and any other services which have been available in the hospital (excluding physicians' services, whether or not provided through a hospital) . A hospital service corporation may also furnish reimbursement for ambulance service expenses.

An interesting aspect of this provision is that it requires approval of New York's Department of Social Welfare for proprietary hospitals but not for other medical care institutions.

The designation of eligible hospitals and the scope of hospital service as outlined in the New York statute are probably typical of such provisions in most acts, with the exception of the allowance for outpatient treatment and convalescent care. Coverage of this type is not generally mentioned in enabling legislation. It is not uncommon for hospital eligibility to be determined by some state agency other than the insurance department.

Most enabling acts restrict Blue Cross plans from contracting with hospitals outside of the state in which the association is operating. Subscribers, however, may have coverage for treatment in hospitals in other states. This allowance facilitates operation of the Inter-Plan Service Benefit Bank.

The purpose underlying a hospital eligibility requirement is the protection of the citizens of a state against inferior medical care. Since the personnel of hospital service associations are not necessarily qualified to evaluate hospital conditions or standards of treatment, the associations could stimulate the use of services from institutions with poor facilities and methods. The states do not have the same concern regarding the hospitals used by policyholders of insurance companies. It is felt that these insureds have a greater freedom in selecting a hospital, inasmuch as insurance policies usually indemnify (up to specified limits) for expenses incurred in any hospital which is "operating legally." The use of member hospitals exclusively is encouraged on the part of Blue Cross subscribers, as it is in these institutions that they receive full service benefits. Regulatory authorities seem to think it is important, therefore, to control the institutions which will be eligible to contract with an association.

Hospitals do not want to become subordinate to a hospital service association, nor do they, in general, want an association to contract with only a limited number of institutions. If Blue Cross plans were to have just a few large hospitals as contracting institutions, smaller hospitals might suffer a decline in their occupancy rate. For this reason hospitals have pressed for statutory provisions which allow a free choice of hospitals by subscribers and policyholders. The institutions have also sought to have legislation passed which would stipulate a minimum number or percentage of hospitals which must cooperate with a Blue Cross plan before it will be allowed to operate. A provision of this type would specify that institutions with a certain percentage of hospital beds must contract with an association before it may enroll subscribers in an area. Illinois was one of the few states to enact this, or any other, type of hospital-participation requirement. The Illinois provision was declared unconstitutional in 1959. The litigated section of the statute had stated:

No corporation which is subject to the provisions of this Act shall solicit, or issue a contract to, any subscriber in any County of this State unless there are at the time in full force and effect contracts . . . between said corporation and hospitals which operate not less than thirty per cent (30%) of the total number of general hospital beds which normally serve the residents of said County.

The director of insurance for Illinois ascertained that the above provision had not been met in thirty-two counties by the Illinois Hospital Service, Inc. (at Rockford, Illinois). He thereupon prohibited the association from operating in those areas. Illinois Hospital Service took the matter to court for a review of the director's decision. The section was held to be unconstitutional by the circuit court, and the director appealed the decision. The circuit court's ruling was upheld.[1]

The appellate court saw no public purpose served by the hospital-participation requirement. The court considered that the provision, in effect, gave hospitals control over the economic life of Blue Cross plans. Inasmuch as the director of insurance had broad supervisory powers over associations by means of the enabling act, there was no reason for hospitals to have additional influence or authority over such operations. The Circuit Court had stated prior to the appeal:

. . . although section 14 gives hospitals ultimate power over hospital service plans, it specifies no standards upon the basis of which that power is to be exercised. So far as the statute is concerned, a single hospital or a group of hospitals may be motivated by caprice or by self-interest. A decision that puts a hospital service plan out of business is not required to be related in any way to the interests of subscribers to hospital service plans, whose in-

---

[1] Several events occurred prior to the court dispute. The two Blue Cross plans in Illinois, operating out of Chicago and Rockford, were—and still are—competing for subscribers. (The Rockford organization is not a currently approved Blue Cross plan.) The Illinois Health Association called the attention of hospitals to the litigated provision, and it was suggested that hospitals contract with only one Blue Cross plan. Thereupon many hospitals did not renew their contracts with the Rockford association. As a result the plan could not meet the 30 per cent requirement of bed capacity in many counties.

terests may—or may not—coincide with those of the hospitals.

If dominion over the economic life of one individual or enterprise is to be given to another, some justification must exist and the conditions upon which control is to be exercised must be stated with at least that degree of precision which is required when comparable authority is given to a public official.[2]

The most stringent requirements concerning hospital participation come from the AHA approval standards. They stipulate that a Blue Cross plan "shall maintain written agreements with *a majority of the hospitals* qualified and equipped to provide the services in the plan's subscriber certificate containing *a majority of the bed capacity* in its enrollment area. . . ."

Participation by Professions in Blue Shield Plans

Enabling acts for medical service associations generally require that participation be open to all duly licensed physicians in the association's area of operation. Some statutes go beyond this and allow, or require, Blue Shield plans to admit dentists, osteopaths, and/or podiatrists in the association arrangement. Dentists actually cooperate in over half of the Blue Shield plans. State statutes are so worded that forty-three of the medical service associations are allowed to include benefits for services rendered by osteopaths. Legislation in the following states appears to limit participation in Blue Shield plans to medical doctors: Alabama, Georgia, Maryland, Minnesota, North Dakota, South Dakota, and Utah.

It should be noted that when statutes require the inclusion of services of dentists and other professions the associations do not have to cover *all* treatments rendered by such individuals. Blue Shield plans themselves determine what benefit structures and coverages they desire to offer. The laws which allow for participation by other than medical doctors merely specify that when an association's benefit

---

[2] *Ill. Hospital Service, Inc., Appellee,* v. *Joseph S. Gerber, Director of Insurance, Appellant,* Sept. 1959.

structure includes treatments which can legally be given by other professions, then individuals from those professions must be allowed to work with the Blue Shield plan.

Twelve of the states which cooperated in the research on which this book is based have legal requirements that a certain portion of physicians must agree to participate in a medical service plan before it may operate in an area. Illinois is the only one of the four largest states with this type of statutory provision. The Illinois act specifies:

> In the county or counties in which a corporation proposes to operate, a majority of the licensed physicians residing in and active in private practice therein [must] have agreed to become participating physicians and to render the medical services for which the corporation agrees to pay.

In addition, the National Association of Blue Shield Plans stipulates that if a plan uses physicians' agreements, no fewer than 51 per cent of the eligible doctors in the plan area must participate. In order to be "approved" by the NABSP, each Blue Shield plan must also have the approval of the local county medical society in each area where it intends to operate. Failure to have endorsement by the local medical profession will deprive an association of the use of the Blue Shield emblem. This stipulation is considered the primary component of the approval program for Blue Shield. The National Association does not grant itself any discretionary or subjective means to side-step the disapproval of an association which does not have the support of the county medical societies.

Capital and Surplus Requirements

Early supporters of the nonprofit hospital and medical service associations' movement endorsed enabling legislation for several reasons. One of the foremost considerations was to avoid the capital and surplus requirements with which associations would have had to comply if they had been organized under the laws for insurance companies. It was noted in a previous chapter that a large number of associations began operation with only meager financial backing. Enabling statutes have generally steered clear of mentioning financial requirements necessary for Blue Cross and Blue Shield plans at their formation.

Among those states whose supervisory authorities submitted information for this study, less than half stipulate that an association must meet any capital requirements before it may commence operation. Most of the remainder tie capital needs into the reserve requisites. Only three—Louisiana, New Mexico, and Ohio—set initial capital limits above $25,000.[3]

California, like a few other areas, has a capital requirement in the nature of a reserve fund which varies from $10,000 to $20,000, depending upon the number of subscribers. Illinois is the only other state among the major four which has a capital requirement. Medical service corporations in Illinois must have "working capital . . . sufficient to carry on acquisition costs and operating expenses for a reasonable period of time from the issuance of this charter . . . [and] not less than $5,000."

Supervisory officials in some jurisdictions are granted authority by the enabling statutes to stipulate what capital an association must have before it is permitted to accept subscribers. Actually, the question of initial capital needs relates to the more basic and long-run issue of financial reserves. For example, lack of initial capital on the part of plans has been justified by the fact that hospitals and doctors often guarantee to provide services to subscribers for the remainder of a contract period even though associations do not have the funds with which to pay for such services. The same logic is applicable to the reserve issue, and it will be discussed thereunder.

If reserve requirements are properly legislated and ad-

---

[3] New Mexico has a $100,000 capital requirement, while Louisiana stipulates that there be $100,000 for capital and $100,000 for surplus. Ohio has a $100,000 capital requirement for Blue Shield plans.

ministered, it does not seem necessary to have capital stipulations in enabling acts. The varying circumstances under which associations are organized argue against capital limits in the laws themselves, although a commissioner should be given the discretionary power to determine that an association has adequate resources to meet the contingencies it will encounter when it begins to operate. These contingencies *are* relatively higher for a new association than for an established organization. Uncertainties are most adequately guarded against by reserve provisions and a supervisory official who can evaluate the hazards which will confront an individual association. Statutory capital requirements would have to treat all organizations the same. Divergent circumstances also include the extensiveness of benefits offered and the nature of medical care costs in an area. In addition, legislated capital stipulations cannot properly consider changing economic conditions. Financial stability must depend upon the adequacy of reserves and not upon dollar limits established by enabling acts as capital requirements.

Territorial Limits

Most state laws do not impose any territorial limitations upon hospital and medical service associations other than requiring that they operate within the boundaries of the state. New York has a more stringent requirement in that it allows such an organization to operate in no more than eighteen counties.

Prohibition against interstate operations is relaxed to allow Blue Cross and Blue Shield plans to cooperate with other associations in covering national groups, and to provide service, or indemnity, to a subscriber who receives medical care outside the state limits or when a nonstate resident obtains treatment within the state. New York is explicit in stating that no foreign nor alien hospital or medical service plan will be allowed to do business in the state for any other reasons. This is the intent of most acts, although few of them state it so directly. (A foreign plan refers to one domiciled in any other state, while an alien organization is one head-quartered outside this country.)

Permits and Licenses for Plans

The jurisdiction of insurance commissioners is established at the time of plan formation through two types of enabling act provisions. One is the condition that all associations offering nonprofit hospital service or medical indemnity must be organized under the enabling legislation and be subject to the supervision of the insurance department. Exemption from other insurance laws is customarily accorded at the same time. This general type of provision often includes a statement similar to that in the Pennsylvania statute:

A nonprofit medical service corporation shall be subject to regulation and supervision by the Department of Health and the Department of Insurance, as provided by this act. It shall not be subject to the laws of this state now in force relating to insurance and corporations engaged in the business of insurance, unless such law specifically and in exact terms applies to such nonprofit medical . . . corporations.[4]

The second manner in which a commissioner's supervision is invoked at the formation stage is through the specification that a permit and/or a license be obtained from him before an association may conduct any business. In order to procure this permit organizations must meet various requirements, most of which have already been described.

Legislation concerning permit and licensing requirements in New York is more extensive than that of many states. New York associations must obtain a permit from the superintendent before they may solicit subscribers. The application

---

[4] New York's enabling act is worded somewhat the reverse of those in most states, but it accomplishes the same purpose: ". . . except as otherwise provided and except as the content otherwise requires, every such corporation shall be *subject to all other requirements* of this chapter [the insurance code] *made applicable to insurance companies generally,* and to the rules and regulations of the Superintendent *except* insofar as said laws, rules and regulations may be inconsistent with other provisions of this act." (Italics added.)

for a permit must include a description of the territory covered and services to be rendered, as well as a $1,000 bond. Apparently the bond is to insure that an organization intends to go through with its arrangements for operation, although the insignificance of the amount seems to negate its usefulness. Blue Cross and Blue Shield plans in the state must also acquire a license to do business from the superintendent. Among the requirements for licensing is a listing of the number of subscribers from whom subscriptions for one sixth of the full coverage payment have been received. The total of these funds must amount to at least $1,800.

Some states require associations to procure a corporate charter from the secretary of state; but before that official can issue the document, the commissioner of insurance must approve the articles of incorporation. California and Illinois, for example, have procedures similar to this for the formation of hospital service associations.

BOARDS OF DIRECTORS

The composition of the governing boards of Blue Cross and Blue Shield plans constitutes an explosive issue. While this would appear an internal problem, it has external implications which center on the philosophical position of hospital and medical service corporations. If associations are social-type organizations, combining *broad* community interests and at least a partial solution to a social problem, it seems reasonable to expect that society's representatives would have a prominent position on boards of directors. If associations, in spite of their social nature, have objectives similar to those of insurance companies, boards of directors need not include a preponderance of public representatives. The specific problem faced by Blue Cross–Blue Shield plans and regulatory authorities is what percentage of the governing board should be lay members. (A lay representative is one who does not come from a hospital or medical group). Subordinate issues concern the eligibility requirements for public representatives and how such individuals should be selected.

Board Requirements Established by the Sources of Regulation

Legal Stipulations. Twenty of the forty-four states cooperating in this study have no provisions in their laws which dictate the composition of boards of directors; six states have either no associations within their area or no enabling acts. The remaining eighteen states have provisions ranging from the requirement that the vendors of association services and the public must both be represented on the board, to the condition that a majority of the governing body be representatives of hopsitals in the case of Blue Cross or doctors in the case of Blue Shield.[5]

Blue Cross. Legislation in ten states which submitted information require public representation on Blue Cross boards.[6] Enactments in Georgia, North Dakota, Ohio, and Rhode Island require that hospital representatives be in the majority on governing boards. Two thirds of a board's membership in California and one half of a board in Illinois must be made up of doctors and hospital representatives. Kansas, Nebraska, and New Mexico require an equal proportion between medical, hospital, and public representatives. New York and Pennsylvania are among the states which do not mention board composition for hospital service corporations.

Blue Shield. Doctors must comprise more than 50 per cent of the Blue Shield boards in the following states: Florida, Georgia, Illinois, Iowa, Massachusetts, North Dakota, Pennsylvania, and Rhode Island. Nine states require public

---

[5] The following states have some type of stipulation for the boards of directors of both hospital and medical service associations: Arizona, Arkansas, Connecticut, Florida, Georgia, Illinois, Iowa, Kansas, Massachusetts, Michigan, North Dakota, Oklahoma and Rhode Island. In addition, California, Nebraska, New Mexico, Ohio, and Wisconsin have requirements which apply only to hospital service organizations.

[6] Arizona, Arkansas, Connecticut, Florida, Kansas, Massachusetts, Michigan, Nebraska, New Mexico, and Oklahoma.

representation on the boards of directors for medical service corporations.[7]

Association Requirements. The approval program administered by the American Hospital Association dictates that a Blue Cross governing board be made up of one-third representation from hospitals and one-third representation from the general public. The AHA has defined a public representative as "one who represents the public in general and is not a practicing physician or an employee or trustee of a contracting hospital." Prior to 1958, the definition accommodated anyone so designated by an association's governing board. The American Hospital Association recognized that boards cannot be changed immediately; an association is not disapproved automatically, therefore, if it fails to meet the one-third requirement for public representation. This makes the determination subjective rather than objective, although the apparent intent is for the requirement to become fixed after a reasonable number of years. A hospital service association which does not have one third of its board as representatives of the public, currently, must show that action is being taken to comply with the stipulation for lay members.

Membership standards of the National Association of Blue Shield Plans do not delineate the groups eligible for membership on boards of directors. These rules do ordain, however, that an association must be approved by the medical societies of the counties in which it operates. This gives assurance that the board membership will be amenable to the desires of the medical profession.

Stipulations in Bylaws of Plans. The bylaws of individual Blue Cross and Blue Shield plans usually include detailed provisions as to the representatives who must be on governing boards, how they are to be chosen, and how long they may serve. These bylaws, though, must meet statutory requirements and be approved by commissioners. Then, too,

---

[7] Arizona, Arkansas, Connecticut, Florida, Illinois, Kansas, Massachusetts, Michigan, and Oklahoma.

they must not conflict with the stipulations set forth by the agencies administering their respective approval programs. Thus, the requirements established by individual associations are subordinate to, and merely an extension of, those set forth by the states and national organizations.

Present Memberships on Boards of Directors

Blue Cross Governing Boards. Statistics on the structure of boards of directors were accumulated by the Blue Cross Commission in 1959 and the Blue Cross Association in 1962. In the early study members were categorized according to whether they represented hospitals, the medical profession or the public. Table 8–1 reveals the results of the survey. There was a total of 1,837 board members for the seventy-nine Blue Cross plans at that time, or an arithmetic average of about twenty-three for each association. The range was from 9 to 122. Of the total membership on the Blue Cross boards, 926, or approximately 50 per cent, were hospital representatives. The study made no differentiation between hospital administrators and hospital trustees. Public representatives accounted for 32 per cent of the total, and 17.6 per cent came from the medical profession. An appraisal of these statistics by a prominent insurance commissioner led him to conclude that twenty-nine of the seventy-nine plans had an undue proportion of hospital representatives. He considered hospital representation excessive whenever it comprised more than 50 per cent of a board's membership. Table 8–1 indicates the proportion of board membership held by public representatives was considerably larger in 1962 than in 1959. The statistics reflect an attitude maintained by a substantial number of those interested in Blue Cross affairs—namely, that hospital representation should be decreased and public representatives given a larger voice.

Blue Shield Governing Boards. The National Association of Blue Shield Plans investigated the internal composition of governing boards for their member organizations in

TABLE 8–1

COMPOSITION OF BLUE CROSS GOVERNING BOARDS
IN THE UNITED STATES, 1959 AND 1962

	1959		1962	
Type of Representatives	*Total Members*	*Percentage*	*Total Members*	*Percentage*
Hospital: administrators			441	23.8
and trustees	926	50.4	217	11.6
Medical	323	17.6	329	17.7
Public	588	32.0	869	46.8
Total directors—				
79 plans	1,837	100.0	1,856	99.9*

* Less than 100.0 per cent because of rounding of numbers.
Source: Blue Cross Commission and Blue Cross Association.

TABLE 8–2

COMPOSITION OF BLUE SHIELD GOVERNING BOARDS
IN THE UNITED STATES, AUGUST 1, 1960

Type of Representatives	*Total Members*		*Percentage*
Hospital administrator	67 }	91	6.8
Hospital trustee	24		
Public—general	309 }		
Public—farm	19 }	350	26.3
Public—labor	22		
Medical	889 }	889	66.9
Total directors, 68 plans	1,330	1,330	99.0

Source: National Association of Blue Shield Plans.

late 1960. A summary of the information gathered may be seen in Table 8–2. The range of board memberships was from five to fifty-eight, with an arithmetic mean of nineteen and one-half members. Of a total membership of 1,330 on the boards, 66.8 per cent were medical representatives. Physicians were in the majority in fifty-seven out of sixty-eight Blue Shield plans in the United States. Public representation accounted for 26.3 per cent of board membership, while 6.8 per cent were hospital representatives.

Six Blue Shield plans had no public representation, and

laymen accounted for less than 10 per cent of the board memberships of three other plans. Twenty-one associations had between 10 and 25 per cent of their board membership composed of individuals from the general public. The California and Pennsylvania Blue Shield plans, as well as two of the Illinois plans, were in this bracket.

Almost half of the associations (thirty-four) had public representatives equal to 26 to 40 per cent of the entire board membership. Included in this category, for example, were all of the New York organizations, plus the Rockford, Illinois, plan. Only four of the associations had public representation of more than 40 per cent.[8]

The Blue Shield Study Commission, under the auspices of the National Association of Blue Shield Plans, recently advocated retaining physician control of boards of directors, but increasing public representation. Regulatory authorities, generally, have stressed to associations the need to increase proportional representation from subscribers or the public. Changes are definitely taking place in this direction.

Present Practices Concerning Nonpublic Representatives

The manner in which hospital and medical members are selected for Blue Cross and Blue Shield governing boards varies greatly as the national associations have no stipulations concerning selection processes; neither do many state laws outline procedures of this type.[9] One prominent method for choosing nonpublic members is to have the "corporation" members elect the directors. Composition of the corporate body, when existent, differs widely, as was discussed in Chapter III. Many other associations have a self-perpetuating procedure for selecting nonpublic representatives, i.e., the board members select those who will fill vacancies.

---

[8] These plans were located in Connecticut, Hawaii, Massachusetts, and New Hampshire.

[9] The problems surrounding qualifications for board members were investigated in Chapter VII.

Issues Concerning the Composition of Governing Boards

Eligibility for Service as Public Representatives. It is generally recognized that hospital administrators and physicians have personal interests which do not permit them to act as true public representatives on Blue Cross and Blue Shield boards. It is less definite, however, whether hospital trustees are qualified to represent the public. These trustees are customarily businessmen who serve on the hospital boards without compensation. Many observers question their ability to work on Blue Cross boards without being influenced by their relationship with hospitals. Supervisory authorities in general feel that no individual should be a public representative if he, or a group with which he is associated, could have a vested interest in a Blue Cross or Blue Shield plan. "Vested interest" refers to benefit as well as profit, since it is recognized that position or authority can be just as important as financial gains. Regulatory officials, therefore, seem to think that hospital trustees should not serve as public representatives in spite of the excellent reputation these trustees may have in a community.

Since there is some question in regard to the qualifications of hospital trustees to serve as public representatives, they should not be allowed generally to act in this capacity. It will be in the best interest of the associations to make every effort to circumvent areas which could result in adverse publicity, even though unwarranted. The highly competitive nature of medical care insurance has caused many issues to be given more prominence than their importance deserves. This is possibly true with respect to the suitability of hospital trustees to serve as lay members. For the reason stated, however, their services should be utilized only where it is absolutely impossible to secure other qualified members.

Selection Procedures for Public Representatives. The question of how to obtain individuals truly representative of the public is a more perplexing practical dilemma than even the conceptual problem concerning the proportion of boards which should be composed of this type of members. Few associations have experimented to any extent in selection methods for public representatives. In most Blue Cross and Blue Shield plans the managing executive or the existing board of directors chooses prominent citizens and asks them to serve as public representatives. Attention is given by the executive or the board, however, to the occupations of the prospective public members. Most associations endeavor to have at least one public representative from a labor organization, one clergyman, and one lawyer, as well as other individuals with vocations in business and finance.

Several procedures might conceivably be used in selecting public representatives. The most democratic approach is for subscribers to elect the lay members. This method is seldom used because it involves the question of whether the majority has the ability to choose those best able to represent it.[10] Many commissioners, as well as executives, fear that subscriber elections could produce unqualified board members who would fail to guide an association properly, with the result that the organization would not achieve its proper

---

[10] This, of course, is one of the philosophical problems faced by a democratic form of government. The Founding Fathers of the United States foresaw such a disadvantage, and the use of the electoral college in the selection of a President was one way they attempted to overcome the weaknesses in the voting arrangement. Theoretically at least, eligible voters selected members of the electoral college and the college elected the President. Then, too, the two-party system modified the possibility that voters would not elect proper officials, inasmuch as some preselection took place within a party before allowing voters to choose from among its candidates at the primary election. Thus, the dilemma democratic elections pose for hospital and medical associations is not completely analogous to the question of whether citizens are qualified to elect their public officials.

In addition, corporate-type elections often use cumulative voting procedures whereby minority groups find it easier to elect representatives. This is not used in governmental elections. Neither are absentee ballots as important in elections of civic officials as are proxy ballots in corporate elections. It is quite easy for most eligible citizens to go to the polls in governmental elections. Most corporations or associations, however, have relatively few eligible voters attend their elections. Often those who do attend are not the average type of member. In many instances, those attending represent special interests and minority groups. Proxy ballots are very important in such elections. Again, the average association member may not vote his proxy, while those with particular interests in the election will.

goals. Practical difficulties are also involved. If cumulative voting or proxy votes are allowed, it is quite possible that a large subscriber group, say of city employees or members of a union, would have enough votes to control a board of directors. Regulatory authorities believe this is not desirable.

At the other extreme, public representatives may be chosen by the existing board or management, which is the most common current procedure. While this manner of selection may obtain individuals who can uphold the public interest, it has brought considerable adverse publicity. It is alleged that the board or association management can choose members of the public who will be most cooperative in agreeing or acquiescing with the desires of the nonpublic representatives. However, extensive interviews have not substantiated this allegation.

Probably the most important recent suggestion for the selection of public representatives is "the governor's committee method." According to one insurance commissioner the procedure here is for the state governor to appoint individuals from specified fields of endeavor to an advisory committee whose function would be to select the public representatives. It has been thought that this would permit the least amount of political interference in the selection process and, at the same time, circumvent the disadvantages considered inherent in the election of public representatives by subscribers. It would also eliminate much of the criticism by insurance companies which claim that lay members are not really public representatives.

A modification of the governor's committee method has been offered by a recent Columbia study which proposes an association accept nominations from the governor but reserve the right to choose from among the nominations.

Composition of Boards of Directors. Dr. C. Rufus Rorem, a pioneer in the Blue Cross movement, has said the Blues must decide whether they want to be "a nongovernmental form of social insurance" or "a nonprofit form of private insurance." This distinction may be applied in principle to the problem of membership on the governing boards of hospital and medical service associations. In the early stages of their development these organizations were considered adjuncts to either the hospitals or the doctors. An association and the vendors of its services were identified *together,* or as one and the same. There is little current agreement among association executives, or others, however, as to the present position of associations in relation to those who render their services. The most common attitude is that contracting hospitals and Blue Cross are partners, regardless of dissensions which may exist between them. A similar, though closer, relationship exists between Blue Shield and doctors. The president of one very large Blue Shield plan expressed the extreme in this alliance when he called his association an "instrument of the medical profession." Often the stationery of Blue Shield organization states, "This is the doctors' plan."

Some indication of the social nature of a Blue Cross or Blue Shield plan may be seen in the proportional representation on its board. If an association is a nongovernmental form of social insurance, then public representatives should be in a majority on its governing board. In this way public confidence will be maintained in the principle that the organization is a community- or social-enterprise arrangement. On the other hand, if the Blues are more like mutual insurers, that is, nonprofit types of private insurers, public representation is not such a vital issue. Mutual health insurance companies, for example, are not expected to let public representatives control their boards of directors.

The question of board representation is all the more pressing in areas where a major portion of the citizens are subscribers of Blue Cross or Blue Shield. If either of these associations offers service benefits, the hospitals and/or doctors become more dependent upon Blue Cross or Blue Shield for their income as the proportion of the population enrolled increases. The issue of representation is not quite as vital where most of an association's subscribers have indemnity certificates, since doctors do not accept stipulated fees in full payment of services rendered under the contracts.

Many executives express doubt as to whether doctors will cooperate in a Blue Shield plan if the medical profession is reduced to a minority on the boards. These executives point to the fact that at least part of the growth of Blue Shield is attributable to the support of doctors. Certainly this factor, plus the concomitant growth of Blue Cross, has fostered the expansion of medical service organizations. The continued cooperation of physicians is certainly encouraged where much of an area's population subscribes since a sizeable portion of a doctor's income would come through the Blue Shield organization. His failure to work with the association could mean an appreciable decrease in personal compensation, assuming many other doctors continued to cooperate with the organization. Also, the widespread refusal of county medical societies to endorse or support Blue Shield plans simply because they do not have the majority of memberships on boards is not likely to be looked upon with favor by regulatory authorities. The medical profession and its affiliated agencies would probably have to publicly justify **any** action of this sort.[11]

Blue Shield and doctors generally need each other. Their interdependence does vary with the number of doctors in a locale and the proportion of the residents who subscribe to medical service organizations. It is likely, nevertheless, that doctors will continue their cooperation with Blue Shield as long as they have an important, though not controlling, position on the boards.

About half of the Blue Cross executives who were queried

---

[11] Indictments have been brought against the American Medical Association and other medical organizations in the past as a result of their relationships with medical care plans. One of the most notable of these occurred in 1938 when the American Medical Association, some county medical societies, and certain physicians were held to be discriminating against the associations. For one account of the indictment see the *New York Times*, December 21, 1938, pp. 20–21.

do not think it necessary to establish definite membership proportions for governing boards. Most of the remainder approve of requirements similar to those established by the American Hospital Association, that is, one third of the membership for hospital representatives and a similar proportion for lay individuals. A majority of the Blue Shield executives who cooperated in the study believe that physicians should have close to 50 per cent, but not a majority, representation on the boards of medical service associations.

The National Association of Blue Shield Plans has taken no official stand on the matter of board memberships. As was mentioned, the organization has urged boards presently composed only of doctors to include laymen.

A general stand in favor of additional, and more representative, public members on boards of directors has been taken in New York by the State's Joint Legislative Committee on Health Insurance Plans. After it conducted hearings in the various Blue Cross areas in New York State in late 1961, the committee commented on the matter in the following vein:

Efforts by Blue Cross (in Albany) to cultivate a favorable public image seem to be not entirely successful. This lack was underscored by labor's representative at our hearing. Several factors are responsible. For example, there is the disinclination, expressed by Blue Cross to agree that the number of hospital representatives on the Blue Cross Board of Directors should be limited to avoid possible conflict of interest.

The board of directors of your Blue Cross plan (Utica), although apparently made up of outstanding individuals, seems unduly weighted against the numerically greatest segment of the community of subscribers. Apparently fourteen have primarily industrial affiliations, three are from banking and only one is from organized labor. Understanding by the community of Blue Cross problems would be increased if several additional spokesmen from labor were added to the board.

Most regulatory officials are of the opinion that a considerable change in board representation is warranted on the part of both Blue Cross and Blue Shield plans, although it is common to hear more stress placed on the matter concerning medical service corporations. Commissioners in most areas lack the power to require these changes. The superintendent of insurance for New York has stated, for example:

> It has been charged that, as presently constituted, AHS[12] is operated by a self-perpetuating board of directors not truly representative of the community which it serves. But so long as it does not contravene existing requirements of law, the choice of AHA management is a subject over which the Superintendent of Insurance lacks supervisory jurisdiction . . . however, the concern of the Superintendent that AHS operate as it recognizes it must—as a "community service"—constrains me to note the obvious desirability both of improving AHS's liaison with all elements properly concerned with its work, and developing closer supervision of its operations by its board.[13]

While supervisory officials may lack legal authority to require changes in the membership of associations' boards, they are not without persuasive powers. Boards can be influenced very pointedly by the manner in which commissioners handle requests for rate approvals, as well as through their jurisdiction over reimbursement schedules, fee schedules, benefit provisions, and examination requirements. In addition, an insurance commissioner can exercise considerable pressure on legislators, other government agencies, and the public itself to make changes which will bring about the action he desires. The insurance commissioner of Pennsylvania has publicly denoted some of these features in connection with a rate hearing for the Pennsylvania Blue Shield plan:

> One basic impression I gained from these hearings is that the Blue Shield organization is more responsive to the views of doctors and the views of the Medical Society of the State of Pennsylvania than to the views of any other group. It was fully apparent during the hearing on Blue Shield's Senior Citizens Agreement

---

[12] Associated Hospital Service, the Blue Cross plan located in New York City.

[13] Adjudication of the superintendent of insurance, State of New York in the *Matter of the Application of Associated Hospital Service of New York,* June 26, 1959.

that the wishes of the Medical Society of the State of Pennsylvania determined the type of senior citizen program which Blue Shield offered for Insurance Department approval. Any views held by Blue Shield management were totally subordinated to the wishes of the State Medical Society. Blue Shield officials stated that The Pennsylvania Medical Society "told us what we should do" in regard to the fee schedule to be used in such a program. They also stated that "the medical society gave us a program and said 'we want your Plan A fee schedule,' that off the bat sets the level of our payment."

It was pointed out by Blue Shield officials that the State Medical Society must have an important voice in such matters since doctors are relied upon to provide service benefits. It was admitted by Blue Shield, however, that persons or groups representing older people and other segments of the public were not consulted at all in the formation of any aspect of the senior citizens' program.

The subordination of initiative and policy by Blue Shield to the Medical Society of the State of Pennsylvania is symptomatic, in my opinion, of a condition which is serious to the extent it exists.

I recognize that Section 510 of the Nonprofit Corporation Law requires that a majority of the members of Blue Shield be doctors of medicine. This fact alone, however, neither justifies nor contemplates that Blue Shield policy and operations be subordinated to the policies and programs of the State Medical Society. It certainly does not justify or contemplate that policy decisions will be made for Blue Shield by the Medical Society and summarily passed on to the Blue Shield organization for implementation. The organized medical profession has no more moral or legal right to control Blue Shield policies than does the Bar Association to control judicial and other offices occupied by members of the legal profession.

The Legislature could reasonably require that a majority of the Board of Directors of Blue Shield be doctors of medicine, while still expecting that Blue Shield would exercise policy free from undue influence from any particular group including the doctors. The doctors of medicine on the Blue Shield Board of Directors should not be serving as members of their medical societies, but should be serving as representatives of the people.

Blue Shield is not the doctors' plan; it is the public's plan. The doctors serving Blue Shield are fulfilling a trust imbodied in them by the Legislature. The nature of that trust is clearly stated in the Enabling Act. . . . In my opinion, Blue Shield, in its dealings with all groups, whether they be medical societies, labor organizations, subscriber groups, employer representatives, or other, must act as an independent public-purpose corporation which will not subordinate itself to any group, but will generously work with all in fulfilling its great public purpose.

Within the framework of the existing law there is room for more public representation on the Blue Shield Board of Directors. While the law requires that the majority of the Board of Directors be doctors of medicine, 18 of the 23 members of the present Board are doctors. It is my firm conviction that the members of the governing body of Blue Shield should be drawn from more than one field of activity. The doctors' point of view is vital in the operation and future development of Blue Shield. But are not other points of view equally as vital? The viewpoints of non-doctor health care specialists would be valuable to Blue Shield as would the viewpoints of labor representatives, industry representatives, and persons capable of expressing the views and aspirations of our ordinary citizens. If the Board of Directors must be enlarged to accommodate such representation, then I recommend that it be enlarged. If the Nonprofit Corporation Law must be amended to assure such broader public participation in the public matters of Blue Shield, then I recommend that such law be amended.

Blue Shield Plans face the greatest challenge of their history. That challenge is to provide ever-broadening medical care to citizens at costs which they can afford. If free voluntary effort through public-purpose organizations cannot meet this challenge, the future of free medicine in America is in danger. The Pennsylvania Blue Shield Plan in facing this challenge must have the sympathetic cooperation of all our doctors, employer representatives, labor representatives, subscriber groups, and the confidence of our general citizenry and its public representatives. To meet the challenge of the immediate future, Blue Shield must return to original and basic concepts. It must identify itself clearly and distinctly in the public mind as the agency empowered and directed by the Legislature to bring adequate health services to our people at prices they can meet within their budgets. I am fearful that Blue Shield will have difficulties meeting this challenge if it retains its present close identity through Board composition and policy with but one, though very important, segment of society.[14]

When the composition of Blue Cross boards was discussed at an NAIC meeting, the director of insurance for the State of Illinois remarked: ". . . I think basically labor, and even management, sincerely believe that if the federal government is to be kept out of this business of insurance, one of the ways to do it is to put these plans in the hands of the people who really own the Plan."[15]

Prescribing Board Requirements. If it is advisable to have definite representation limits for boards, how should this be accomplished—by statute or through association bylaws? As might be expected, the majority of association executives feel the problem can be handled adequately through the bylaws. They indicate that the bylaws of most Blue Cross and Blue Shield plans must be approved by the appropriate insurance commissioner; thus, there is no need, they say, to embody membership requirements in enabling acts. Regulatory officials, generally, and some association managers do not concur with this attitude. These individuals point out that variances in statues and their administration preclude accomplishment of the desired result, even though bylaws need prior approval before becoming effective. They also feel there is not the same compulsion to meet bylaw pro-

---

[14] Adjudication of Francis R. Smith, insurance commissioner of the Commonwealth of Pennsylvania, in the *Matter of Filing No. 1-H, 1960, of the Medical Service Association of Pennsylvania,* February 2, 1961, pp. 5–8.

[15] Statement by Joseph S. Gerber, director of insurance, State of Illinois, before the Subcommittee to Study the Problem of Reimbursement Formulas between Hospitals and Service Associations, contained in the minutes of the NAIC meeting at San Francisco, California on May 30, 1960.

visions as there is to comply with state statutory requirements. Many supervisory officials are of the opinion, therefore, that membership proportions for boards of directors
should be prescribed by the enabling acts.

Recommendations Regarding Board Representation

The most appropriate long-run solution to the entire problem of board representation is for statutory provisions to
stipulate that "less than the majority of the governing board
at any official meeting will be representatives of the vendors
of association services." A related provision in the definitions
section of laws should define "vendors of association services"
to include hospital administrators, hospital trustees, and
members of any segment of the medical profession. This
should in no way result in the control of doctors' diagnoses
or treatment of their patients, nor should it have a detri-
mental influence on the standards of hospital care. There will
be adequate representatives from both the hospital and
medical fields to grant the board the benefit of their vast
knowledge; and, at the same time, such representatives
should be able to appropriately uphold the interest of these
two professions. Associations cannot help but benefit by such
membership proportions, inasmuch as they will be able to
avoid much of the disadvantageous publicity which has attended their operations. When a Blue Cross or Blue Shield
plan can point to half of its governing body as prominent
laymen from various segments of community life, not associated with the medical or hospital fields, the citizens can
have greater assurance their interests are being properly
served. The social nature of plans will be maintained and
supported.

As a final point, it is probably best that statutory requirements and bylaw provisions not impose limits on the number
of years a director may serve. It takes a period of time for
even astute businessmen to become attuned to the operation

and problems of a Blue Cross or Blue Shield plan, and rapid turnover of board personnel accentuates this problem.

ENROLLMENT REPRESENTATIVES

Blue Cross and Blue Shield plans consider the individuals performing sales functions for their plans to be different from agents who are the sales representatives for insurance companies. This has been true from the very inception of the associations when they decided to call their salesmen "enrollment representatives." The approach of these individuals was held to vary from that of their counterparts in health insurance companies, in so far as those associated with the Blues were considered to be *spreading* the *benefits* of a social movement more than they were *selling* insurance coverages. Individuals in insurance company ranks customarily look upon this expressed difference as terminological "gibberish."

It has been widely publicized that enrollment representatives are paid on a salary basis only, as contrasted with the commission method of compensation for insurance agents. Some observers feel this has meant Blue Cross and Blue Shield representatives were of "lower caliber but higher character" than insurance agents. The "lower caliber" is apparently in reference to their formal education while "character" concerns their sincerity and unusual devotion to the social purposes of the associations. It is undoubtedly true that the men have been motivated, at least in the past, by more than financial objectives. Some individuals have pointed out that the educational qualifications of enrollment representatives are rapidly improving and they should no longer be considered inferior to insurance salesmen in this respect.

The two questions to be answered regarding regulations for enrollment representatives are whether there should be licensing requirements for them and whether it is necessary to limit the methods by which they are compensated.

Licensing

Insurance salesmen are licensed in order to provide some control over the quality of those who represent insurance companies and, thereby, to protect the citizens of the state. It was felt from the time that Blue Cross and Blue Shield plans were inaugurated that limiting the compensation of salesmen to a salary basis would, in effect, reduce the pressures and misrepresentations which the incentive basis encourages in some insurance agents.

Licensing does permit a more direct control of salesmen by the regulatory authority than if the official worked through the agent's principal. Particular difficulties are involved when a salesman represents several insurance companies and the supervisory official is trying to determine the principle through whom to exercise control. Enrollment representatives present a different situation in that they generally work for two organizations at the most (a Blue Cross plan and a Blue Shield plan) , and the principal is in a better position to account for them. Thus, the reasons for licensing have not been thought to apply to enrollment representatives. Associations themselves and the salary basis of compensation have been considered adequate controls. Then, too, the somewhat disappointing results licensing has had in raising the caliber of insurance agents, or controlling them, probably has discouraged the use of licenses for enrollment representatives. Very few insurance commissioners feel anything would be gained by instituting a licensing procedure for enrollment representatives.

Compensation

Most plan executives think it is becoming necessary to determine a portion of enrollment representatives' wages on an incentive basis. The incentive feature would vary with the amount, and possibly with the type and quality, of business the individuals secured for the association. Executives indicate generally that motivation presented by promotional opportunities for those who are particularly successful is insufficient. A large number of associations, therefore, are either considering or offering some types of financial incentives. Associations in Pennsylvania and Illinois are notable among those now using incentive compensation.

Some state statutes preclude the use of any basis of compensation other than straight salary. New York, for example, stipulates that: "Every medical expense indemnity corporation, dental expense indemnity corporation and hospital service corporation is prohibited from employing solicitors or accepting business from brokers on a commission basis but all solicitors shall be paid on a salary basis only." The regulatory authority in New York has determined that a "salary basis" may possibly include the granting of bonuses, as long as they are actually a part of a salary which is withheld temporarily to encourage maximum efficiency.[16] Other than the limitation of compensation to a salary basis, the superintendent of insurance in New York has no power to fix the salaries of any organization. As is true in most other areas, the superintendent only has control over the total expenses of an association.[17]

Twenty-one states which cooperated in this research have no limitations on the method or amount of compensation for enrollment representatives. The majority of the remaining areas require the supervisory official's approval on the bases for wage determination. It is possible that authorities with approval powers over methods of compensation would allow some types of incentive pay. Officials from Arizona, New

---

[16] Considerable adverse press coverage was given to the Blue Cross plan in New York City because it granted bonuses to its employees for Christmas, 1960. The association had done so in previous years and employees apparently came to consider this as part of their salary. Without the bonuses they could have obtained jobs elsewhere which were more desirable financially. The fact that New York Blue Cross requested a rate increase just prior to the payment of these bonuses furnished ripe material for the press. The bonus was actually an unimportant part of the rate increase. Regulatory officials of the state seem to concur that the bonus did not violate the statutory section. Nevertheless, the attendant publicity resulted in an investigation on the part of the Joint Legislative Committee on Health Insurance Plans of the State.

[17] Expense limitations are appraised in Chapter XII.

York, and Rhode Island were the only ones who stated that their legislation stipulated a salary basis.[18]

A straight salary is probably still the typical means by which enrollment representatives are paid. It is logical to believe, though, that competition for good men will encourage the utilization of incentive bases for compensation on the part of more and more Blue Cross and Blue Shield plans. Representatives were fundamentally order takers for new groups in the early days of Blue Cross and Blue Shield. Even at the present time it is customary for enrollment representatives to work only on group cases. Nongroup subscribers enroll through the mail or by going personally to the offices of the association. The last two decades have seen much keener competition and a greater percentage of the population is enrolled. As a consequence, it is more difficult to obtain new subscribers. In fact, many associations have not been able to maintain their former memberships. The changed competitive environment probably merits some type of incentive wage. Additional encouragement for the use of this type of compensation will be obtained if enrollment representatives start to solicit nongroup subscribers. Incentive compensation is not expected to approach the full commission basis maintained by most insurance companies. It should be noted, however, that the laws of most states do not preclude straight commission unless the regulatory authority deems it improper. Similarly, the National Association of Blue Shield Plans has stated that medical service associations could provide straight commissions and still meet the approval requirements. The AHA approval requirements for Blue Cross plans state, "No employee of a plan shall be paid principally by commission or on a production fee basis." This standard does not prevent an approved plan from using some incentive compensation.

The proposals which seem to be most acceptable to associations provide for base salaries plus additions, either for

---

[18] Rhode Island may deviate from the salary basis upon approval from the regulatory authority.

each application beyond a specified number or for subscription income above certain amounts. Several executives indicated that, as a rule of thumb, the incentive proportion should be limited to between 15 and 25 per cent of a man's income.

ADVERTISING

Advertising has been one of the most highly litigated areas of health insurance operations in the past decade. While few of the legal controversies have involved nonprofit associations, the decisions which have been rendered, and the laws which have resulted, apply to Blue Cross and Blue Shield as well as to insurance companies.

The most intriguing aspect of disputes concerned with advertising has been the involvement of the federal government. The Federal Trade Commission entered the arena in 1954 by indicting seventeen insurance companies, charging false and misleading advertising. There followed a succession of events involving further complaints by the FTC against insurance companies and decisions by several courts. The Supreme Court of the United States handed down a unanimous decision on June 30, 1958, that no authority over health insurance advertising may be exercised by the FTC in states which have passed laws of their own regarding advertising. In so doing the court upheld similar decisions by two circuit courts of appeal. The court relied upon several portions of the McCarran-Ferguson Act:

Sec. 1. . . . Congress hereby declares that the continued regulation and taxation by the several States of the business of insurance is in the public interest, and that silence on the part of Congress shall not be construed to impose any barrier to the regulation or taxation of such business by the several States.

Sec. 2. (a) The business of insurance, and every person engaged therein, shall be subject to the laws of the several States which relate to the regulation of taxation of such business.

(b) No Act of Congress shall be construed to invalidate, impair, or supersede any law enacted by any State for the purpose of regulating the business of insurance, or which imposes a fee or tax upon such business, unless such Act specifically relates to the business of insurance: Provided, that after June 30, 1948, the Sherman Act, . . . the Clayton Act, and . . . the Federal Trade Commission Act . . . shall be applicable to the business of insurance to the extent that such business is not regulated by State law. . . .

The Supreme Court held that these provisions withdrew from the FTC the authority to regulate advertising practices in states governing such practices under their own laws. The second portion of the decision indicated that the FTC could not enter the picture once a state had advertising laws, even if there were no administrative supervision in accordance with such statutes:

. . . [FTC] urges that a general prohibition designed to guarantee certain standards of conduct is too "inchoate" to be "regulation" until that prohibition has been crystallized into "administrative elaboration of these standards and application in individual cases." However, assuming there is some difference in the McCarran-Ferguson Act between "legislation" and "regulation," nothing in the language of that Act or its legislative history supports the distinctions drawn by [FTC].

The furor created over health insurance advertising resulted in adoption of an advertising code by the National Association of Insurance Commissioners in December, 1955.[19] The definitions section of the NAIC code states:

. . . shall include any policy, plan, certificate, contract, agreement, statement of coverage, rider or endorsement which provides accident or sickness benefits, whether on a cash indemnity, reimbursement, or service basis, except when issued in connection with another kind of insurance other than life and except disability and double indemnity benefits included in life insurance and annuity contracts.

---

[19] Appendix C contains the NAIC Advertising Code.

This obviously includes the protection and coverages available through hospital and medical service plans. Some of the major states had statutory requirements regarding advertising prior to the NAIC enactment. Other states have either legislated this code into their insurance laws or utilized it as an administrative standard. In either case, the advertising regulations of states are generally considered to apply to the associations.

The development of advertising regulations has undoubtedly influenced the national, but not the local, advertising of Blue Cross and Blue Shield. The advertising agency of one of the national organizations has pointed out that statements cannot be made about benefit programs and practices of associations because of their great diversity throughout the country. For this reason the national advertising utilizes individual testimonials and there is no implication that benefits in one area will apply elsewhere. Some plan executives feel the FTC investigation helped Blue Cross and Blue Shield by bringing the advertising methods of renegade health insurance companies more into line.

In addition to their advertising codes, many states place over-all limitations on funds used for this purpose. These provisions will be discussed in Chapter XII.

chapter IX

SUBSCRIBER CONTRACTS AND BENEFITS

Control over benefit structures is a most important responsibility for any person, group, or agency which possesses regulatory powers. This undoubtedly justifies the check-and-balance system of control over benefits whereby an association's management and board of directors determine the benefit structure submitted to the supervisory official for approval. Obviously, a commissioner can exert subtle pressures for changes in coverages. By and large, however, the nature of benefits is determined by financial considerations, competition, the fear of additional regulation, and the extent of true community interest of an association's governing officers. Many executive directors think that extensions in benefits have been motivated more by competition than by pressures from the state regulatory bodies. In those aspects of coverage where there is little or no competition, e.g., the over-65 market, apprehension about a possible change in tax position or other regulatory feature, as well as a sincere desire on the part of many associations to help solve a social problem, has done much to project benefits into actuarially undesirable areas.

The concern of state officials and those associated with Blue Cross and Blue Shield plans should be particularly keen in areas where a large percentage of the population is enrolled. Benefit structures in these locales are a major force in establishing the quality of medical care available on a "prepaid" basis. Similarly, the quality of care could be sorely affected if inadequate reimbursement is made for services rendered.

FILING AND APPROVAL OF
BENEFIT STRUCTURES

The great majority of states require both Blue Cross and Blue Shield plans to file the benefits they intend to offer group and nongroup subscribers with the state supervisory department. Thirty-one states have indicated that "prior approval" of benefit structures is necessary, in addition to "filling." Thus, *before* benefits may be offered to members or potential enrollees, they must be passed upon affirmatively by the supervisory authority.

The provision of the enabling act which requires contracts to be filed and approved in New York reads as follows:

No medical expense indemnity, dental expense indemnity corporation or hospital service corporation shall enter into any contract with a subscriber unless and until it shall have filed with the superintendent of insurance a copy of the contract or certificate and of all applications, riders and endorsements for use in connection with the issuance or renewal thereof, to be formally approved by him as conforming to section two hundred fifty-three [which delineates specific inclusions] of this article and not inconsistent with any other provision of law applicable thereto. The superintendent shall, within a reasonable time after the filing of any such form, notify the insurer filing the same either of his approval or of his disapproval of such form.

Some states have an automatic approval procedure. California, for example, allows a hospital service association to use the forms it has submitted for approval either after thirty days have expired without notice from the commissioner or upon specific notice prior thereto that the commissioner has approved the contract provisions. Thus, approval is automatic after thirty days, if disapproval has not been expressed by that time.

It is not uncommon for states to have "subsequent disapproval" requirements for group benefit structures. According to these procedures, an association may commence using group benefits as soon as they have been filed. Such benefits are subject to possible disapproval by the commissioner, however, after they have been extended to group subscribers. The difference in approval requirements between group and individual contracts is accounted for by the fact that group buyers are supposedly more knowledgeable regarding insurance contracts and coverages than are individual enrollees.

Enabling acts which require that benefit structures be approved by the supervisory authority usually allow considerable discretion on the part of an official in evaluating the benefits. The law to which Blue Cross plans in Illinois are subject is more specific than most states regarding the reasons the regulatory official may disapprove benefit structures:

> It shall be the duty of the Director of Insurance to withhold approval of any contract filed with him if it violates any provision of this Act, contains inconsistent, ambiguous or misleading clauses, or contains exceptions and conditions that unreasonably or deceptively affect the hospital service to be provided in the general coverage of the contract. In all other cases the Director of Insurance shall give his approval.

Almost all enabling legislation allows an association a court review of a commissioner's disapproval of benefit structures. Some statutes provide for recourse to the courts in the same section that delineates the requirements for approval of benefits, while other laws have a general provision for court review of any acts of the regulatory authority.

CERTIFICATE PROVISIONS

Statutory provisions concerning the inclusions required in Blue Cross and Blue Shield subscriber contracts may be classified as to the certificate form and its use; nongroup terms and conditions; group terms and conditions; and the nature

of benefits. Most states have adopted stipulations for Blue
Cross and Blue Shield contracts identical, or very similar, to
those for health insurance companies. The basis for these
was the work of the NAIC in developing standard provisions
for health insurance contracts. Where enabling acts are of
more recent origin, as is particularly true of those for medical service associations, contract stipulations of some sort are
usually a part of the law. Some of the older enabling statutes
have not been amended to include standard provisions; the
regulatory authorities in such areas, however, generally use
the NAIC provisions as unofficial requirements.

Certificate Form and Its Use

Certificates are usually required, either by law or administrative ruling, to be in writing in those states which
regulate Blue Cross or Blue Shield plans. All subscribers,
but not their dependents, usually must be given certificates.
It is also common for the statutes to outline the manner, and
possibly the size of type, in which exceptions to the contract
will be printed. A brief description of inclusions must
be enumerated on the front and back of a certificate.

When part of a corporation's charter or bylaws are incorporated into a certificate, the full context of the section
so included must be stated. Like insurance policies, certificates stipulate that the document with endorsements constitutes the entire contract. No statement by a subscriber in
an application may be used against him unless the statement
is in the contract. In the absence of fraud, statements by
enrollees are considered representations and not warranties.
As representations, statements may render a contract void-
able at the option of the association only if the declarations
are both false and material. Only officers of an association,
and not its agents, can waive any contract provision.

Terms and Conditions—Nongroup

Length of Contract and Renewability. New York's statute
requires, as is typical of enabling acts, that certificates must

be effective for a period of a year. Benefits granted by associations in the state may not commence more than one year from the contract date. The unusual feature of New York's requirements is that after two years nongroup contracts become guaranteed renewable up to age limits specified by the association. Specifically, the nonprofit association cannot fail to renew the coverage of a nongroup enrollee unless there is:

. . . fraud in applying for the contract or in applying for any benefits under the contract, moral hazard, overinsurance or duplication of benefits according to standards on file with the superintendent of insurance, discontinuance of a class of policies, and such other reasons, including but not limited to, the filing of false or improper claims, as the superintendent of insurance may approve; however after such two year period in no event shall any corporation refuse to renew any such contract because of a change in the physical or mental condition or the health of any person covered thereunder.

Riders or endorsements which would limit benefits are also precluded after the two-year period.

The entire guaranteed renewability provision was part of New York's "Metcalf Legislation," enacted in 1958 and made effective July 1, 1959. It applies to contracts issued, amended, or altered after the effective date by insurance companies or nonprofit associations. A guaranteed renewability provision has more significance in connection with hospital and medical service plans than with insurance companies since most hospital associations and many medical associations offer service benefits. If contracts must be renewed and rate increases are not approved by a commissioner, an association can encounter financial difficulties when the costs of services are rising. Indemnity contracts do not have this built-in disadvantage. Their guarantees are in terms of dollars and the size of their financial commitments under a contract do not vary with changing costs.

The principal means by which an association may refuse to renew guaranteed renewable certificates is to discontinue an entire class of certificates.[1] Needless to say, public hearings and adverse publicity would occur if an association tried such action in connection with a widely-held-certificate. The head of a Blue Cross plan having several million subscribers remarked that anytime his organization tampers with rates or benefits on certificates affecting more than 15 per cent of all subscribers the association is subjected to wide press coverage. This does not allow for unpublicized changes on the part of a very large portion of enrollees.

Neither California, Pennsylvania, Illinois, nor other major states have enacted guaranteed renewability stipulations up to the present time. Nevertheless, New York could be starting another important trend with its requirement.

It is common for enabling acts to require that the first page of a certificate must specify any age or period beyond which the coverage will not be renewed. States using the standard provisions include a ten-day examination period after delivery, during which a direct-pay member may cancel the coverage and have his premium returned.

Convertibility and Overinsurance. Family contracts usually contain a provision that when a child attains age nineteen he is no longer eligible for coverage under the family-group. Such children have a right to coverage under the type of certificate most similar to the family contract. They must apply for the converted certificate within thirty-one days after they become ineligible as family members. No evidence of insurability can be required, nor may pre-existing conditions be excluded. Conversion may be denied in New York if there is evidence it will facilitate overinsurance:

Such corporation shall not be required to issue an individual converted contract . . . if it appears that the person applying

---

[1] A "class" of certificates refers to all of an entire type of subscriber contracts. Some associations have a high and a low benefit certificate between which individual enrollees may choose. If a high-option contract was designated as an "A" certificate, for example, an association would have to discontinue all direct-pay Class "A" certificates, in order to cancel any guaranteed renewable contracts of this type, except for fraud, etc.

for such contract shall have at that time in force another hospital service or medical expense indemnity corporation contract or an insurance policy providing similar benefits or is covered by or is eligible for coverage by a group insurance policy or contract providing similar benefits or shall be covered by similar benefits required by any statute or provided by any welfare plan or program, which together with the converted contract would result in overinsurance or duplication of benefits according to standards on file with the superintendent of insurance relating to individual contracts. . . . If any such person is so covered or so provided and fails to furnish the details of such coverage when requested, the benefits provided under the converted contract may be based on the hospital surgical or medical expenses actually incurred after excluding expenses to the extent they are payable under such other coverage or provided under such statute, plan or program.

The broad question of overinsurance is supposed to be analyzed for the NAIC by an unusual assemblage of individuals. This group is comprised of representatives from health insurance companies and Blue Cross–Blue Shield plans. The liaison conference was established in 1958 as a result of the reimbursement squabble then occurring in the association. Overinsurance is the only topic before the liaison conference. Although both groups are highly competitive in the market, there is *some* realization at a higher, philosophical level that they are in a common endeavor. The conference has no absolute authority but it possesses important powers of persuasion.

Provisions Regarding Subscriber Payments. The amount and frequency of payments required of a subscriber must be stated in most certificates. Many laws allow a ten-day grace period for payments, as well as the provision that acceptance of a remittance by an association or its agent after the grace period suffices to reinstate the certificate.

Hospital-Patient and Doctor-Patient Relationships. Some of the legislative enactments for hospital and medical service associations contain a specific prohibition against any practices of these organizations that might disturb either free choice of a hospital or doctor or the personal nature of relationships between hospitals or doctors and their patients. The California directive, for instance, is that no contract between a hospital service corporation and a subscriber shall be entered into unless it:

. . . contains in black-face type not less than 10-point the following provisions:

Nothing in this contract contained shall in any way or manner restrict or interfere with the right of any individual entitled to hospital service and care hereunder to select the contracting hospital or to make a free choice of attending physician, who shall be the holder of a valid and unrevoked physician and surgeon's certificate and who is a member of, or acceptable to, the attending staff and board of directors of the hospital in which said hospital services are to be provided and rendered.

Terms and Conditions—Group

Group coverages must meet the same contractual requirements as for nongroup subscribers with the exception of the differences elaborated below.

Eligibility. Most enabling laws prescribe that associations must comply with the minimum group limits established for health insurance companies. Recent years have seen a lowering of these minimums. The majority of states now require a minimum of ten lives for a single employer group. Some states stipulate, and most plans provide in their underwriting requirements, that 75 per cent of those eligible to participate must do so when employees contribute in the premium payment. Different requirements often apply to business and professional association groups. Associations in California, for example, must cover not less than 50 per cent of all eligible members, in addition to meeting the normal group requirement of ten members. Most jurisdictions specify that a group must have been organized for purposes other than the obtaining of insurance in order to be eligible for group coverage.

Benefit Limits. Enabling acts prescribe directly, or by incorporating provisions of the insurance code, that group subscribers may not individually determine the extent of their coverage.

Certificates. States stipulate that group enrollees must be given an individual certificate which outlines the basic coverages and exclusions granted by the group contract. California defines an "individual" certificate as one which either contains the name of the covered member or makes it possible in some other way for the person to determine that it is his certificate.

Convertibility. Blue Cross and Blue Shield certificates are generally required by statute to grant conversion rights to a group member upon the termination of his employment, if he was covered for at least three months. Conversion must be requested within thirty-one days after termination. These rights are also extended to the dependents of a deceased group subscriber. The conversion privileges are similar to those available for individuals who reach the children's age limit under a family certificate.

Nature of Benefits

Blue Cross. The difference between benefits offered in terms of services and those stated in dollar amounts is one important feature which separates Blue Cross–Blue Shield and health insurance companies. It is natural, then, that enabling acts should establish the nature of benefits to be offered by associations. Most acts do not specifically preclude indemnity benefits. The consistent use of the term "hospital service" in enabling statutes, however, seems to indicate that service benefits are intended. The superintendent in New York interprets the law in that state to mean that as long as base contracts offer service-type benefits, minor features may deviate therefrom. New York allows Blue Cross certificates to include such indemnity benefits as cash payments or allowances for hospitalization received in nonmember institutions, and dollar credits when a subscriber chooses to have a private room. Dollar limitations on maternity benefits also modify the service concept.

Since the applicable statutes are often vague as to whether indemnity benefits may or may not be provided by a hospital service association, this becomes an area subject to regulatory interpretation by the supervisory official. Commissioners seem to feel that they may allow a small portion of the benefit package to have an indemnity basis, similar to the interpretation in New York, even when service benefits are specifically contemplated in the law.

The problem of rising costs has repeatedly focused attention on the structure of service benefits. There have always been maximum limitations on coverages of this type, generally stated as the total number of days of hospitalization which will be provided. Additional limits are established by prescribing the services other than room and board which will be covered or excluded. Several associations have also used the deductible and coinsurance features adopted by many health insurance companies. The managements of a number of plans feel that service benefits are compromised if any contractual provisions require contributions from the subscriber for covered benefits. This is where the idea of prepayment becomes entangled with the service approach. Some consider that subscribers "prepay" their hospitalization expenses and no additional funds can be required of them other than for excluded services or when they receive more than the allowable maximum of hospital days.

Commissioners are showing increased willingness to grant modifications of full service benefits. Hospital utilization studies have startled many supervisory officials into concluding that deductibles at least are going to be necessary elements in controlling noninflationary aspects of rising hospital-medical costs. This tolerance on the part of state officials indicates it is not likely that deductibles or coinsurance provisions will be considered to violate the statutory requirements for "service" benefits.

An interesting situation concerning deductibles arose in Virginia where, for a while, they were a required contractual feature for associations. The circumstances, as well as an indication of the underwriting problems which accompany deductibles and the effects of regulatory methods thereon, are succinctly reported by a plan manager in Virginia.[2]

We first issued the $50 Deductible in June of 1958—on an optional basis—at a $4.50-group and $5.40 non-group family rate. These rates were only a couple of dollars lower than the simultaneously approved new Standard Contract rate, and we had hardly any $50 Deductible takers—only 8,000 out of 160,000 contract-holders.

But then in June of 1959 we had to have another increase (49%) in the rates for the Standard Contract, at a time when our good loss-ratio experience with the 8,000 Deductible Contracts precluded approval of any concomitant increase in the Deductible rates. Thus, in June of 1959 family subscribers had the choice of a $50 Deductible at $4.50 and $5.40 and a Standard Contract at $9.40 and $11.72 (group and non-group) respectively.

The significant rate differential caused transfers in droves, by September we had 60% of all small-group subscribers and 66% of all pay-directs under the $50 Deductible. The lack of any underwriting control to the option available hurt us. The original rates for the $50 Deductible became inadequate; the new and very high rates for the Standard also immediately proved inadequate as concerns pay-directs and small group members because the folks in these categories who stayed with the Standard were "poor risks."

As soon as we recognized what had happened, we "hinted" that a mandatory $50 Deductible at new rates for all pay-directs and small-group members would help our situation, and in November the State Corporation Commission partially took the hint. With an official Order to justify the procedure we "forced" all of these people to the Deductible. It was considered best to "force" 34% to where 66% had voluntarily gone, and to "force" from an expensive contract to an inexpensive contract, in order to regain a proper spread of risk. However, we had no opportunity to increase the $50 Deductible rates, so we "forced" subscribers to an inadequate rate.

---

[2] Letter from Dr. Richard J. Ackart, executive director, Virginia Hospital Service Association and Virginia Medical Association, Richmond, Virginia, dated February 6, 1961.

Then in January, with no warning at all, the Commission issued a 2 to 1 decision that *all* our contracts, starting April 1 would have to have a Deductible—no exception whatsoever.

We could picture ourselves losing just about all groups in which organized labor is involved, and many others besides, not to mention being a monkey-wrench in the machinery of National Accounts. And so we went to work with an appeal to the State Supreme Court and, as a second string to our bow, with a change in our enabling legislation. Fortunately the General Assembly was in session, and we were successful in getting our law changed and getting out from under the State Corporation Commission as concerns approval of contracts and rates! [3]

Philadelphia Blue Cross and other large associations have had successful experience with deductible and coinsurance provisions. The approach in Philadelphia is not to use an absolute dollar amount initially borne by the subscriber before his Blue Cross coverage takes effect. Rather, hospitalized persons pay $5 of their charges each day, up to a maximum of 15 days. Thus, the maximum amount a subscriber may have to bear is $75. This is a somewhat unusual coinsurance requirement in that it employs a dollar amount per day rather than a percentage of the hospital bill.

The experience in Virginia calls attention to the fact, however, that panaceas for association problems are not easy to locate. The use of deductibles, nonetheless, is on the increase. When bolstered by adequate experience and proper underwriting techniques, they should have an efficacious part in solving the problem of unnecessary rises in benefit utilization. The need for deductibles can be sensed more closely when the never-ending pressure from labor groups to have employers bear the full cost of Blue Cross–Blue Shield group programs is considered. Unwarranted medical care seems all the more possible when employees have full service benefits and, at the same time, do not contribute to the subscription charges.

---

[3] The General Assembly of Virginia transferred responsibility for administering the laws to the Bureau of Insurance, a division of the State Corporation Commission, on March 29, 1960.

Blue Shield. Service benefits are not as much a part of benefit structures for Blue Shield plans as they are for Blue Cross organizations. Neither does there appear to be as much legal necessity for Blue Shield in most states to use the service approach. For instance, even the title of New York's enabling act—"Non-Profit Medical and Dental *Indemnity* or Hospital Service Corporation"—alludes to the difference in types of benefits available from Blue Cross and Blue Shield plans. The National Association of Blue Shield Plans encourages associations to utilize the service-benefit method more extensively, and they report that some associations are tending to do so.

When a Blue Shield corporation is said to be a service-type association, however, its actual position depends upon the income limits in the benefit structure. The specified income levels may be so low that only a minor portion of the enrollees actually receive services without having to make additional payments to the doctor. Income limits are established in very few enabling acts, one of which is the statute in Pennsylvania.[4] Associations in the state are given the right to determine whether a subscriber is in the low-income brackets established, and the determination is final. This is another indication of regulatory controls granted by law to the associations. The current practice in Pennsylvania is for the Blue Shield plan to submit desired income limits to the commissioner for his ratification. The original levels established by law are changed in this manner.

Neither Pennsylvania nor Illinois allows cash payments to subscribers of medical service organizations as a general procedure. In Pennsylvania the statutory section reads:

No contract by or on behalf of any nonprofit medical (and osteopathic and dental) service corporation shall provide for the payment of any cash or other material benefit by that cor-

---

[4] The original act described those of low income as having an average income during the preceding twenty-five weeks of not less than $30 for individuals, $45 for those with one dependent, and $60 for subscribers with more than one dependent.

poration to a subscriber on account of illness or injury, nor be in any way related to the payment of any such benefit by any other agency.

Illinois requires that certificates include the statement: "Indemnity in the form of cash will not be paid to any subscriber except in reimbursement for payments made by the subscriber to a physician and for which the corporation was liable at the time of such payment." These stipulations do not preclude the payment of indemnity benefits inasmuch as they refer to payments by an association to a subscriber. A subscriber could be required to pay additional amounts to doctors for services received and still not violate the provision.

It was mentioned previously that coverage from Blue Shield plans in recent years has been extended in many states to include the services of dentists, osteopaths, and podiatrists. It has not been the intent of associations, however, to include in their benefit structures all of the services provided by these professional men. In 1954, the New York enabling act was amended to read that medical expense indemnity *may* consist of reimbursement for podiatrical care. The statute was altered in 1957, after which it stated that medical expense indemnity *shall* include podiatrical care. The terms "may" and "shall" have since been the subject of litigation in the state to determine whether they imply a mandatory or permissive meaning. The original case of this type concerned dental care.[5] It was established in the dispute that where a medical expense contract includes services of a kind recognized as common to both the medical and dental professions, the service to a subscriber should be reimbursed if provided by a physician *or* a dentist. The issue over podiatry arose when United Medical Service (the New York City Blue Shield plan) attempted to remove some of the coverage it had granted for foot care prior to 1957. The Podiatry Society of the State of New York challenged this on the basis

---

[5] *Matter of United Medical Service, Inc.* v. *Holz* (5 Misc. 2d 999, 4 App. Div. 2d 1017).

that the previous court decision had given the word "shall" a mandatory construction. *UMS* v. *Holz* had, however, decreed that the mandatory aspect applied only to the rendering of services by either a physician or a dentist. It was not mandatory for an association to continue providing forever a benefit it had once included in contracts. Even the guaranteed renewability legislation in 1958–1959 allowed an association to cancel all benefits for an entire class of certificates. The conclusion, based on the *UMS* v. *Holz* decision, was that the Blue Shield plan must grant payment to podiatrists only if the services granted by a certificate include those legally rendered by podiatrists.

While the final determination of benefit structures may depend upon the approval of a commissioner or a court's interpretation of statutory provisions, associations themselves will undoubtedly continue to be the prime sources of innovations and extensions in Blue Cross and Blue Shield benefits and coverages.

chapter X

REIMBURSEMENT SCHEDULES AND
FEE SCHEDULES

Hospital reimbursement schedules and doctors' fee schedules are at the core of the relationship between associations and those who render services for subscribers; at the same time, certain aspects of the hospital reimbursement schedules are the source of some most bitter attacks from insurance company organizations. Shifts in the ties between Blue Cross plans and hospitals, as well as between Blue Shield organizations and doctors, have been reflected in the nature of the payment schedules. Where the two parties to a schedule have become identified as separate entities, rather than being closely related, the reimbursement arrangements have come to use more definite and statistical bases. Disputes over these contractual features have been most widespread between Blue Cross and hospitals; in fact, several hospital service associations and some of their contracting institutions have recently severed connections, amid considerable clamor, when reimbursement agreements could not be reached. Less than 10 per cent of the hospitals and doctors, however, have failed to cooperate with the associations in recent years.

Schedules are a regulatory problem because over 80 per cent of the expenditures of most associations are made on the basis of these contracts. The financial position of an organization is thus significantly influenced by such arrangements. In addition, there is the supervisory problem of seeing that schedules do not contribute to a misuse of subscription funds, particularly when the institutions or individuals who provide services for associations might be in a position to dictate the financial terms.

HOSPITAL REIMBURSEMENT SCHEDULES

Bases for Reimbursement

The individual arrangements for determining how associations will pay their contracting hospitals are many and varied. All, however, are modifications of three major categories: the so-called per diem charges; hospital retail charges; and hospital costs.

Negotiated Per Diem Reimbursement. The term "per diem," as used by Blue Cross, refers to a dollar amount plans agree to pay contracting hospitals for each day of covered hospital care provided for a subscriber.[1] The per diem figure is arrived at by negotiation and need not be directly related to hospital charges or costs. Actually, "negotiated per diem" is a more appropriate term, inasmuch as the retail-charges and hospital-costs methods arrive at a daily rate, i.e., "per diem" in the broad sense. Plans, however, use the term "per diem" to mean the negotiated rate. The principal variation of a straight per diem reimbursement is called the "per diem sliding scale." Under this basis the daily reimbursement decreases as the days of hospitalization increase until a lower dollar limit is reached. For example, payments might be made at the rate of $25 for the first day of hospitalization, $24 for the second day, down to $10 for the sixteenth day and thereafter. The sliding scale takes into account that a hospital incurs lower average daily costs on behalf of a patient as the period of hospitalization increases, until a cost plateau is reached.

Per diem types of reimbursement were used extensively during the early years of Blue Cross. Financial statistics were not needed to determine these reimbursement rates. The fact that many hospitals did not maintain detailed records

---

[1] It is now common procedure to charge for the day of admission but not the day of discharge.

undoubtedly encouraged the use of per diem schedules. Then too, the process of negotiation between associations and hospitals was not exactly an arms-length transaction. Because of their close relationship, it was not too difficult in earlier years for the two parties to arrive at a mutually agreeable price for reimbursement. Often all hospitals contracting with a Blue Cross plan would use the same per diem price.

Per diem schedules have advantages other than not needing detailed cost data to arrive at the reimbursement rate. Rising costs can be anticipated in a per diem rate, and a sufficient projection for cost changes may preclude the need for rate increases at the end of every contract period. Efficient hospitals may also benefit by a per diem rate that applies to all contracting institutions. The well-organized hospital with costs lower than average will profit more from a per diem rate than will a high-cost institution. Unfortunately, low-cost hospitals which provide a below-average quality of medical care will be rewarded in the same manner.

The lack of statistical foundation, the major procedural advantage of the per diem method, is also the main disadvantage of per diem as a principle. The negotiated figure is hard to explain and justify, particularly to regulatory authorities. The diverging interests of Blue Cross plans and member hospitals, as well as the increased concern of the supervisory officials, have tended to bring reimbursement arrangements closer to statistical foundations. Per diem has thus become relatively unimportant as a distinct method of reimbursement. While twenty-five associations were using a per diem basis in 1950, only eight of seventy-nine Blue Cross plans utilized it in 1959.[2]

The superintendent of insurance for New York has made the following statement regarding a uniform and per diem reimbursement rate:

Ideally, it might seem like hospital care should receive like compensation. Not only does long-established variation in inde-

---

[2] See Table 10-1, page 196.

pendently established "retail" charges make this administratively difficult but even more basic an impediment is posed by the fact that hospital care is not a fungible commodity. For the same disease, different patients require different care, and different doctors may diagnose and prescribe differently for the same patient, with consequent disparity in daily "retail" charges for similarly afflicted patients in similar accommodations in the same hospital.

. . . Desirable though it might be from an insurance standpoint, it must be concluded that the use of a uniform rate of payment to all participating hospitals is not only impracticable, but also—from the hospital standpoint—inequitable.[3]

Reimbursement Based Upon Hospitals' Retail Charges.
In 1959, twenty-two of the seventy-nine Blue Cross plans in the United States were paying hospitals on the basis of their individual retail charges. "Retail charges" refer to the regular room rates and normal billings for special services any patient, insured or noninsured, would pay. The actual relationship between a hospital's costs and its charges to patients has changed radically in the past two decades. During the early years of Blue Cross operations, gifts and endowments were a substantial source of hospital income. Room rates and charges for services were frequently less than the actual cost of providing them, with the differences made up through philanthropy. Gifts to hospitals have declined in recent years and income from endowments is becoming relatively less significant, so hospital charges have had to be raised. Retail charges are now construed to mean a price at least equal to, and most probably above, the actual cost per patient day of providing hospital accommodations.

Retail charges are the maximum reimbursement limits. An association could not be expected to reimburse at a higher rate than nonsubscribers would pay. Several variations of normal retail charges are used in paying hospitals. An institution might contract to accept a fixed proportion,

---

[3] Adjudication of Thomas Thacher, Superintendent of Insurance, State of New York in the *Matter of Two 1960 Applications of Associated Hospital Service of New York,* August 3, 1960, pp. 9–10.

such as 90 per cent, of its regular charges. Some hospitals have agreed to a payment procedure based upon a varying proportion of their retail charges. Under this method, the percentage is determined by the ratio the total income of an association bears to the total regular charges for hospital services rendered subscribers during a particular period.

It is not uncommon to find the average retail charge for *all* hospitals contracting with a Blue Cross plan used as a reimbursement limit. For example, an association might agree to pay each individual hospital's retail charges as long as such rates do not exceed the average daily charge for all contracting hospitals, or a percentage thereof, e.g., 110 per cent. The rationale of this procedure is to restrain institutions from charging in excess of a norm, since no justification of the reasonableness of charges is required. At the same time it allows reimbursement at a rate approximately adequate. Inefficient hospitals are supposedly penalized by the procedure. In a few associations the average daily charge, or a proportion of it, for all contracting hospitals is the rate of reimbursement for individual hospitals.

Reimbursement schedules based upon retail charges, like per diem schedules, have the advantage of simple derivation. Intricate statistical techniques are not required to determine the price to be paid by an association. In addition, reimbursement based upon a hospital's charges prevents non-Blue Cross organizations and patients from feeling they are receiving discriminatory treatment. This method has the obvious advantage for hospitals that they themselves dictate the terms of reimbursement.

A disadvantage of basing payments to hospitals on their retail charges is the constant possibility that some institutions will overcharge. To preclude this, review and audit committees are necessitated. Reimbursement on retail charges also allows some hospitals to gain a profit from their relations with Blue Cross. In addition, Blue Cross plans have the primary obligation of restraining unnecessary rises in hospital rates when the reimbursement is on hospital charges.

Finally, a major conceptual issue is involved. By paying retail charges an association is assuming part of the community's financial burden for the free care given to medically indigent. This occurs because the difference between hospital costs and charges for paying patients is used to provide the free care.[4] Many observers question whether a contribution of this sort is equitable for associations when these organizations already cover an important portion of those who would probably otherwise be receiving "free" hospital treatment.

The use of retail charge schedules appears to be decreasing. The number of Blue Cross plans with this type of arrangement declined from twenty-nine in 1950 to twenty-two in 1959. Over half of the associations which used retail charges were located in the South; only two were in the East. This is undoubtedly influenced by the fact that regulatory authorities are tending to look less favorably upon retail charges as a reimbursement method. An example of this attitude may be seen in a detailed review of hospital payment schedules by New York's superintendent of insurance in August, 1960:

> Observance of this principle [that retail charges should be the maximum payment made by Blue Cross], it might be urged, is all that should be looked to by the Superintendent of Insurance in determining the reasonableness of the reimbursement rates of a New York hospital service corporation, such as AHA. But, while, with appropriate discount to recognize the advantage of "wholesale buying" and the avoidance of collection expenses and bad debts, hospital "retail" charges may properly serve as a ceiling for Blue Cross reimbursement rates, the disparities in their composition appear to me to preclude their meaningful use as an accurate gauge of the reasonableness of Blue Cross payments to hospitals.[5]

Reimbursement Based Upon Hospital Costs. Use of hospital costs as the basis for reimbursement has been increasing.

---

[4] "Free" care is now defined in many areas as the hospitalization received by patients who pay less than $10 per day for such treatment. Thus, the term does not mean that such medical care is *completely* free of charge.

[5] Adjudication, New York, August 3, 1960, p. 8.

By this method a Blue Cross plan undertakes to reimburse a contracting hospital for the actual costs the institution incurs in providing services to subscriber-patients. Hospital costs, as allocated to subscribers, provide the theoretical minimum reimbursement figure, inasmuch as no institution would intentionally lose money by providing hospitalization for Blue Cross members.

Considerable judgment must be exercised in allocating expenses between subscribers and nonsubscribers. One such determination which cost-based formulas necessitate is to differentiate between the expenses a hospital incurs in providing private, semiprivate, and ward care. The procedure is to assign a weighting to each of these classes of care. The distribution of costs between categories is based upon many subjective factors, at the present time. No weighting is equally appropriate for all hospitals, but approximate valuations have had to be accepted, pending more objective techniques. For example, the insurance department of New York has agreed upon a weighting of 115:100:90. First, the average daily costs for hospital care are determined by dividing the total *allowable* expenses by the total patient days. Then, private-room care is assumed to account for expenses equal to 115 per cent of average daily costs; semiprivate patients are considered responsible for costs just equal to the average daily figure; and ward care is treated as contributing to over-all expenses in the proportion of 90 per cent of average daily costs. The department declined a suggested ratio of 115:100:85 because it felt costs commensurate with providing ward care were closer to those for semiprivate than this weighting indicated. Many variations are in this method as the relationships between the classes of care are not the same in all areas. There is a strong indication that ward care is more costly than 90 per cent of semiprivate-care costs. Many observers feel the cost of providing ward care is actually higher than the related figure for semiprivate accommodations and possibly greater than the expenses incurred in rendering care in private rooms.

Once the elements included in allowable costs have been agreed upon, the only major alterations are concerned with minimum and maximum limits for total costs. Minimum-cost stipulations are termed "floors" and, where used, are a certain percentage of the average rate of each size or locational grouping of contracting hospitals. Maximum allowable costs are referred to as "ceilings." These are normally a stated proportion of average costs among hospitals of similar nature and size, although ceilings are sometimes stated as a percentage of regular retail charges. The Joint Committee on Hospital Rates in New York uses a ceiling of 110 per cent.

The effect of a floor is to reward hospitals with costs below this level. The inference is that the reward is due to efficiency, although the low costs could be caused by an inferior quality of medical care. Ceilings penalize high-cost institutions by allowing them less than their full cost if the figure is too far out of line with those of related hospitals. The difficult feature in arriving at these minimums and maximums is the hospital groupings used. If large hospitals with specialized facilities are grouped with smaller hospitals having less apparatus and personnel, obviously the reimbursement floors and ceilings will be higher than if the latter type of institution is grouped alone.

Analysis of Internal Factors of Cost-Based Reimbursement. Some guideposts for allocating the internal cost elements attributable to subscribers were established in 1953 by the American Hospital Association as "Principles of Prepayment of Hospital Care" (hereafter referred to as the "Principles"). Minor revisions in the "Principles" were adopted by the AHA House of Delegates in January, 1962, and it is anticipated that further changes will be proposed by early 1963. The AHA standards for prepayment and their revisions have been discussed at several meetings of the NAIC Subcommittee on Reimbursement Formulae between Hospitals and Nonprofit Hospital Service Associations. Supervisory authorities have often relied upon the "Principles" because the NAIC has not reached any decisions on cost factors.

A. Depreciation of Building and Equipment. The amount to which any asset deteriorates during a period of time is subject to conjecture. Those who pay for part of the depreciation, i.e., Blue Cross plans, are likely to place a lower evaluation on the wear and tear than are hospitals who receive the payments. The "Principles" merely state that depreciation must be considered as a part of reimbursable cost, and the funds therefor should be used for capital purposes.[6] Greater mutual agreement on the part of hospitals and Blue Cross plans in this respect was originally facilitated by AHA's "Handbook on Accounting, Statistics and Business Office Procedures for Hospitals," which listed the anticipated life of various hospital apparatus. More recent AHA publications, "The Uniform Chart of Accounts and Definitions for Hospitals" and "Cost Finding for Hospitals," have been of considerable value in determining rates of depreciation in current agreements.

The Joint Committee on Hospital Rates in New York City determined that depreciation for a group of Blue Cross contracting hospitals in New York in 1959 amounted to an average charge of 3.1 per cent of all other reimbursable expenses. An average proportion of 4 per cent was charged by hospitals which had depreciation allowances.[7] The superintendent in New York has approved a flat 5 per cent of the semiprivate rate as an allowable amount for depreciation "on the condition that the allowance be funded by the recipient hospital and used only to defray the costs of replacement of equipment or the modernization and replacement of existing buildings."[8] In granting a flat rate not

---

[6] American Hospital Association, *Principles of Prepayment for Hospital Care* (Chicago: American Hospital Assn., 1953, rev. 1962) , p. 11. Current repairs which do not add to the value of hospital property or equipment are not a part of depreciation. Total expenditures of this sort are allowable as current costs.

[7] Adjudication, New York, August 3, 1960, p. 37.

[8] Adjudication of Thomas Thacher, Superintendent of Insurance, State of New York, in the *Matter of Two Amended 1960 Applications of Associated Hospital Service of New York,* September 12, 1960, p. 9.

specifically related to the cost structure of any particular hospital, the superintendent noted that more accurate determination was impossible on the part of many institutions because they had not kept adequate records to determine depreciation.

The solution to the problem of cost allocation is at least partially dependent upon uniform definitions and accounting procedures. Some associations have asserted, for example, that hospitals are including donated items when they determine depreciation other than with a flat percentage. In many cases neither side can substantiate its position because of inadequate financial records.

The federal government has established some standards for possible use in uniform hospital accounting. These are referred to as "The Hospital Statement of Reimbursable Costs, Joint Hospital Form #1."[9] With reference to depreciation, Joint Form #1 allows 6 per cent of other reimbursable expenses for those hospitals that have not kept sufficient records to determine their specific depreciation figure. It should be noted that any percentage of this nature involves two hazards: if the base to which the percentage is applied is incorrect, the error is magnified in the same direction; and although a hospital with less than 6 per cent actual depreciation could profit from the flat proportion the more probable result is that hospitals with high cost due to inefficiencies would profit while the lower cost, more efficient institutions would not so benefit. Insurance commissioners are about evenly divided in their attitudes toward allowances for depreciation charges on improvements financed by tax funds.

Not only is the amount of depreciation a subject of controversy, but also whether the funds so delegated and paid by Blue Cross should be set aside in a special account or commingled with general hospital funds. Blue Cross plans are of the opinion, and commissioners are beginning to concur with them, that segregation of depreciation funds is

---

[9] Often called "Joint Form #1."

desirable.[10] In this manner assurance exists that reserves are actually used to replace the present plant and not for other hospital needs. Some associations even go so far as to state that their approval, or that of some community agency such as a hospital planning commission, should be required prior to utilization of depreciation funds.

An example of this type of action occurred when the supervisory authority in New York agreed to establishment of a special committee by the New York Blue Cross plan. One of the functions of the committee has been to review requests by hospitals to use replacement-account funds for noncapital purposes. The commissioner in Pennsylvania has also considered this issue. In an "Order on the Reduction of Hospital Costs," in connection with a rate hearing, he stated, "Where hospital reimbursement payments contain an amount for depreciation of capital assets or equipment, the hospitals receiving such monies shall be *requested* to fund them by establishing proper reserves, so that these monies shall be used for the purposes for which they have been paid."[11]

B. Interest on Capital Projects. Another controversial item of cost is the interest many hospitals pay on bonds sold to finance capital projects. Although this is an obvious expense, a question of discrimination is involved. Some hospitals seek to amortize their buildings and equipment by establishing depreciation fund accounts. The principle behind this action is that the costs of facilities are included as a part of total hospital expenses and are, in turn, reflected in the charges of hospitals. When plant and equipment must be repaired or replaced the required money will be available from the

---

[10] Insurance commissioners insist that in their activities they are not "controlling" hospitals nor entering the realm of hospital regulation. When hospitals must make a public accounting as to depreciation funds they have received, however, this is certainly an aspect of control. It is justified by officials on the basis that citizens have the right to expect that hospital facilities will not be depleted. One manner of protecting such interests of citizens is by assuring that depreciation funds are actually spent for replacement needs.

[11] Adjudication, Pennsylvania, April 15, 1958, p. 17. Italics added.

depreciation fund and it will not be necessary to float a bond issue or seek public contributions. However, swings in economic conditions, mounting hospital costs, pressures against increases in hospital charges, and other factors have often made it difficult, if not impossible, for some institutions to amortize their facilities as they intended. At the same time, many hospitals have not attempted to obtain the return of capital funds out of the sale of services. As a result, a majority of the hospitals have had to obtain capital funds from the community. The question then arises whether hospitals which incur interest charges on bonds should be reimbursed by associations when other hospitals that have constructed the same type of facilities avoid such expenses through successful amortization procedures. The possibility exists in this respect that some hospitals which do not receive allowances for interest are more efficient than institutions that obtain such credits.

The current trend is to allow interest as an eligible item in costs. The AHA "Principles" recognize this treatment, and the statement is added: "If the public has not provided a debt-free institution, either through extended purchase of care or through public fund-raising campaigns, it must assume responsibility for the payment of debt service charges added to its bill for hospital care." The comment does not take into account that some hospitals could provide in advance for such funds through segregated amortization accounts.

C. Expenses for Outpatient Treatment. The problem of how to allocate expenses is encountered again in reference to inpatient versus outpatient care. Only a few Blue Cross plans currently offer outpatient benefits; a valuation of expenses a hospital has incurred on behalf of subscribers, therefore, should exclude expenditures made for this type of service.

The supervisory authority in New York allowed the inclusion of some outpatient expenses in a hospital reimbursement formula in 1960. He noted that, ". . . literal application of that principle at this time could result in unfair discrimination against non-Blue Cross patients and reduction of essential community services. . . ."[12] The need for reappraising the methods of financing this element was also mentioned. The recognizable portion of outpatient expenses was restricted to 5 per cent of total reimbursable expenses for each hospital.

Joint Form #1 assumes an average outpatient charge of $3 per visit. The presumption is that outpatient costs approximate the charges for such treatment. Thus, a hospital which has not kept sufficient records to allocate expenses between inpatient and outpatient care merely multiplies the number of outpatient visits by the set dollar amount. The product of this multiplication is assumed to be the total expense incurred in providing outpatient treatment, and the amount is therefore deducted from total costs. This is the most frequent method used by associations in an attempt to exclude outpatient costs. There is considerable variance from the $3 figure, however.

D. Research Expenditures.   The AHA "Principles" exclude major expenditures for medical research from the compilation of reimbursable costs. In so prescribing, the remark was made:

> Research ultimately results in better patient care; its benefits usually are derived over long periods of time and are not always of direct benefit to patients in the hospital at the time the research is being conducted. It is therefore reasonable that such desirable pioneering efforts be financed from sources other than the patients being served in a particular hospital. Such other sources might be eleemosynary foundations, philantrophic contributors, and tax-supported agencies.[13]

E. Training of Doctors and Nurses.   Another issue associated with cost reimbursement concerns the allocation of expenses for training medical personnel. While the whole

---

[12] Adjudication, New York, September 12, 1960, p. 8.

[13] American Hospital Association, *op. cit.*, p. 8.

community ultimately benefits from these expenditures and thus should pay for them, it is common for patients to bear much of the educational and training costs. The "Principles" state in this respect:

> In determining reimbursable cost, a reasonable amount for medical, nursing and other education not reimbursed through tuition, or through scholarships, grants or other community sources is a legitimate inclusion in the interest of continuing to upgrade quality of service to the community.
>
> Comment . . . It will be necessary . . . that the cost of such programs be considered as a factor in determining reimbursable cost of hospital service until the community is prepared to assume this educational responsibility.[14]

Further justification for the inclusion of expenses incurred in the training of residents and interns has been based upon the idea that this training will: "(1) provide services to assure continuous 24-hour medical supervision of the care of patients, (2) encourage high standards of medical staff performance, (3) enhance the knowledge, ability and technical skills of physicians who will be serving the community."[15]

The desirability of at least limiting the inclusion of training expenses has been noted by the insurance commissioner in Pennsylvania: "Through . . . negotiations, the Blue Cross Plan shall seek to adjust hospital payments which include the cost of medical research and the cost of maintaining nursing schools to an amount commensurate with the services received by Blue Cross patients from such [activities]."[16] Other commissioners are not in unanimous agreement with this attitude, although there is general support of it.

F. Evaluation of Services by Members of Religious Orders. There has been some dissension in the past over the cost allowances for members of religious orders who work in hospitals. The purpose of cost schedules is to reimburse

---

[14] *Ibid.,* pp. 8–9.

[15] Statement by the Associated Hospital Service of New York in Adjudication, New York, August 3, 1960, p. 32.

[16] Adjudication, Pennsylvania, April 15, 1958, p. 17.

a hospital for expenses it has incurred on behalf of the association, but oftentimes these religious members (primarily Roman Catholic Sisters) receive little or no compensation. The situation is particularly touchy for Blue Cross plans in locales where religious institutions provide an important portion of subscriber hospitalization.

The logic now generally used is that members of religious orders are donating their time and services to their church. Theoretically, these individuals could work for a normal salary, then turn it over to the institution of which they are a member. Just because they agree to forego their compensation or, in effect, to "return" it to the institution, does not mean they should not be accorded average wages for their endeavors. Thus, most Blue Cross plans do pay a hospital for this type of donated work. The amount of such remuneration is determined by negotiation, and it approximates what is received by nurses providing similar services in similar institutions in the community. The AHA "Principles" sanction this procedure. Expenses for maintaining the sisters are not includable costs for a hospital under this approach, inasmuch as the approximate market value of contributed service is used.

Most of the regulatory authorities who answered an NAIC questionnaire in late 1961 concerned with reimbursement were of the opinion that the only cost item which should be included for contributed services is the cost of maintenance.

Advantages and Disadvantages of Cost-based Reimbursement. Schedules based upon hospital costs are amenable to the nonprofit status of Blue Cross plans. The cost method also provides in principle that hospitals will receive adequate amounts to cover the expenses they incur in providing hospitalization to subscribers. The audits, uniform accounting, and other procedures which establish this adequacy assure that a Blue Cross plan is not being overcharged. Then too, the hospital knows in advance it will receive payment for the services rendered to association members, many of whom might otherwise be recipients of "free" care because of their inability to pay for hospitalization.

However, several disadvantages are associated with cost-based schedules. The high-cost hospital may not be operating as efficiently as a lower-cost institution, yet the former is reimbursed at a higher rate. There is some question, therefore, as to whether reimbursement based upon costs might not encourage inefficiency. If so, such schedules would also encourage increases in the cost of hospitalization. (Ceilings on cost schedules attempt to prevent this.) Then, too, associations have the responsibility, as was true under the retail-charges method, for identifying the causes of rising hospital costs. Commissioners seem to feel, however, that publication of costs for individual hospitals will help reveal unnecessary expenses and, at the same time, encourage efficiency.

Practical problems are also a part of the cost-based payments. Extensive audits, internal standards, and controls become necessary. In addition, there must be agreement as to the expenses and allowances included and excluded from costs.

Attitudes toward Cost-based Schedules. Insurance companies naturally dislike any use of the cost basis by associations. They feel it gives Blue Cross an undeserved financial advantage. The American Life Convention, the Health Insurance Association of America, and the Life Insurance Association of America have therefore proposed, on behalf of their member companies, revision of the "Principles of Prepayment for Hospital Care" to include the following overriding principle:

A third-party agency contracting with hospitals for benefits to be rendered hospital-using beneficiaries or subscribers should be expected to pay "full cost" defined and prorated in such a way that the books of the hospitals, taken collectively, would balance if the entire bill-paying public were beneficiaries or subscribers of such agency.[17]

---

[17] *Proceedings, the National Association of Insurance Commissioners, 1962,* Vol. I, p. 176.

This suggestion would in effect eliminate the current concept of cost-based reimbursement since associations would be forced to share in the payment of charitable care.

The first principle in the AHA standards, in the most recent revision, is: "The amount and method of payment to hospitals should be such as (1) to pay fairly and adequately for *services purchased* [italics added], (2) to maintain essential services, and (3) to encourage the development of higher standards of service to meet the needs of the community." The "Principles" currently justify the cost approach to reimbursement in the following manner:

Under the principle of free enterprise, individual full-pay patients would expect to pay approximately the same amounts for the same services in the same community. But in the long run, established charges to individual patients cannot be expected to control the amounts paid by large-scale contractors who guarantee definite payments for all their clients. The amount paid by such a contracting agency will tend to equal the cost of the services rendered to its clients.

Since the American Hospital Association represents the bulk of the country's hospitals in many matters and also looks out for the best interests of the institutions, AHA's support of the cost approach is having a profound influence on regulatory attitudes.

The reimbursement dispute was at one time referred to the Liaison Conference between the Health Insurance Association of America and Blue Cross–Blue Shield. This group realized no agreement would ever be reached, so they "agreed" not to consider the matter further. The NAIC subcommittee which is trying to resolve the reimbursement issue has reached no conclusion, as yet. In late 1961, the subcommittee sent a questionnaire concerned with attitudes and statistics about reimbursement to all Blue Cross plans and state insurance commissioners. Returns from the questionnaire revealed that respondents felt reimbursement schedules should be flexible in recognizing the needs of different types of hospitals. The problem in this respect is how to categorize the institutions. Classifications by urban and rural locality, bed capacity, and public versus private ownership were not acceptable to the associations nor to the insurance commissioners who answered the NAIC query. Most did agree that hospitals with associated medical schools should be in a separate category. If any stand is taken by the NAIC after its investigation, it is probable that most of the suggestions of insurance company organizations will be rejected and approval will be given to at least a modified cost basis of reimbursement.

While reimbursement formulas now generally differ among hospitals within a plan area, as well as within states where more than one association is located, most plans and regulatory authorities indicated that institutions within a plan area and within a particular state should have the same formula arrangements.

Both associations and supervisory officials favor the cost-based schedules. Fifteen of the thirty-three commissioners who responded to the NAIC questionnaire preferred the audited hospital-costs method to any other basis, while four favored costs with an imposed ceiling. Three of the thirty-three officials advocated a negotiated per diem arrangement, two would use a per diem sliding scale, and seven suggested using charges billed to patients. Two of the commissioners favored a schedule which would discount retail charges.

Two reasons were among those given for the cost-based schedule preference: first it would be most equitable for plans, the public, and hospitals alike, and second, it automatically incorporates cost-level changes, thus diminishing the need for constant renegotiation on schedule conditions. An indication of the somewhat-common regulatory attitude toward cost-based schedules may be observed in a 1960 declaration by the superintendent of insurance for the State of New York:

Reimbursement on the basis of an individual hospital's costs
. . . appears to be the only method by which to obviate under-

payment of individual hospitals and overpayment of others (as on a flat or index-based rate) and to avoid potentially persistent overpayment by a Blue Cross plan (as on a "retail" charge basis). But the success of any cost-based system is in turn dependent upon the propriety of the value judgments used in the identification of costs referable to subscriber inpatient care and in their allocation as between services covered as service benefits by the subscriber contract and those handled thereunder by way of indemnity or not at all.[18]

Regulatory authorities are of the general opinion that reimbursement of proprietary hospitals should be on other than a "cost-plus" basis. They also definitely feel that all hospitals reimbursed on a cost arrangement should be required to maintain uniform accounting procedures.

Trend in Use of Cost-based Schedules. There is a pronounced trend toward cost-related schedules, as may be seen in Table 10–1. Associations covering 63 per cent of total sub-

TABLE 10–1

HOSPITAL REIMBURSEMENT METHODS, 1950–1959

	Number of Plans			Number of Subscribers			Percentage of Total Enrollment		
Year	*Cost Related*	*Retail Charges*	*Per Diem or Other*	*Cost Related*	*Retail Charges*	*or Other Method*	*Cost Related*	*Retail Charges*	*Per Diem or Other*
1959	49	22	8	34,153,462	11,479,422	8,068,657	63.60	21.38	15.02
1957	37	30	12	30,628,208	12,458,337	8,624,477	59.23	24.09	16.68
1955	37	29	13	28,349,128	10,850,854	8,080,433	59.96	22.95	17.09
1950	25	29	25	15,540,000	8,384,974	11,914,564	43.36	23.40	33.24

Source: Blue Cross Commission.

scribers used cost-type methods for paying hospitals in 1959, as contrasted with 43 per cent in 1950. Eleven of the sixteen Blue Cross plans in the four largest states had schedules based upon hospitals' costs in 1959. Nine of the thirteen associations with more than a million members were using this type of formula.

The pressure by associations for cost-based schedules is less

---

[18] Adjudication, New York, August 3, 1960, p. 10. Parenthesis in the original.

pronounced in areas with special government hospitals for the medically indigent, such as in California. In these areas other hospitals do not have the burden of providing care for the needy. Any endowment income of nongovernmental hospitals may then be used to reduce the charges to *all* patients and not solely to pay for the care of the poor. It also appears that the reduced bargaining position of plans in areas where only a small percentage of the population is enrolled has tended to make institutions more hostile toward cost-based schedules in such locales. (This, too, is a part of the California situation.)

Regulatory Control over Hospital Reimbursement Schedules

About half the state laws place reimbursement schedules under the jurisdiction of the supervisory official. New York requires the approval of the commissioner of social welfare as to the adequacy of payment rates to hospitals, while the superintendent of insurance rules on the reasonableness thereof. California, Pennsylvania, and Illinois are among the many states which prescribe that the commissioner of insurance must give approval to reimbursement contracts with hospitals prior to their use.

Attitudes vary as to whether it is appropriate for regulatory authorities to have controls over reimbursement schedules. Most associations apparently feel this is desirable, and a definite majority of the commissioners think it necessary. The reasons advanced against such controls are that they are either unnecessary or not within the jurisdiction of state insurance officials. Those who feel it is not necessary for insurance departments to have jurisdiction over reimbursement schedules argue that a commissioner's authority over rates is sufficient. The commissioner can hold down any unwarranted rise in hospital costs paid by associations, they say, by refusing rate-increase requests. Associations will then be unable to increase the level of payments under the schedules. This attitude, however, fails to reconcile the possibility that hospitals would refuse to accept a contract with reductions. Such action is certainly possible in institutions with a high bed-occupancy rate attributable to non-Blue Cross subscribers. The increase of arms-length dealings also contributes to the possibility. Associations could be left in the lurch if pressured by an adamant commissioner who would not agree to rate increases and hospitals which would not continue to provide services unless the reimbursement were raised.

It appears that final approval of these schedules by the commissioner is most desirable. This does not impair the ability of hospitals and associations to negotiate mutually the schedule inclusions and amounts. If they are justified and well reasoned, particularly through uniform accounting methods, supervisory officials may be expected to accept the schedule arrangements. Probably only inefficient institutions and those without proper records need have any real fears.

Hospital personnel have questioned whether an insurance commissioner's authority over reimbursement schedules is legal. It is an obvious control over part of a hospital's income, and Blue Cross can be a substantial source of hospital receipts when subscribers account for an important part of the bed occupancy. Still, no hospital is under compulsion, other than economic, to contract with a Blue Cross plan. Nor can any regulatory official require a hospital and an association to deal with each other on a stipulated rate basis. He can only tell them that if they do contract, it must be on terms agreeable to him. This is considered legally proper. If an institution does not agree with a commissioner's edict concerning the rate of payment, it can sever its connections with an association. An alternative would be to appeal to the courts, since the commissioner's actions are normally subject to judicial review.

Several experiments in process attempt to make hospital reimbursement more objective, and among the most interesting are those instituted by insurance commissioners. The need for new procedures in the area of reimbursement has been expressed by one supervisory official as follows:

I realize that there is suspicion of collusion. Yet in its dealings with the hospitals, Blue Cross has been tending to go the opposite of what the public thinks. Blue Cross may be trying to drive too hard a bargain with the hospitals. . . .

In order to convince the public that someone is looking out for its interests and to make certain that hospitals are not overcharging, it is my belief that [there should be] an independent agency representing the Blue Cross, the hospitals and the State Government, which would employ "hospital examiners" similar to bank and insurance examiners, to examine and audit hospital records and accounting procedures and satisfy everyone that the hospital costs are honest and fair.

While most people still would not understand the complexities of hospital financing, the same people do not understand banking or insurance financing either, yet they trust their banks and their insurance companies because expert examiners certify the bank and insurance records. It is my further belief that the hospitals would gain similar public confidence if they were certified by competent examiners for this special hospital work.[19]

A new organization has been created in Maryland to do the things viewed as necessary by the commissioner quoted above.

Partly as a result of the interest in Blue Cross problems, and partly because of the interest of the State of Maryland in the cost of its program for hospitalization for indigent persons, the State Health Department and the State Insurance Department have sponsored a new organization—The Hospital Cost Analysis Service. It will be the purpose of this organization to try to establish proper methods of uniform accounting for hospitals. We hope this will permit us to arrive at a better understanding of hospital costs.

This non-profit organization will operate as an entirely independent body. The initial Board of Directors were [*sic.*] chosen by the State Department of Health, the Insurance Commissioner, the Hospital Council of Maryland, the Maryland Blue Cross, the State Bar Association, and the Maryland Association of Certi-

---

[19] Letter from Mr. Alfred N. Premo, Commissioner of Insurance, State of Connecticut, to Mr. F. Douglass Sears, Insurance Commissioner, State of Maryland, dated April 18, 1960.

fied Public Accountants, each of whom designated one Director. Four Directors representing the general public were named by the Governor. . . .

The cost of operating the service is to be borne jointly by the State Health Department, the Hospital Council, and the Blue Cross. . . .

The organization will conduct systematic, on-the-site examinations of financial and statistical records at hospitals throughout the State of Maryland to determine actual patient care costs. These cost figures will be used by the State as the basis for payment for care rendered indigent and medically indigent patients and by Blue Cross for determining payments to hospitals for the care of subscribers.[20]

The NAIC is watching the development in Maryland with considerable interest, and the Subcommittee to Study the Problem of Reimbursement Formulas is compiling information on this and other experiments. A report of the subcommittee was approved at the December, 1961, meeting of the NAIC, when it was decided to continue the study of the present bases of payment. The returns from the NAIC questionnaire on reimbursement will undoubtedly influence future NAIC deliberations on this subject. Some of the responses to the questionnaire have been—and will be—discussed in this book.

Critique of Hospital Reimbursement Schedules

The nature of an association's responsibilities to contracting hospitals and the dependency of hospitals upon hospital service associations are influencing factors in reimbursement arrangements. Since the schedules are generally established by negotiation between the associations and the hospitals before being passed upon by the regulatory authority, the relative bargaining power of each side plays a large part in determining the final terms. It is true that many hospitals are dependent upon associations for their very existence in areas

---

[20] Report of the Subcommittee to Study the Problem of Reimbursement Formulas between Hospitals and Service Associations, contained in the minutes of NAIC meeting at San Francisco, California, May 30, 1960.

of high population enrollment. Inadequate reimbursement will impair the quality of medical care, unless outside funds make up the deficit. Blue Cross plans do not want to bankrupt the hospitals, nor do most hospitals want to impair the financial condition of the associations. One needs the other. This does not eliminate the fact, however, that both parties do, and should, look out for their own interests.

In areas with a large number of hospitals and a major portion of the population covered by Blue Cross, the association is likely to be in the superior bargaining position. Doctors are most likely to select or suggest member hospitals where a potential patient will be able to receive full service benefits. Subscribers themselves will show obvious preference for co-operating institutions. And when a sizeable segment of a community is enrolled in Blue Cross, a "renegade" hospital may see a decline in its bed-occupancy ratio. Hospitals in such locales are prone to agree to cost-based schedules rather than refuse to contract with an association.

The justifications for giving a Blue Cross plan so-called hospital "discounts" have been: that the associations are purchasing large blocks of service and should be entitled to a wholesale price; that a hospital is guaranteed prompt and adequate payment for services rendered; and that many Blue Cross patients would have received "free" care from the hospital if they had not been plan members. Commissioners generally reject the idea that a discount should be allowed just because plans relieve hospitals of collection difficulties. Many of the regulatory officials agree with the other arguments in favor of the cost basis, however.

Blue Cross plans feel, with considerable justification, that many lower-income groups have built-in adverse selection factors. In accepting low-income members, associations think they are not only making financially responsible patients out of such enrollees but at the same time accepting high loss-ratio groups. Why then, associations reason, should they pay for the care given by hospitals to those with low incomes who are not Blue Cross members? If reimbursement were on a charge basis, associations would obviously be contributing to the payment of the medically indigent. Since there is no important difference between the income levels of groups covered by Blue Cross and those with insurance company protection, the significance of this sentiment on the part of Blue Cross would be diminished for those plans whose enrollment is largely on a group basis *if insurance companies customarily granted group conversion privileges.* Although more carriers are now offering conversion rights, they have not generally done so in the past. As a result, the aged have not been able to retain their protection upon retirement when covered by insurance companies. If carriers were to provide conversion privileges, the use of experience-rating techniques by Blue Cross would further reduce the distinction between the two types of organizations.

The real issue involved in cost-based schedules is whether paying patients should bear costs institutions have had to incur on behalf of nonpaying patients. Since hospitalized policyholders have had this cost of care for the medically indigent included in their charges, insurance companies have felt the same treatment should be imposed upon associations. The more narrow basis for differentiation in payments has thus relied upon associations' acceptance of nongroup subscribers without stringent underwriting practices, as well as upon the group conversion privileges traditionally available in Blue Cross.

When the NAIC was considering this topic, a leading spokesman for the health insurance companies expressed their sentiment very clearly.

The principles under consideration by your subcommittee as published by the American Hospital Association contain a statement in the introductory comment which indicates that there is a differential between established charges to individual patients and the amounts paid by large scale contractors who under certain conditions guarantee payment for all their clients for the same accommodations. These principles, therefore, by encouraging the exclusion of specific operating cost items from the hospital's

reimbursement formula would support this differential produc-
ing a different rate of reimbursement to the hospital for the same
type of care to the public with the controlling variable being the
patient's status in financing such care. This is inequitable to the
public since it supports a discriminatory pricing policy which
may either ultimately place the hospital in an unstable financial
position or financially penalize the patient who pays for his hospital care at the higher level of reimbursement.[21]

Preceding discussions have attempted to analyze this difference in philosophy to an extent sufficient for the reader to
see the divergencies. On the basis of these it appears that cost-
based formulas are justified. It is regrettable and unfair that
insurance companies and noninsured paying patients are
forced to assume part of the over-all community burden
brought by the medically indigent. Reforms should be instituted to correct this type of abuse. Regulatory authorities,
for example, are in general agreement that the eventual solution should involve a governmental subsidy for hospitals.
The commissioners feel that such a subsidy should reflect the
principle that responsibility for capital improvements of hospitals, as well as for treatment of the medically indigent, lies
with the public and not with those who are hospitalized. The
fact that insurance companies are currently wronged, however, is in no way a vindication of similar improper treatment for Blue Cross plans.

FEE SCHEDULES

Fee schedules establish the rates of payment by Blue
Shield plans to physicians, and other allowable practitioners,
for rendering services to subscribers. These instruments
have a purpose similar to that of hospital reimbursement
schedules. It has been pointed out, however, that the financial arrangements doctors have with many associations do

---

[21] Mr. J. F. Follmann, Jr., Director of Information and Research, Health
Insurance Association of America, in a statement before the NAIC Subcommit-
tee to Study the Problem of Reimbursement Formulas between Hospitals and
Service Associations, June 10, 1957.

not make fee schedules the only basis of payments for given services. Where indemnity benefits only are provided, or where a subscriber's income is in excess of income limits, a doctor may receive payment from the patient for any difference between the rates established in the schedule and his normal fees.

Blue Shield plans have been reticent to enter into deliberations concerning fee schedule relativities. It has been frequent practice for medical socities in an area to determine the relative values of various medical treatments and services, primarily those of a surgical nature. In the past, these weighted values were generally accepted by an association. Now Blue Shield plans often have fee schedule committees composed only of doctors to consider these issues. Associations generally determine the dollar value of a unit in negotiation with the medical profession. The unit dollar value multiplied by the number of units assigned for a particular operation determines the fees doctors will receive for treating subscribers.

Fee schedules are often referred to or categorized by their uppermost limit. A schedule which allows a top fee of $300 for the most difficult surgical procedures is called a "$300 schedule." The unfortunate implication is that a $500 schedule automatically pays higher fees to doctors than does, say, a $300 schedule. Actually, a $500 schedule may have considerably lower rates of compensation for most operations than a $300 schedule.

There is no uniformity within state boundaries as to the rates set by fee schedules. Nor is there concurrence among states as to the relative values of various medical procedures.

Regulatory Control Over Fee Schedules

About half of the enabling acts in states which regulate Blue Shield plans contain provisions for regulatory approval of rates of payment between associations and physicians. This is similar to the proportion of laws granting controls over payments to hospitals. Although statutes do provide a commissioner with approval power, in many states it is a perfunctory process. At least there is much less extensive determination of the propriety of these schedules than is true of arrangements with hospitals.

The medical profession as a group, and doctors individually, take offense at the prospect of controls over any feature of the practice of medicine. This attitude is present when supervisory controls are placed on the fee schedules of associations which offer service benefits. Pressures from various sources have been successful in preventing regulatory supervision of fee schedules in many areas. The insurance department of New York, for example, with all of its power and prestige, has not been granted the right to approve the fee arrangements Blue Shield plans make with contracting doctors. California does not regulate medical service plans, so fee schedules obviously are not subject to approval from any governmental agency in that state. The statutes of Pennsylvania do prescribe approval of fee schedules from the insurance commissioner before they can become effective, and the department is being watched throughout the country as to how it effects these controls. The Pennsylvania provision states: ". . . all methods and rates of payment by such corporation to doctors of medicine (or doctors of osteopathy or doctors of dental surgery) serving its subscribers . . . shall be approved by the Insurance Department before they become effective."

In a 1961 adjudication of a Blue Shield rate case in Pennsylvania, the insurance commissioner of the commonwealth outlined the position of a regulatory authority in reference to fee schedules. At the same time his remarks point to several attitudes which have compounded the difficulties of supervision in this area.

It may very well be that the Blue Shield Board of Directors, aided by its Fee Schedule Committee, thoroughly reviews requests from doctors . . . for revisions of fee schedules. It may very well be that Blue Shield gauges such requests for revisions against sound standards and submits them to the Insurance Department for approval only when such revisions are eminently justified or required. The testimony submitted at the hearing, however, could not fail but give the impression that in some instances such thorough review is not made. . . . [The] Chairman of the Fee Schedule Committee, stated with respect to the changes proposed for radiation therapy that he did not know how the proposed new fees were arrived at by the roentgenologists and that he would take no responsibility for these fees being appropriate. . . .

Witnesses for Blue Shield did not specify what criteria or standards were applied to determine whether the upward revision of fees was proper and justified. . . .

Blue Shield, in its brief, repeatedly stated that such revisions must be accepted by me where there is no medical testimony contradicting their reasonableness. This is a strange position for Blue Shield to take when it also argues that I, as Insurance Commissioner, have no right to take testimony from any one other than Blue Shield representatives and that the holding of any public hearing is improper. More important, however, Blue Shield's position, if true, would for all practical purposes deny me, as Insurance Commissioner, the express authority placed in me by Section 12 of the Blue Shield Regulatory Act to approve all methods and rates of payments by Blue Shield to doctors serving its subscribers. If Blue Shield is correct, I could never reject any proposed fee until I . . . had elicited and obtained medical testimony challenging its reasonableness. Furthermore, I would doubt the readiness of many doctors to testify against the reasonableness of fees worked out by Blue Shield and committees of the State Medical Society. This fact is very evident when the State Medical Society rejected an opportunity to have a representative appear at these hearings for the very purpose of testifying upon the reasonableness of proposed fees. If, as Blue Shield contends, a proposed fee must be accepted when not contradicted by medical testimony, it would not be the Insurance Commissioner who would be empowered to approve or reject proposed fees, but rather, it would be the medical profession. This interpretation I must summarily reject as being contrary to the clear intent of the Blue Shield Regulatory Act.

. . . If the Chairman of Blue Shield's Fee Schedule Committee cannot personally vouch for the fairness of a fee submitted to me, how can I vouch for it before the general public of Pennsylvania?[22]

The commissioner then set down factors which must be considered and established before the proposed reimbursement schedule could be approved.

I recommend that Blue Shield consider the following factors in making such revision and be prepared to demonstrate to the Insurance Department the effect of such factors upon each revision which it proposes:

1. Time and skills involved in the procedure being revised in relation to comparable procedures.

2. The average fees paid doctors in Pennsylvania for the procedure being revised and the average fees paid for comparable services in terms of time and skill.

3. The aggregate fees paid by Blue Shield to doctors for the procedure being revised and the number of doctors receiving such aggregate payment.

4. Comparable data relating to fees for similar services paid by public agencies such as the United States Veterans Administration to Pennsylvania doctors.

5. Data showing the aggregate instances where the revised fee will be in full payment for the procedure and data showing the aggregate instances where doctors will bill patients for additional amounts together with aggregate estimates of such additional billings.

6. The estimated average income (and basis of evaluation) of the Blue Shield subscribers directly affected by such revised fee.

7. The submission of a formula, factor, or explanation showing to what extent the proposed fee is less than the average or reasonable fee for the same procedure which would properly be charged over income patients.

8. Such other data as will enable me to determine the reasonableness of such proposed revision. . . .

A comprehensive review of all Blue Shield fee schedules taking into consideration the above factors is in order.[23]

---

[22] Adjudication, in the *Matter of Filing No. 1–H, 1960, of the Medical Service Association of Pennsylvania,* February 2, 1961, pp. 13–15.

[23] *Ibid.,* pp. 15–16.

The laws of Illinois stipulate that, "Payment for medical services may be made to participating or non-participating physicians at rates adopted by the board of trustees." Thus, control over fee schedules is delegated by law to the governing boards.

Several executives report that the very fact a commissioner has power over fee schedules is often a stimulant for boards of directors to inquire into these payments with more detail and interest.

Some executives, particularly of national organizations, say that the only concern of regulatory authorities over fee schedules should be in determining that subscriber rates are not excessive. This, of course, amounts to no control at all over the payments to doctors and is in direct opposition to the attitude of such officials as the commissioner of Pennsylvania.

Summary Concerning Fee Schedules

Physicians, like hospitals, are not obligated to perform services for Blue Shield plans. If a commissioner's decree concerning a fee schedule is not considered tolerable, doctors can refuse to contract with the Blue Shield organization. Mass refusal on the part of doctors could actually stifle the operations of medical service associations in more ways than one. The associations need doctors to provide services guaranteed to subscribers, and, equally important, the approval of local medical societies is a necessary requirement for an organization to be approved as a Blue Shield plan. In addition, some state laws require an association to have the cooperation of a certain percentage of doctors in order for it to function within the jurisdiction.

As in the case of hospitals, effective control of Blue Cross rates necessitates a regulatory official having authority over fee schedules. This provides him with a weapon against unwarranted advances in costs and removes the possibility that elements of the medical profession will be able to dictate to

Blue Shield plans. Still, commissioners must walk the high wire of discretion in order to retain the active cooperation of doctors in medical service plans and, at the same time, prevent regulatory actions from encouraging a reduction in the quality of medical care.

chapter XI

RATES

Scholars often characterize the "rate" as "the heart of the insurance transaction." It is understandable, then, that regulatory problems concerned with Blue Cross and Blue Shield rates are as old as public supervision of the associations. In fact, much of the logic behind governmental authority over hospital and medical service associations is the alleged undesirability, or inability, of these organizations to "regulate" their own rates. Blue Cross plans, for example, had a monopoly in the hospital prepayment realm in the early 1930's. To give an association free rein over the rates it would charge subscribers was considered by some states as possibly subjecting enrollees to the same type of overcharges characterizing monopolies. In many areas Blue Cross and Blue Shield plans themselves requested governmental supervision. This would help assure subscribers they were being treated fairly.

RATE MAKING AND RATING METHODS

Community Rating

One early goal of Blue Cross and Blue Shield was to make hospital service available to all segments of a community. To do so involved covering poor risks as well as average and better risks. This was considered in the community interest, and all covered elements of the community were averaged. All subscribers supposedly paid the same rate, and, about two decades after the inception of associations, this technique became known as "community rating."

Actually, at no time have all subscribers paid identical rates. Most associations have differentiated between single subscribers, those with one dependent, and families. As Blue Cross and Blue Shield plans expanded their enrollment methods to embrace nongroup members, a different rate was used for these direct-pay subscribers. Conversion privileges, a traditional feature of group certificates, developed another type of member, the group conversion subscriber. The higher claim costs incurred by those who convert have often been felt to necessitate a special rate for this membership category.

From the very beginning, then, departures have been made from the principle that each subscriber should pay the same rate regardless of his claim potential. A pure community rate would probably have been one whereby each spending unit made the same contribution to an association without such payment being influenced by any other factor.[1] Thus, "community rating" becomes a matter of definition.

The concept of community rating was first considered an *actuarial-statistical technique.* In this rate-making sense it implied a pooling of risks among the members of a community, with the "community" including either all of the citizens in an association's area or all of the subscribers. Averaging resulted in the low-loss subscribers subsidizing the high-loss members.

"Community rating" came to mean more than a method for determining rates, however. Hospitals were in the social and community interest and the medically indigent presented a social problem. Since Blue Cross and Blue Shield were able to assume part of this social burden, the community-rating concept they employed began to take on *sociopolitical overtones.* In the latter context community rating has received adverse as well as favorable comment. When combined with the nonprofit characteristic of associa-

---

[1] Some observers feel that a rate based on ability to pay would be more equitable than even a pure community rate, i.e., a rate based on the benefit structure. The judgment and administrative problems connected with rates determined by ability to pay have prevented their serious consideration by associations.

tions, community rating has implied to many that socialistic principles are being utilized and that the entire process is against the American ideal of private enterprise.

Internally, community rating is a critical issue because those who abandon its use are considered by some other associations as having compromised a basic characteristic of the Blues' movement. At the same time the mavericks are felt to have moved closer to insurance-company-type operations. Community rating has become an external problem because most associations are competitively handicapped with it.

Experience Rating

"Experience rating," also called "merit rating" or "self-adjusting rates," is a method evolved to deal with the inadequacies of the community-rating technique. The "new" device goes beyond the deviations for family composition and type of membership used to modify a pure community rate. It allows, in addition, the actual loss experience of a group, and sometimes the expense experience as well, to influence the rate paid.

State laws often prescribe who may be considered a "group" for health insurance purposes. Generally allowable are employees of a common employer, members of a labor union, those who belong to an association not created for the purpose of obtaining insurance, and trusteeships of multiple employers-employees. In this latter arrangement small groups of certain sizes, such as between ten and twenty-five members, are combined and a collective group rate is determined. The same might be done for groups with twenty-five to fifty members, for example, and all over fifty would be individually experience rated.

An experience rate is determined through the application of three, or possibly four, elements: the class rate (often known as the community rate), group experience, and group credibility. The fourth element is an allowance for contingencies. By taking into account the anticipated loss or claim costs, expected administrative costs, and contingency reserve requirements for each class—e.g., single group subscribers, family group subscribers, etc.—the community rate is ascertained basically by dividing the total of these amounts by the total subscribers in the class. A prospective determination is involved in that last year's class experience plus trend factors are used to compute the rate for the coming year. The three primary trend factors for Blue Cross are changes in hospital admissions, length of stay, and hospital costs. The adjustments for Blue Shield are utilization of doctors' services and changes in medical-surgical costs.

A group experience trend is then estimated by comparing the group's actual loss ratio with its expected loss ratio for the past period. Actually, the statistics from several past periods may be utilized. Loss ratios are essentially the proportion incurred claim costs, actual or expected, bear to earned subscription income, actual or expected.

The degree of reliability of the expected experience loss ratio is determined by the group's credibility factor. A controlling determinant of this factor is the size of the group. The larger the group, the more trustworthy its experience. A credibility factor may vary from 100 per cent for groups of possibly a thousand or more members, down to 5 or 10 per cent for small groups, such as twenty-five members. The greater significance attributed to the experience of a large group means that its actual loss ratio is more likely to be free of accidental fluctuations and to represent its probable prospective loss ratio. Limitations imposed by the credibility factor stabilize the rates for smaller groups. Without these the widely fluctuating experience from year to year in small groups would call for unduly frequent rate changes.

Once the credibility factor is determined the final rate construction is carried out. If group size suggests a 30 per cent significance figure, then 30 per cent of the rate is based upon the specific group's expected loss ratio and 70 per cent is determined by the expected loss ratio of the class. The expense portion of the rate is generally added separately for small groups, inasmuch as such groups can do little to affect expenses upward or downward. In some instances larger groups are allowed experience modifications of the expense element based generally on the proportional size of the case.

Some associations modify the experience-rating process by basing part or all of the credibility upon the total group payroll or upon the total premiums for medical care coverage.

The rate-making process described here is applied to all categories of a group's members: the single class, those with one dependent, and the family class.

The experience modifications may be made on a prospective basis, as described, or retrospectively. With the latter process, a group's actual rate is determined after the period of protection is completed. Thus, for groups with 100 per cent credibility, retrospective rating amounts to a cost-plus arrangement, with the "plus" the expense portion and any amount included for contingencies. (New York law limits the retrospective period to one year.)

Some associations apply the retrospective rate modification if it will result in a *lower* group payment; otherwise, the prospective experience rate is used. This is, of course, a competitive inducement. At first glance it would appear to encourage over-all rate inadequacy for an association since groups with poor experience would make no additional retroactive payment while those with favorable experience would be granted a retroactive credit. Aggregate rate inadequacy is averted when this provision is employed by including a contingency factor for such credits in all group rates.

It is possible for an association to lose money through experience rating. One large eastern Blue Cross plan recently lost $1.8 million on experience-rated business. Improper trend analysis in the *prospective* rate contributed to the loss, although the actual cause has not yet been determined with certainty. The association suspects utilization of outpatient diagnostic benefits is partially responsible.

Stimuli for Experience Rating. The growth of experience

rating was fostered by insurance companies after World War II when increased intensity of business competition forced an emphasis on cost reductions. At the same time, the upsurge in utilization and cost of associations' benefits caused many groups to change their former support of the community-rating principle and its associated high-cost elements. Groups with favorable experience saw the opportunity to obtain hospital and medical insurance coverage at a reduced outlay if such cost were based upon their own losses rather than those of an entire class. Insurance companies developed experience rating partly as a means of providing rate equity and also because many employers and unions were threatening to self-insure if experience rating techniques were not adopted. Blue Cross and Blue Shield thus had some of their largest groups switch to coverages offered by insurance companies. A perplexing enigma developed. The departure of low-loss groups would leave Blue Cross–Blue Shield with predominantly high-loss elements. Rates would have to be increased. Higher rates in themselves would discourage the continuation of favorable groups remaining with the Blues, as well as deter those considering membership. Further losses of subscribers to insurance companies would ensue. This pattern actually occurred, and the proportional loss of subscribers discussed in Chapter II is partially explained by the failure of associations to utilize competitive rating methods.

A further dilemma appeared. The supposed goal of Blue Cross and Blue Shield was to enroll elements of the community for whom coverage was otherwise not obtainable. Generally those citizens lacked coverage because they could not afford to pay for protection. Blue Cross and Blue Shield were able to include a portion of these elements because their rates were subsidized by low-cost risks. If favorable risks moved out of the Blue Cross–Blue Shield system, the accompanying rate increases would preclude high-cost elements from retaining, let alone expanding, their membership.

It has become evident, therefore, that community rating, even with its modifications, can include the major part of *all* segments of the community only if it has a virtual monopoly in the area.[2] The aged, in particular, have so few funds with which to purchase medical care protection that it requires the inclusion of a great proportion of low-cost subscribers to offset the adverse selection the elderly present and at the same time to bring the rate within their financial means. Governmental contributions at some level would undoubtedly be necessary before all of the aged could be covered.

Competition has not been the sole mover behind experience rates. It is no secret within associations that many organizations have used experience rating as a means of *circumventing rate hearings.* About 60 per cent of the executives contacted in associations which used experience-rating methods said that the prime motivator for the adoption of the technique was to by-pass public hearings. Organizations with enrollment among the state population as high as 80 per cent have implemented experience rating. With this just short of a monopoly in hospital and medical prepayment, certainly something more than present competition must have encouraged a change in rating methods.

Whenever a community rate is altered, most commissioners feel state statutes give them the authority to hold public hearings if they deem it necessary in evaluating the propriety of rate changes. In the case of experience rates, however, the regulatory authorities are usually concerned only with the initial experience formula. Once this is approved, it may be applied year after year without investigation by the supervisory official. Only when an experience formula is modified does a commissioner enter the scene again in most jurisdictions.

---

[2] The federal government, for example, uses community-type rating—considering all the insureds as the "community"—in its disability income program under the social security system, and the same would presumably be true for any system of socialized medicine.

There is not an automatic by-passing of all hearings, however, just because a plan employs experience-rating techniques. The application of individual experience as a modification of rates is limited to subscriber *groups;* direct-pay subscribers and those who are group conversions are still rated on a community basis even when experience rates are used for group risks. (Classifying memberships as to direct-pay, group conversion, etc., is more appropriately considered class rating rather than experience rating.)

It should also be mentioned that even the approval of an original experience formula is not as thoroughly scrutinized by most commissioners. They feel group buyers are more capable of looking out for their own interests than are direct-pay members. The responsibility of attending to the public interest is focused primarily on the direct-pay and group-conversion rates.

In addition to the fact that competition and the possibility of circumventing rate hearings have stimulated the expansion of experience rating, Blue Cross and Blue Shield plans have looked upon the technique with favor for other reasons. First, experience rating will ward off many pressures by employers and unions[3] to pay noncovered services and overpay claims. Second, rates influenced by individual group experience will focus attention on the high-cost elements. Third, experience rates can be a factor in controlling unwarranted increases in hospital and medical costs. As more and more groups, particularly those of large size, see that approximately 90 per cent of their medical care insurance costs are determined by expenditures to hospitals and doctors, they are going to become much more concerned with the "whys-and-wherefores" of such payments. Direct accounting to groups as to the nature of these costs is already a reality. They themselves can quite conceivably exert pressures on associations, vendors of association services, and regulatory officials to rectify abuses in the use of benefits and to correct

---

[3] In most cases unions are more concerned with rates if employees contribute in the premium payment.

what they judge improper increases in the medical care costs. It will be surprising if uniform accounting, central purchasing by hospitals in a community, and other features which may foster economy are not brought about more readily through the influence of group buyers.

Utilization of Experience Rating. Blue Cross. Approximately two-thirds of the Blue Cross plans in the United States allow experience rating for at least some groups. A

TABLE 11–1

THE USE OF COMMUNITY RATING AND EXPERIENCE RATING BY
BLUE CROSS PLANS, 1959

Rating Method	Plans Number	Plans Percentage	Total Subscribers Number	Total Subscribers Percentage
Community rating only *	35	44.9	18,819,247	36.2
Community rating with experience rating available	26	33.3	19,504,371	37.5
Experience rating required for groups above minimum size	17	21.8	13,643,705	26.3
Total	78	100.0	51,967,323	100.0

* Thirteen of these plans, with an enrollment of 6,579,553, will use experience rating for national accounts.

Source: Blue Cross Commission, *Research and Technical Assistance Service Bulletin*, Number RT – 59–1, p. 1.

study by the Blue Cross Commission in 1959 revealed that 64 per cent of the subscribers were in associations which employed experience rating to some extent. Part of the commission's study is summarized in Table 11–1. It should be noted that enrollment statistics refer to total subscribers and not just to group members although the latter would be those to whom an experience rate would apply. The actual proportion of group subscribers whose rates were influenced by individual group experience is not known.

The Blue Cross plans in California and Illinois are among those which require experience rating. Associations in New York and Pennsylvania are about split as to the use of only a community rate or experience rating on an optional basis.

Associations which compel the use of experience rating do so only for groups above specified member size. The requirement to use this rate-making method does not apply to direct-pay subscribers, group conversion members, or non-eligible groups.

A total of fifty-six of the seventy-eight Blue Cross plans used experience rating for national accounts. Thirteen of these organizations would not allow self-adjusting rates for local accounts. National accounts extend beyond the borders of any individual state and thereby involve more than one hospital service association if their members are to be covered by Blue Cross. Where an association refuses to base the rate for members of national groups within its area on the over-all national experience, the community rate is the payment which must be made if such members are to be covered. The variance of rates by associations, when they refuse to experience rate, has been of more competitive disadvantage than even the refusal of some organizations to cooperate in offering a uniform benefit structure throughout the country.

An indication of the size limits placed upon experience-rated groups may be seen in Table 11–2. The wide range of these restrictions imposed by Blue Cross plans indicates that most state laws and regulatory officials have either not resolved the size limitations desirable for group rating, or else they have not done so with any degree of uniformity.

TABLE 11–2

Size Limits for Experience-rated Groups in Blue Cross Plans, 1959

Minimum Number of Contracts	Experience Rating Required Number of Plans	Percentage of Plans	Experience Rating Optional Number of Plans	Percentage of Plans
25 or less	9	53	3	11
50	1	6	6	23
75	1	6	1	4
100	6	35	11	42
250			1	4
500			2	8
Other			2	8
Total	17	100	26	100

Source: Blue Cross Commission, *Research and Technical Assistance Service Bulletin*, Number RT–59–1, p. 2.

Blue Shield. Statistics are not available on the total number of medical service associations allowing experience rating. Information has been obtained from the largest Blue Shield plans, and it is summarized in Table 11–3. The giants among Blue Shield plans are, it may be seen, on both sides of the rate fence.

TABLE 11–3

THE USE OF COMMUNITY RATING AND EXPERIENCE RATING BY BLUE
SHIELD PLANS HAVING OVER ONE MILLION SUBSCRIBERS, 1962

Area	Local Groups Community Rate Only	Local Groups Experience Rate Available	Percentage of Area Population Enrolled, December 31, 1961*	National Groups Community Rate Only	National Groups Experience Rate Available
New York City		X	41.10		X
Pennsylvania		X	37.37		X
Michigan	X		41.67	X	
Columbus, Ohio	X		32.26	X	
Massachusetts		X	46.62		X
Chicago		X	22.20		X
New Jersey	X		35.41	X†	
Indiana		X‡	30.37		X
Texas		X	13.90		X
Connecticut	X		47.29	X	
Cleveland, Ohio			52.64		
California		X	6.41		X
Total	4	7		4	7

* Source: Blue Shield Medical Care Plans, *Enrollment Reports, Blue Shield Plans, December 31, 1961*, pp. 2–3.

† Special legislation was enacted to allow the plan to participate in the Federal Employees Health Benefits Program which uses an experience-rating system.

‡ On January 1, 1961, the plan adopted an experience-rating program for all groups above fifty. The plan considers the new program basically still a community-rating technique, however, because the rate variations are so small.

Source: National Association of Blue Shield Plans and correspondence with some of the plans

The proportions of enrollment do not give any clear indication as to variances in the use of experience rating with changes in subscriber percentages. Nor is there any apparent geographic pattern in the use of rate methods.

Problems Associated with Experience Rating. Contingency Factors. One debatable issue in the construction of experience rates is whether there should be any contribution to a contingency reserve. A reserve of this type is used to off-set the higher claim costs an association incurs on behalf of high-loss subscriber segments, particularly the aged. When an employee with Blue Cross–Blue Shield group protection re-tires from a company, three choices are available regarding his coverage. First, the firm may keep him on the subscribers list and pay the enrollment fees for him. Experience-rated group employers who retain retired employees' coverage for them obviously have their premiums increased. Premiums rise more than the per capita subscription cost because the aged have both a higher incidence of hospitalization and a longer average stay once they are confined to a hospital. Simi-larly, their utilization of doctors' services is higher. Several associations grant special experience-rate credits to encourage employers to retain the coverage of retired employees. For example, double credit may be given for additional payments made on behalf of the pensioners. Credits, however, do not generally keep the premium per subscriber from being above what it would have been if pensioners had been excluded. Thus, employers who are motivated more by economic con-siderations than social and labor pressures are likely not to retain retired employees on subscriber rolls.

Retired employees not kept in the subscriber group may convert to an individual member basis. In this event they are called "group conversion" subscribers. Benefits under a con-verted contract are similar to those of group members. The rates for group conversions, however, are generally higher than they would have been under a group certificate, even if the employer had not contributed any portion of the premi-ums. Table 11–4 reveals that while the rate relationship be-tween group conversions and original direct-pay subscribers is close, the difference between group conversion and group rates is considerable. Single group converters included in the table had a median rate 24 per cent higher than the single group members. In the family category there was approxi-mately a 16 per cent increase from the median group rate to the group conversion median.

The final "choice" for pensioners is to terminate their coverage if the employer does not continue the protection for them or if they do not, or cannot afford to, convert to an individual subscriber basis.

TABLE 11–4

COMBINED ANNUAL PREMIUMS FOR BLUE CROSS AND/OR BLUE SHIELD HOSPITALIZATION AND SURGICAL-MEDICAL INSURANCE FOR GROUP, GROUP CONVERSION, AND NONGROUP CONTRACTS, 1957

Type of Contract and Coverage*	Number of Combined Plans †	Annual Premium	
		Median	Range
Group contract:			
One person	82	$ 38.40	$24.60 to $ 72.00
Family	82	97.40	67.80 to 145.80
Group conversion contract:			
One person	82	47.80	30.60 to 82.80
Family	82	112.50	79.80 to 165.60
Nongroup contract:			
One person	77	48.00	31.20 to 82.80
Family	77	110.20	78.60 to 165.60
Additional annual costs of group conversion over group contract:			
One person	82	9.00	−0.10 to 25.80
Family	82	14.40	−10.80 to 46.20

* Under each plan the contract selected was that offering most nearly comparable benefits to group, group conversion, and nongroup subscribers.

† A "combined plan" represents either a coordinated Blue Cross–Blue Shield organization in the same area (74 cases), or a Blue Cross plan (5 cases), or Blue Shield (3 cases), which offers protection against the cost of both hospitalization and physicians' services. If a Blue Cross plan were coordinated with two or more Blue Shield plans or vice versa, each "coordination" was counted as a "combined plan." For example, in New York State where there are eight Blue Cross plans and seven Blue Shield plans, a total of eight "plans" was used. Three Blue Shield plans were omitted because the surgical-medical plan was "coordinated" with a hospitalization plan that was not a member of the Blue Cross commission. Four Blue Cross hospitalization plans were omitted because of uncertainty about the source of surgical-medical insurance for their members. Under five of the plans' (as defined) nongroup contracts either were not offered or did not provide insurance protection against both hospitalization and physicians' charges.

Source: U.S. Department of Health, Education and Welfare; Social Security Administration, Division of Program Research, Research and Statistics Note No. 33–1957. Data were obtained from *Blue Cross Guide*, January, 1957, and from *Blue Shield Manual* as revised to June 1, 1957.

Since employers are not compelled to retain retired employees on the subscription rolls (no state is known to so dictate) should employers be required to contribute to a contingency fund for pensioners? A majority of executives who use experience rating believe the technique is applied equitably only if the same percentage for contribution to the aged's contingency reserve is put in the rate for employers who do not retain pensioners in their group as is in the community rate.[4] Experience-rated groups, as well as community-rated subscribers, would thereby be compelled to share the burden of coverage for the aged. Commissioners generally concur. This seems fair since many of the aged were formerly group members. The problem, however, is that health insurance companies do not include a contingency factor for pensioners in their rates. If such a factor is too large in Blue Cross or Blue Shield experience rates, there will be the same motivation for good groups to obtain coverage from insurance companies as existed before the associations utilized experience rating.

Influence on Enrollment. The Blue Cross Commission concluded after its 1959 survey that no generalization was possible regarding the effect of experience rating on enrollment. Still, some executives believe growth in the number of subscribers is hampered by this technique. Experience rating is utilized, nevertheless, by some of the largest Blue Cross and Blue Shield plans. The reply of a New England manager typifies the opinions of many associations which use this method:

. . . We prefer to look at our enrollment success as being "because of our experience rating." It became apparent many years ago that the purchasers of our services were becoming very well versed in their own needs. Unions became experts on prepayment-for-health costs; some of the larger and better management teams, realizing the importance of this fringe benefit, also became expert in these matters. We therefore found ourselves in the position of dealing with experts who were conversant not only with the benefits but with the various methods of financing these plans. It was through close work with them that we developed our present experience rating method. Beyond any doubt

---

[4] It should be noted that experience rates which are a modification of community rates do not necessarily contribute funds for the aged, even though the aged are covered by the community rate. For example, groups with full credibility use no part of the community rate under such a system.

if we were unwilling to work with them in the area of financing their program, they would have sought coverage through other carriers.

It is our considered opinion that our present experience rating program maintains and actually enhances our basic principle of community rating. Considered as one category, groups subject to experience rating are self-supporting . . . the additional income from surcharges is offset by the discounts granted to other groups. Such groups, however, do contribute to the community by a subsidy of non-group members, a significant contribution to statutory reserves, and a reduction in our operating costs through greater volume.

Rate Cutting.   The theory behind experience rating is that groups which pay less than the community rate will be offset by groups which pay more. The total subscription income is supposedly identical under either rating method. The hazard involved, though, is that groups will want experience rating only when they have a favorable loss picture. If an association allows groups to move in and out of experience rating, the method becomes merely a means for procuring rate decreases. Table 11–1 revealed that seventeen of the forty-three Blue Cross plans which use experience rating require that groups above a certain size must have their rates determined at least in part by their own experience. This eliminates the possibility of obtaining rate reductions by going from experience rating to community rating.

Regulatory Attitudes Concerning Rating Methods

Very few enabling acts mention the types of rating methods a Blue Cross or Blue Shield plan may use.[5] The issue is therefore left to the discretion of the insurance commissioners. Of the commissioners who would make unequivocal

---

[5] New York is the only state among the four largest which mentions experience rating in its enabling act. The New York provision states: "Any such contract may provide for the adjustment of the rate of premium based upon the experience thereunder at the end of the first year or of any subsequent year of insurance thereunder and such readjustments may be made retroactive only for such policy year."

statements, nine said that experience rating is consistent with Blue Cross and Blue Shield philosophy, while twelve responded in the negative. The remainder gave qualified replies. Many thought merit-type rating was a modification of an original Blue Cross–Blue Shield characteristic, but most of those who held this view felt competitive struggles would warrant partial abandonment of the community-rating feature. Several commissioners reported tremendous public pressure had been exerted on their departments by associations and groups to allow experience rating. Most large states have approved use of this technique, at least on an experimental basis.

Summary of Rating Methods

The severe competitive environment and the expansion of public hearings forecast a continuation of the trend toward rates influenced by individual group experience. Where, then, does this leave community rating? A prerequisite before an association may implement self-adjusting rates should be that such rates include the same contingency factor as does the community rate for contributions to segments with adverse selection features. By so doing, the community rate will not be raised unduly by having to bear the complete burden of high-cost elements, a portion of whom were placed upon the community when they converted from group certificates. The major high-cost areas may be identified as the aged, lower-income subscribers, and small groups in particular occupations which have an abnormally high utilization of plan services. If the community rate does not have to assume the full financial responsibility for these high-cost subscribers, it can still compete effectively with insurance companies.

Dr. Duncan M. MacIntyre, who has been conducting a study on community rating and experience rating for the Health Insurance Foundation, states that community rating can never, in itself, bring all segments of the community onto the Blue Cross rolls.[6] The incomes of the aged are too meager in many instances for them to purchase Blue Cross and Blue Shield coverage, regardless of the rating method utilized. It is inappropriate, therefore, to retain community rating resolutely and reject experience rating on the premise that only the former will enable all elements of the community to procure coverage. Dr. MacIntyre is of the same opinion. Competition will win the good experience groups from associations if they do not experience rate, and the community rate thereafter will be out of the financial range of many individuals anyway.

Dr. Ray E. Trussell, study director for the Columbia Report of New York's Blue Cross plans, is one who objects vehemently to experience rating:

> The New York City Blue Cross Plan which now experience rates part of its group contracts does so at the expense of the rest of the subscribers and contrary to the principle of community-wide spreading of the risk and cost of illness. Many experience-rated groups are overpaying for care received. Others are refusing to be a part of the community by demanding and receiving special rates. Neither situation is desirable. Blue Cross was never intended to merely provide office services for the purpose of self-insurance regardless of legislative permission.[7]

Dr. Trussell seems to ignore the fact that community rating without deviations can quite conceivably ruin some associations, no matter how philosophically desirable the idea back of an average rate for the entire community. He also seems to disregard the possibility of a community rate not being adversely affected to a great extent by experience rating, if these self-adjusted rates were mandatory for groups above a certain size and if they were also required to include a contingency

---

[6] Duncan M. MacIntyre, Professor of Industrial and Labor Relations, Cornell University, in a a paper given at the 1960 Annual Conference of Blue Cross Plans, Los Angeles, California, April 6, 1960.

[7] School of Public Health and Administrative Medicine, Columbia University, *Prepayment for Hospital Care in New York*, p. 2.

factor for the community's high-cost segments. Thus, experience rates could be above and below the community rate. The over-all association income could be identical with what would occur if only community rating were present; the community rate could be relatively the same. In fact, it could be lower than would be the case if good groups were lost along with contributions they make to contingency reserves and expenses. It is possible that the only major rate changes would be for experience-rated groups.

There is justification for the disapproval expressed in the Columbia Report over experience rating of very small groups. It is also true that experience rating has not been much of an incentive toward reduced hospitalization, although this does not mean it will fail to contribute to a control of hospital costs and overutilization in the future. Community rating without any experience-rated groups could survive against the competition in the long run only if insurance companies were compelled to use similar rating techniques. "Continuous and intensive public educational programs," as recommended by the Trussell Committee, will not suffice to stave off the vigorous competition insurance companies present for Blue Cross and Blue Shield plans.

The Columbia Report suggests that experience rating encourages abuses, including "unequal treatment of groups because of such factors as the pressure of agents, or the bargaining power of large policyholders."[8] These are matters for supervision both at association and state regulatory levels. Contrary arguments might also be advanced that community rating exerts pressures to provide services not covered by certificates or to overpay claims. A reduction of these possibilities was listed among the advantages of experience rating.

Extensive experience rating would place Blue Cross in the same position as now prevails for the insurance companies. Such a destruction of the community purpose of Blue Cross would

---

[8] *Ibid.*, p. 94.

properly raise questions as to the public need for the Plan and its favored status.[9]

The acceptance of experience rating on the part of Blue Cross and Blue Shield by an important portion of state regulatory authorities, even if it does modify an original characteristic, does not seem to support the assumption of the quotation. With proper regulatory controls on the self-adjustment rating techniques of both associations and insurance companies, hospital and medical service organizations can still pursue their purposes of community enrollment on a wide, although not all-inclusive, scale.

APPROVAL OF SUBSCRIBER RATES

Statutory Requirements Regarding Rate Approval

The most accurate present information indicates that thirty-four states require the supervisory authority to give his approval of subscriber rates before they may be implemented. New York, California,[10] Pennsylvania, and Illinois are among these. For the sixteen states which appear not to have prior approval stipulations,[11] five do not regulate any phase of associations' operations and two have neither Blue Cross nor Blue Shield plans within their borders.

In some areas nongroup and group-conversion rates must have prior approval, while group rates are subject to subsequent disapproval requirements. The reason for this divergent approach is akin to that advanced for similar differences in the treatment of group and nongroup benefits, a topic discussed in Chapter III. It is presumed that the group pur-

---

[9] *Ibid.*

[10] Blue Shield is not regulated by the commissioner in California.

[11] The following states were determined not to have prior approval requisites for rates: Arizona, Colorado, Delaware, Louisiana, Minnesota, Missouri, Montana, Nevada, North Dakota, Oregon, Texas, Vermont, Virginia, Washington, Wisconsin and Wyoming. This information was obtained from questionnaires completed by the state regulatory officials, except for Missouri and North Dakota where data were obtained from the Blue Cross Commission booklet, *Public Regulation of Hospital Service Plans Approved by the American Hospital Association*, May, 1960.

chaser has more information and knowledge about insurance, and is in a better position to fend for himself when dealing with an association, than is the individual subscriber.

Enabling acts are not characteristically detailed as to conditions upon which rates will be approved or disapproved. New York law prescribes: "The superintendent may refuse such approval if he finds that such rates are excessive, inadequate or unfairly discriminatory." This is a common statutory provision for any kind of insurance rates. It is less prevalent in enabling acts than in the general sections of insurance codes. The statute in New York also states, "Any rate approved by the superintendent shall make provision for such increase as may be necessary to meet the requirements of a plan approved by the superintendent in the manner prescribed . . . for restoration of the special contingent surplus fund required. . . ." This order refers to the requirement that any reduction in the contingent surplus must be restored within three years in a manner approved by the superintendent. The details of surplus regulations will be discussed in the next chapter.

California has an unusual statutory feature regarding the basis upon which rate-change requests will be approved or disapproved. The commissioner in that state cannot renew an association's certificate of authority until:

. . . a schedule of the rates, dues, fees or other periodic charges to be paid by subscribers has been filed with the commissioner and the same are not such as will, after providing for legal reserves . . . , result in profit to, or in the accumulation of excessive reserves or surpluses by such corporation and are such as will enable such corporation to furnish or provide the hospital services which it proposes to make available to its beneficiaries and subscribers without impairment of its legal reserves and without a constant depletion of the assets of such corporation. A reserve or surplus over and above all approved and required reserves in an amount in excess of the average annual gross income of such corporation for the immediately preceding three calendar years shall be prime facie an excessive accumulation.

Regulatory Attitudes Concerning Rate Approval

As might be expected, commissioners consider recent experience, trends, benefit changes, and the solvency of associations among the primary factors in appraising rate-change requests. The numerous questions commissioners seem to have about claim costs of associations indicate this aspect is coming under closer scrutiny. The propriety of expenditures for services to subscribers is questioned with reference to the possibility of abuse of benefits by subscribers, and the causes of increases in hospital and medical costs. Both of these areas are investigated as "Problems" in Chapter XIV. Commissioners indicate that statistical data and judgment have about equal weight in their final determinations on rate requests. Most supervisory authorities assess rate changes with the view they will be adequate for a two-year period. The futility felt by commissioners when they look at their responsibility for rate approval was expressed by one such official who remarked, "Rates must be adequate and reasonable . . . at the same time the Commissioner is concerned with solvency. With no ultimate loss ratio for Blue Cross, it becomes an impossible task."

Fifty-seven per cent of the commissioners who mentioned their recent rate dealings said they had either declined rate-increase requests from plans within the last two years or had approved lesser increases than submitted.

It should be reiterated that courts are not likely to set aside the action of a commissioner unless he very obviously has gone beyond his official boundaries. This has been pointed out in numerous cases, such as in an action brought by the cities of Pittsburgh and Philadelphia against the insurance department and the insurance commissioner of Pennsylvania. Although the case concerns fire insurance rates, the decision is appropriate for actions of the commissioner with any type of rates.

In our judgment, the power of the Insurance Commissioner to approve or disapprove the filing of rates under the Rate Regulatory Act necessarily calls for the exercise of administrative discretion on the part of the Commissioner. This power to approve rates submitted by the insurers, or by the filer in their behalf, is in contrast to action taken by some administrative bodies which exercise quasi judicial powers and legislative functions as rate making or price fixing agencies. . . .

The general rule is that where an administrative agency is clothed with discretion in the discharge of its duty, the Court will not interfere with the manner in which that agency has exercised its discretion, unless the record clearly establishes that there has been an arbitrary, capricious or unreasonable determination or a clear violation of positive law. . . .[12]

Public Rate Hearings

A prior-approval requirement over rates formerly meant rate changes would be filed with the state regulatory official; the official, in conjunction with his departmental technicians and assistants, would then pass upon the desirability of such changes from the point of view of public interest. In many areas approval was—and to a limited extent still is—a matter-of-fact occurrence. A commissioner considered he could determine within the confines of his own department what changes were in the best interests of the state's citizens. Any communications a commissioner had with subscribers, or other parties at interest, were on an unofficial and nonpublic basis.

This approval procedure has been altered in several states by adoption of public hearings under the auspices of the regulatory official. The purported purpose served by hearings is to enable a supervisory authority to hear all sides on whether rate changes, that is, rate *increases*, should be granted. (Hearings are also held to consider the approval or disapproval of hospital reimbursement schedules, doctors'

---

[12] *Insurance Department of the Commonwealth of Pennsylvania and Francis R. Smith, Insurance Commissioner of Commonwealth of Pennsylvania v. City of Philadelphia*, 309 Dauph. 1959, July 25, 1960 and *Insurance Department of the Commonwealth of Pennsylvania and Francis R. Smith, Insurance Commissioner of Commonwealth of Pennsylvania v. City of Pittsburgh*, 312 Dauph. 1959, July 25, 1960.

fee schedules, and benefit structure changes, as well as for over-all rate alterations.)

Rate hearings have had notoriety not only because they represent a major change in the manner in which Blue Cross and Blue Shield rates receive regulatory approval. They have also fostered serious questions by association executives, officials of national organizations, regulatory authorities and legislators: Does a supervisory official have the legal power to hold public hearings? Even if hearings are legal, are they a desirable feature of regulation? What about the effects of hearings on associations' operations? Finally, there is considerable interest in whether public hearings are likely to become more widespread.

Legality of Public Hearings. The insurance departments of Pennsylvania and New York have been among the major proponents of public hearings. There have been no rate hearings in Illinois, for example, because of the large amount of experience-rated groups in that area. It appears that hearings might be held in Illinois if sizeable rate increases are requested on contracts affecting an important portion of direct-pay or group conversion subscribers.

The New York statute does not address itself to the legal basis for hearings. The superintendent has reported, however, that the statute provides him with broad general powers which would include the right to hold hearings.

Legal authority for public hearings is probably more definitive in Pennsylvania. The commonwealth's Casualty, Surety and Title Insurance Act specifies:

Every insurer shall file with the Commissioner every manual of classifications, rules and rates, every rating plan and every modification of any of the foregoing which it proposes to use. Every such filing shall state the proposed effective date thereof and shall indicate the character and extent of the coverage contemplated. When a filing is not accompanied by the information upon which the insurer supports such filing, and the commissioner does not have sufficient information to determine whether such filing meets the requirements of the Act, he may require such insurer to furnish the information upon which it supports such filing. Any filing may be supported by (1) the experience or judgment of the insurer or rating organization making the filing, (2) the experience of other insurers or rating organizations, or (3) any other factor which the insurer or rating organization deems relevant. *A filing and any supporting information shall be open to public inspection after the filing becomes effective.*[13]

The question presented by this law is whether rates shall be open to public inspection *before* they become effective. The insurance commissioner of Pennsylvania feels the law should be interpreted to mean a *permissive* allowance of public inspection *before* rates are effective and mandatory examination *thereafter*. Others construe section 4 to mean a public inspection of rates is *prohibited before* they become effective and mandatory after they are approved. To circumvent any problem of legality over an interpretation of section 4, the commissioner has approved rate filings perfunctorily, then *immediately suspended* them. This is in agreement with either interpretation of the law, inasmuch as the rates are in effect, though suspended, and the statute permits "public inspection after the filing becomes effective."

In areas where rate hearings have been adopted, commissioners view them as a procedure that may be used at their discretion. If a supervisory official feels public proceedings are uncalled for with reference to a particular rate-change request, it is his prerogative to approve or disapprove rates without a hearing.

Insurance companies have not been subjected to rate hearings for initial approval of rates. In fact, *the entire rate-approval process is more routine in most states for insurance companies than it is for Blue Cross or Blue Shield plans.* In nearly all areas the rate-approval procedure for companies

---

[13] Public Law 538, Sec. 4 (a), of June 11, 1947 of the Commonwealth of Pennsylvania. Italics added. The essence of this provision is also in the Fire and Marine Insurance Act (Public Law 551, Sec. 4, of June 11, 1947).

in effect amounts to the mere filing of rates. Approval is customarily automatic.[14]

The reason given by several supervisory officials for the differential regulatory procedures is that an individual Blue Cross or Blue Shield plan often has a larger portion of the population enrolled than does any one company.[15] If an association has an almost monopolistic position in an area, the possibility of unreasonable rates does exist. Commissioners probably also want to make sure subscriber rates are not increased automatically just because hospitals or doctors desire higher reimbursements for their services. In areas where associations compete actively with insurance companies, however, it seems an unfair competitive advantage for the rates of insurance companies to have less surveillance. In many areas the protection of the interest of citizens would seem to require similar treatment regarding approval of rates for associations and companies.

The broad wording of provisions in enabling acts regarding rate approval, and the liberality of courts in assessing the legality of actions by supervisory officials, support the postulation that hearings can be held legally in most states where Blue Cross and Blue Shield are regulated.

Evaluation of Rate Hearings. Sixty per cent of the commissioners who chose to appraise the desirability of public hearings as a feature in rate regulation supported them.

---

[14] The insurance department of New York feels that it has the power to hold hearings concerning insurance company rates as well as subscription charges of associations. Actually, the law requires such hearings when approval is withdrawn for a rate which previously had the superintendent's ratification. The attorney general of Pennsylvania has handed down the opinion that the insurance commissioner has approval powers over the rates of insurance companies in that state. This has not been tested in the courts, however, and there is some feeling that the attorney general's opinion would not be substantiated. It is apparent that insurance department staffs would have to be augmented considerably if rates of all companies were to be given regulatory treatment similar to that for hospital and medical associations. One commissioner observed he would have to make approximately eighty adjudications each day if all insurance companies were supervised as are associations in rate considerations.

[15] Insurance companies in the aggregate, however, have a larger percentage of the population under coverage.

Some plan executives and officers of national associations also think rate hearings are of benefit to the organizations. One mentioned that associations which are truly "community plans" should not object to public inspection. Another manager thought hearings are beneficial in keeping Blue Cross, Blue Shield, doctors, hospitals, and the public alert.

Most derogatory comments about rate hearings come from executive directors of associations, although it was surprising to find that 40 per cent of the commissioners do not feel hearings are desirable. The remark was made by one regulatory authority that the "attendant publicity often creates a circus atmosphere and makes objective consideration of the issues more difficult." Primary objections to hearings are: no information is developed in addition to what a commissioner already has available; a public place is provided for those with axes to grind; adverse publicity may be given to associations by newspaper reporting; large financial expenditures by associations are required; and an unwarranted delay in approval of rate increases may result.

The means customarily used by commissioners to obtain information are triennial examinations, annual reports, and visitation of associations. A supervisory official can also approach different sources on a nonpublic basis to obtain their opinions, such as by publicizing the fact that interested parties are welcome to contact the insurance department regarding contemplated rate changes. These possibilities, however, are not as likely to bring out all elements as are public hearings. It should be assumed, therefore, that regulatory officials possess the ability to ascertain what method for obtaining information is most appropriate for the protection of the public interest. In so doing, officials should consider the following potentially adverse features of public hearings.

Rate hearings, up to this time, have provided an arena for many witnesses who are not typical subscribers. Almost all rate hearings have had some representatives of older subscribers, for example, who decry increases because they cannot afford to pay them. Although this is pitifully true, it is not news to associations nor to commissioners, and it is of little value if an association is encountering financial difficulties—often because of unanticipated utilization by just such groups. One commissioner felt these public "trials" provide the opportunity for many power seekers and publicity grabbers to gain the spotlight with little accompanying illumination for the regulatory authority.

Another bad feature of rate hearings has been improper press reporting of radical views. The testimony of emotional witnesses has been the source of misleading headlines and stories which have not assessed the entire situation. Evidence upon which newspapers concentrate is often from non-credible witnesses or those who speak for only a very small portion of subscribers. Even credible witnesses can slant statistics. Newspapers have the ethical responsibility to evaluate the true merit of statements made at hearings.[16]

Most commissioners evaluate the adequacy of rate requests for a period of approximately two years after they have been granted. The public often considers Blue Cross and Blue Shield one and the same; hence, if each type of organization requests a rate change every two years the public feels rate increases for its hospital-medical protection are being required on the average of once a year. Hearings emphasize the changes and can cause these subscriber misunderstandings.

Many insurance departments operate financially from fees obtained from regulated organizations. Thus, associations must often supply funds for holding hearings. Considerable

---

[16] An example of this type of sensationalism occurred in New York where newspapers concentrated on the testimony of individuals who assailed the New York Blue Cross plan for its expenditures for television advertising. Regulatory authorities, as well as Blue Cross executives, felt this emphasis was not appropriate inasmuch as advertising expenditures were a minute part of total disbursements by the organization. If abandoned, the saving of these advertising costs would have amounted to a few cents per subscriber. In addition, the insurance department felt there was merit in the statement that the association would have lost subscribers and suffered increased per capita costs if they did not use some means to keep the Blue Cross name before the public.

time and money must also be expended to prepare for a hearing. Several Blue Cross and Blue Shield plans reported they have been kept from implementing experimental benefit features—major-medical-type coverage and programs for the aged were those mentioned—because the drain of funds and management talent hearings caused.

Another feature associated with rate hearings is that they may bring about delays in effecting increases in subscriber charges. Unwarranted delays could result in rate increases being inadequate when granted; otherwise a larger rate increase is necessitated.

One unfair aspect of hearings is associated with the fact that health insurance companies have not been subjected to public examination regarding rates as yet. Thus, even though many of the statements made at hearings could apply with equal force against insurance companies, associations are held out as the sole villain. Hearings imply to some observers that associations might be operated unscrupulously when insurance companies are not treated accordingly. It is impossible, of course, for a regulatory authority to hold a hearing for each rate-change request of all insurance companies and all hospital and medical service associations. Commissioners do, however, need the discretion to hold hearings for either type of organization.

Future Position of Hearings. The use of rate hearings as a regulatory method will almost surely be extended. At least this is the opinion of three fourths of the commissioners. Many feel hearings are inevitable because of the continual rise in hospital-medical costs and the increase in utilization of plans' services, both of which foster successive boosts in Blue Cross and Blue Shield rates.

chapter XII

FINANCIAL STANDARDS

Although Blue Cross and Blue Shield plans may be social in nature and influence, they are, without question, business operations. Unlike a governmental social scheme, they do not have recourse to tax funds if their financial position becomes imperiled. Like insurance companies, associations endeavor to make their assets approximate their liabilities through adequate rates and investment income. This struggle is complicated by the volatile and subjective aspects of their obligations to subscribers. As a result, actual potential liabilities are difficult to determine with complete assurance. It is possible that income received during a particular period may be insufficient to cover the liabilities incurred during that time. This hazard is all the more probable when it is recalled that associations generally do not have complete control over either the rates they will charge or the prices they must pay hospitals and doctors. Reserves are the bulwark against bankruptcy when rate structures prove insufficient and financial obligations extend beyond anticipations. State laws, supervisory officials, national organizations to which Blue Cross and Blue Shield plans belong, and the managements and governing boards of associations are all concerned with the resolution of reserve problems.

Additional measures to thwart financial adversity on the part of associations have been instituted through regulatory requirements concerning investment limitations and stipulations for maximum allowable expenses. At the same time, most enabling acts have granted supervisory authorities the right to ascertain the actual financial position of associations through annual reports, periodic examinations of records, and perusal of their operations whenever it is desired.

If it becomes impossible, or inadvisable, to salvage a financially embarrassed hospital or medical service association, the laws prescribe procedures for liquidating the organization.

RESERVES

Early Attitudes toward Reserves

During the early years of Blue Cross and Blue Shield, those who organized associations, as well as regulatory authorities, placed a minor emphasis on the reserves an association should accumulate and maintain. Surplus and capital requirements were viewed in a similar light. These were financial safeguards for insurance companies but not vital for Blue Cross and Blue Shield organizations. The social constitution of associations and the methods by which they operated seemed to obviate the need for financial stabilizers.

Hospitals by and large agreed to provide services for subscribers even if funds were not available to reimburse the institutions. Doctors who contracted with Blue Shield plans often assented to similar arrangements. Thus, the need for a reserve fund which could be called upon when financial obligations proved excessive was questionable. Subscribers would continue to receive the services they had been promised whether a financial reserve existed or not. It was commonly stated that "hospital guarantees" and "physicians' guarantees" constituted the contingency or surplus "reserve."

Associations, like insurance companies, had generally evaluated their *incurred* liabilities, such as for claims—known or unknown—and for unearned premiums. These determinations were not approached in identical fashions by all Blue Cross and Blue Shield plans or by all supervisory officials, and they were—and still are—a source of strife. The issue of maternity reserves, for example, has never been resolved to the satisfaction of all associations. An appraisal of losses and claims outstanding, however, does not involve as extensive a practical dilemma as does a determination of *contingency* reserves.[1] The latter are to protect against hazards which have not been contemplated.

Many who observed Blue Cross and Blue Shield operations during their incubation period came to wonder if hospital and doctor guarantees were sufficient to circumvent the need for financial reserves. These doubts were fostered when fewer hospitals and doctors granted guarantees and when it was recognized that guarantees, even where existent, gave shorter reprieves for financial afflictions than would dollar reserves. As over-all costs rose for associations during the 1940's, additional concern was directed toward the reserve element by associations and regulators. NAIC committees included the subject on their agendas. By 1944 there was at least general agreement that financial reserves, in some form, were necessary. This need was beyond the stability furnished by "normal" reserves. The unearned premium reserve (UPR) of associations, for example, is usually not of appreciable size. This is because an important part of the business of most Blue Cross and Blue Shield plans is written on a group basis and with monthly subscription payments. The UPR on such business would be approximately one twenty-fourth of a year's subscription income. In addition, the low expense

---

[1] Accountants might define all reserves as "contingency" reserves inasmuch as they are to reduce the effect of associations' contingencies. For the purpose of this section, though, contingency reserves will not be considered to include the provisions made for various types of expected or incurred liabilities. Hereafter, the term "reserves" will include only contingency reserves, unless otherwise indicated.

While a contingency reserve appears on the liability side of a balance sheet, it is not a liability in the normal sense but rather a surplus item. Considerable confusion arises over this fact, as the word "reserve" often leads to the inference that it is a liability. A contingency reserve is probably most easily understood if viewed as similar to the policyholder surplus of insurance companies. A legislated or administered contingency-reserve requirement would appear in a statement as an allocated surplus (or reserve).

The term "reserve fund" also causes misunderstanding. While there are no assets in such a "fund," the reserve is, of course, *offset* by assets. Occasionally, a contingency reserve is offset by specific assets, rather than by the general assets of the organization.

ratios of associations give them a smaller equity (through prepaid expenses) in the UPR than is true for health insurance companies.

The Extent of Current Reserves

Blue Cross. The average reserves possessed by Blue Cross plans in the United States on December 31, 1961, amounted to 2.5 months of monthly hospital and operating expenses. Reserves for all the hospital associations totaled $410 million, or 42.2 per cent of total liabilities. One year prior to

TABLE 12–1

RESERVE POSITIONS OF BLUE CROSS PLANS IN THE UNITED STATES,
DECEMBER 31, 1961

| Size of Plan Membership | Number of Plans | Months of Average Monthly Claims and Operating Expense in Reserve | | | |
| | | Range | | | |
		High	Low	Mean*	Median
More than 1,000,000	14	7.30	0.22	2.29	1.87
500,000–1,000,000	19	4.68	0.94	2.80	2.75
200,000–500,000	26	9.50	0.60	3.03	2.62
100,000–200,000	7	2.78	−0.39	1.18	1.25
50,000–100,000	6	7.80	1.59	2.88	2.65
Less than 50,000	5	6.23	0.46	3.98	2.56
Total	77			2.50	2.17

* The means for enrollment classifications up to 500,000 members are based upon slightly different groupings of the plans than are the other statistics.

Source: Blue Cross Association, *Financial Reports of Blue Cross Plans, Year of 1961.*

that time the financial safeguards equaled 2.48 months of average total expenses, while at the end of 1959 reserves were at a level of 2.26 months' needs. Table 12–1 classifies the reserve positions of associations according to the size of their subscriber rolls.

It is apparent that no generalization is possible concerning a correlation between association size and reserve position. Neither does there appear to be a relationship between geographic location and reserve size. Obviously, local conditions are the major determinant. Seven of the sixteen Blue Cross plans in New York, California, Pennsylvania, and Illinois had reserves within the range of 1.5 and 2.07 months of average monthly claims and operating expenses; thirteen of the organizations were within the range of 1.5 and 2.84 months' requirements. Throughout the entire country, forty of the seventy-seven associations had between one and three months of average expenses in reserve. Eleven of the organizations had less than one month's reserve (two were technically insolvent), and twenty-six had more than three months' average needs.[2]

Blue Shield. On December 31, 1961, the average reserve position of the Blue Shield organizations (including six Canadian plans) was 3.3 months of average monthly claims and operating expenses. Blue Shield reserves totaled $255 million, which was 53.05 per cent of over-all liabilities. The combined reserve status of these associations declined from 3.47 months' requirements at the end of 1960 and 3.72 months' needs at the end of 1959. Table 12–2 summarizes the reserve standings of the Blue Shield plans as of December 31, 1961.

Only one medical service association in the United States had less than one month of average monthly claims and operating expense needs, while twenty-seven had between one and three months' requirements. Twenty-nine organizations had more than four months of average monthly expenditures, and nineteen of these were above the five months' figure.

Blue Shield organizations generally have higher reserve levels than do Blue Cross plans since the latter often have more difficulty in keeping their surpluses from being depleted. This is largely explained by the greater preponderance of indemnity contracts in the medical service plans, and, as a result, Blue Shield generally is not as adversely affected

---

[2] The Norfolk, Virginia, association had the lowest reserve position in the United States with minus 0.39 months' requirements, while the figure for the Fargo, North Dakota, association was minus 0.12. These plans are technically insolvent. Blue Cross plans with more than five months' average hospital and operating expenses in reserve included Portland, Ore., 5.18; Parkersburg, W. Va., 6.23; Boston, 6.28; Seattle, 6.38; New Haven, 7.30; Wheeling, W. Va., 7.80; and Omaha, 9.50.

in times of rising prices. An association with service benefits will usually have an increasing average claim expense in periods when medical care costs are mounting as there is an accompanying rise in the cost of providing services for subscribers. The increase in claims expense may be forestalled during the time old reimbursement and fee schedules are in

TABLE 12–2

RESERVE POSITIONS OF BLUE SHIELD PLANS IN THE UNITED STATES
DECEMBER 31, 1961

| Size of Plan Membership | Number of Plans | Months of Average Monthly Claims and Operating Expense in Reserve | | | |
| | | Range | | | |
		High	Low	Mean*	Median
More than 1,000,000	12	8.40	0.19	3.13(1)	3.78
500,000–1,000,000	16	6.61	1.84	3.39	3.29
200,000–500,000	19	7.53	1.18	3.65(4)	3.81
100,000–200,000	4	6.42	1.83	3.72	4.74
50,000–100,000	6	8.62	1.33	3.67(1)	3.71
Less than 50,000	11 †	11.32	1.62	3.81	4.14
Total	68 †				

* Includes Canadian plans shown in parentheses.
† The merger of the Fairmont and Wheeling, W. Va., plans results in their treatment as only one association in these figures. In the enrollment statistics they were considered separately.
Source: National Association of Blue Shield Plans, *Financial Reports, Blue Shield Plans, Year 1961,* pp. 5–9.

effect. Associations with indemnity provisions have upper dollar limits on benefits beyond which they will not reimburse. These organizations will be affected by advancing prices only if previous average claim costs were considerably below the maximum indemnity level. In this case the average claim figure will rise as prices increase until the reimbursement level is reached. The relationship between benefits and reserves may justify lower reserve requirements for associations with indemnity provisions than those which offer service contracts.

Laws and Regulatory Stipulations for Reserves

Nineteen states are known to have some type of reserve requirement for hospital service associations, while twenty-five

states do not.[3] Medical service organizations are required to
maintain reserves in at least twenty states; a minimum of
twenty-four states have no such stipulations. Regulatory authorities use rules of thumb to prescribe reserve levels in
eight states which have not legislated such requirements for
either Blue Cross or Blue Shield.

It is difficult to classify the reserve provisions in enabling
acts because there is so little similarity among states in this
respect. The broadest breakdown would separate reserve requirements as to whether they are stated in subjective or objective terms. A subjective provision merely mentions that
reserves will be maintained, or that reserves will be approved
by the regulatory authority. Objective reserve requirements
either specify definite dollar amounts which must be maintained, or the law incorporates a formula by which the necessary reserve limits, or contributions toward reserves, are determined.

Another type of classification for reserve requirements
would differentiate between provisions for "normal" reserves
and stipulations concerning "contingency" or excess reserves.
Normal reserves include those for losses and claims outstanding and for unearned premiums. The primary concern of this
discussion is with contingency reserves, which are surpluses
over and above normal reserves.

Seven statutes requiring Blue Cross plans to maintain reserves are of the subjective type. The twelve statutes of objective nature generally compel Blue Cross plans to maintain
specified dollar amounts as reserves. Those laws which outline a reserve formula customarily have a dual approach in
that they prescribe a rate of contribution to contingency reserves and a maximum number of months of financial needs

---

[3] Six states did not submit information. The following states have provisions concerning reserves for both hospital and medical service associations:
Alaska, Arizona, Arkansas, Georgia, Hawaii (there is presently no approved
Blue Cross plan within the state), Kansas, Louisiana, Massachusetts, Michigan, Nebraska, New Jersey, New Mexico, New York, North Carolina, Oklahoma, Pennsylvania, South Carolina, and Wisconsin. In addition, California
has a reserve provision which applies to Blue Cross plans while Illinois and
South Dakota have requirements for Blue Shield plans.

which may be held. Some formulas stipulate a minimum percentage of subscription (premium) income which must be maintained. Since there is a relationship between expenditures and income, the two types of formulas use basically the same approach. The laws with subjective or general requirements for reserves are usually worded so that a supervisory official may require contingency-type reserves. Similarly, the purpose of most formula stipulations is to provide for reserves in addition to those of the normal accounting variety.

Seven of the twenty reserve enactments applicable to Blue Shield plans are subjective. Four statutes for Blue Cross and a similar number for Blue Shield are concerned only with "normal" reserves.

As a broad generalization, reserve requirements are prescribed by law in approximately 40 per cent of the states, and the majority of these are stated in objective terms with a purpose of establishing contingency reserves.

Of the four largest states, California has no regulation of Blue Shield reserves while Illinois law makes no mention of reserves for hospital service associations. New York's reserve requirement applies to either Blue Cross or Blue Shield plans:

Every such corporation which was incorporated prior to the effective date of this amendment *shall maintain a special contingent surplus fund which shall* from time to time during *each calendar year be increased* in an amount equal to *at least two per centum of the net premium income* of such corporation during such whole calendar year, provided however, that if such corporation reinsures part of its risk under any or all of its contracts by means of reinsurance approved by the superintendent as an appropriate substitute for the special contingent surplus fund, then the required increase to the special contingent surplus fund at the end of any calendar year shall be reduced by the amount of the premium paid by such corporation for such reinsurance during such calendar year or by two per centum of the net premium income received by such corporation during such calendar year on its contracts so reinsured for the period during which they are so reinsured, which ever amount is the lesser, and further *provided,* however, *that the special contingent surplus fund at the end of any calendar year shall not exceed fifteen per centum of the net* premium income of such calendar year. . . . *Such special* contingent surplus *fund may not be reduced* below the amount required to be maintained hereunder *except in the event of an epidemic or other catastrophe* resulting in extraordinary hospital or medical utilization. In such event *the superintendent may authorize reduction* below the amount required to be maintained hereunder, *provided the amount of reduction shall be restored with a period of not more than three years in accordance with a plan submitted by the corporation and approved by the superintendent.* A corporation incorporated after the effective date of this amendment shall after the first calendar year of doing business set aside and accumulate a special contingent surplus fund in accordance with the requirements of this section. [Italics added.]

The New York provision was enacted into law on April 16, 1959. Prior to that time associations were required to contribute to a special contingent surplus at the annual rate of 4 per cent of net premium income until a fund with a maximum of 25 per cent of net premium income was obtained. The original law gave the superintendent discretion over the use of the reserve and how it would be reinstated. On very few occasions were the reserves used, and it came to be felt such a high maximum was no longer necessary to cope with usual demands, such as epidemics. (Actually, neither the old 25 per cent maximum nor the new 15 per cent limit were based upon specific experience figures as most reserve stipulations rely heavily upon judgment.) While the New York insurance department has said that no groups pressed for the reduction, rate increases in the state called attention to, and brought a reappraisal of, the old 25 per cent figure.

The new law in New York severely limits the superintendent's discretionary powers over the use of the reserve. Another new feature is the three-year requirement for restoration. The regulatory attitude in New York is that an association should have a "reasonable" amount of "free surplus" over the 15 per cent of premium income required. Since the special contingent surplus cannot be invaded under normal conditions, an additional surplus account is thought necessary. The department aims at a free surplus of not less than one-half month's needs at the end of a rate projection period of two years. New York officials do not think it desirable to have the reserve formula vary by size of association, percentage of population enrolled, or other factors.

California's reserve requirement for nonprofit hospital service associations is of the fixed-dollar type, and it commands that such organizations:

. . . at all times maintain a reserve fund equal to the following minimum amounts in relation to the number of individuals entitled to hospital benefits under contracts issued by such corporations:

Number of Individuals Entitled to Benefits	Amount of Reserve Fund
2,500 or less	$10,000.00
2,501 to 3,500 inclusive	12,500.00
3,501 to 4,500 inclusive	15,000.00
4,501 to 5,500 inclusive	17,500.00
5,501 and above	20,000.00

In computing said reserve fund, the commissioner shall include the amounts agreed to be paid by contracting hospitals to the corporation or its equivalent value of hospital service to be rendered without charge by the contracting hospital to the hospital service corporation.

The California statute requires, in addition:

If any corporation subject to this chapter has a reserve of admitted assets over all liabilities in excess of two hundred fifty thousand dollars ($250,000), upon its written request the commissioner shall issue to it his certificate stating such fact. Whenever the commissioner finds such fact does not exist he shall revoke and require the surrender of such certificate. Upon such revocation the corporation shall cease to enter into or to renew any contracts . . . except that it may continue to carry out in good faith its obligations under any such contract which was entered into prior to such revocation up to but not beyond the date of the next annual renewal of such contract.

The enabling act for hospital service associations in Pennsylvania does not provide a basis for determining reserves. The law specifies only that reserves are subject to prior approval by the insurance department. Pennsylvania's non-profit medical (and osteopathic and dental) service act stipulates that reserves will be maintained "in such form and amount as the Insurance Commissioner may determine, to insure its subscribers against loss through the failure of the corporation to furnish the services agreed to in its contracts." It is the regulatory attitude in Pennsylvania that associations should probably use three months of financial needs as a goal for reserves, although no official opinion has been promulgated concerning the level to be maintained nor restrictions on the use of the reserves.

A Blue Shield plan in Illinois, "after its first full calendar year of doing business shall accumulate and maintain a special contingent reserve over and above its reserves and liabilities at the rate of two per centum (2%) annually of its net premium income so long as the special contingent reserve does not exceed fifty-five per centum (55%) of its average annual income for the previous five years." The accumulation factor in Illinois is identical to that required in New York. The maximum fund size in the former state is almost four times higher, however. Illinois also decrees that "average" premium income will be determined over a five-year period, rather than for the previous year as in New York.

NAIC Actions on Reserves

Reserve levels and determinations constitute one of the most perplexing issues facing the NAIC in recent years with respect to hospital and medical service associations. This may be observed in the following statements by NAIC committees.

1944: Your committee recommends that proper reserves be required at all times for unearned subscription fees and unpaid hospital bills, including provision for unreported and undischarged hospital cases. In addition, contingency reserves or surplus should be accumulated at the rate of *not less than 5%* of earned, *subscription income.* When such contingency reserve or surplus equals *five months subscription income or seven months hospitalization expenses,* we believe that each Blue Cross Plan should give consideration to the possibility of increasing current benefits or reducing their subscription rates.[4]

1945: The consensus of opinion of this Committee agree that a surplus equal to *five months utilization* cost is entirely adequate, and when such surpluses reach the equivalent of six months utilization, consideration of plans for furnishing additional services to subscribers without additional cost should be submitted by said plans: When such surpluses drop to the equivalent of four months utilization cost, it is a definite danger signal to said plans, and when the surpluses drop to the equivalent of two months utilization cost, it is definite notice to the commissioner supervising the plan that rates should be given his careful study and attention.[5]

By these standards, at least sixty-two Blue Cross plans and thirty-nine Blue Shield plans are in the danger zone, while the rates of thirty-two Blue Cross organizations and fourteen Blue Shield associations need "careful study and attention" by the respective commissioners.

1945: Special problems posed by the service contract character of the Blue Cross Plans in the period of rapidly rising cost of the services offered makes your Committee suggest that this reserve be permitted to rise to *eight times the monthly hospitalization expense.*[6]

1952: Your committee feels that it is important to reaffirm the action of the (June) . . . 1945 N.A.I.C. meeting (". . . *five months utilization cost* is entirely adequate. . . .")

---

[4] Report of the Joint Meeting of the Subcommittee of Group Hospitalization and Medical Service Committee of the NAIC and representatives of Blue Cross Plans, Harrisburg, Pennsylvania, May 15, 1944. Italics added.

[5] Group Hospitalization and Medical Service Committee's report at the 76th session of the NAIC, St. Paul, Minnesota, June 4–6, 1945. Italics added.

[6] Group Hospitalization and Medical Service Committee's report at the 77th session of the NAIC, Grand Rapids, Michigan, December 2–5, 1945. Italics added.

It is to be pointed out that the contingency reserve requirements referred to in the 1945 report are considered to be reserves in addition to those necessary reserves for known and unknown liabilities such as unearned premium reserves, reserves for insured not reported claims and those reserves which are necessary to reflect liability of a Blue Cross plan for incurred maternity coverage. These latter reserves are to be considered as existing liabilities and not as part of excess or surplus funds.[7]

1953: It is urged that each Commissioner require the systematic *annual accumulation* of a contingency reserve by Blue Cross–Blue Shield Plans of *not less than 2% to 3% of earned premiums* until a *certain maximum* is reached, with the proviso that such contingency reserve may not be used for claims or expenses except with the consent of the Commissioner and then only under a plan acceptable to him for the restoration of the amount so used.[8]

1953: [The Subcommittee accepted a proposal, made by the Blue Cross–Blue Shield Commissions, which reaffirmed the earlier 1953 limits, but changed the provisions regarding consent to use the fund to read] . . . with the proviso that the Guarantee Fund may be used by a Plan for claims or expenses upon notice to the Commissioner of its intent to do so together with a Plan for corrective steps, such as a premium increase, or a contract change.

The establishment of such a Guarantee Fund shall not be a segregated item of surplus in the presentation to the public of policyholders' surplus, but the surplus shall be so separated in the financial statement furnished to the Insurance Department.[9]

1957: [The subcommittee recommended it undertake an extensive review and reappraisal of the formula for reserve policies.][10]

---

[7] Report of the Subcommittee on Blue Cross–Blue Shield at the 83rd session of the NAIC, Chicago, Illinois, June 23, 1952. Italics added.

[8] Report of the Subcommittee on Blue Cross–Blue Shield at the 84th session of the NAIC, San Francisco, California, June 8–12, 1953. Italics added.

[9] Report of the Subcommittee on Blue Cross–Blue Shield at the 85th session of the NAIC, Miami Beach, Florida, November 30–December 4, 1953.

[10] Report of the Subcommittee to Study Greater Standardization of Blue Cross and Blue Shield at the 93rd session of the NAIC, New York City, December 2–6, 1957.

NAIC deliberations resulted in some agreement that reserves should be accumulated at not less than 2 to 3 per cent of earned premiums, with five months of utilization costs being proper as a maximum. Obviously, few states have followed this suggestion. Several commissioners say they are waiting for the NAIC report—from the action instituted in 1957—prior to invoking or proposing revisions in their reserve stipulations. Some NAIC members state the necessary statistics are being obtained for consideration of this problem. A prominent member of the committee, however, has maintained the reserve question has been by-passed because of more important Blue Cross–Blue Shield issues. There are no indications the NAIC committee has given further study in recent years to the reserve issue.

Executives of some associations are disgusted by what they call NAIC's "wishy-washy" attitude toward reserves. They feel the group is avoiding the question because certain commissioners want to prevent rate increases; a definitive reserve requirement could necessitate substantial rate alterations, particularly if it were five times monthly claim needs.

Reserve Requirements Established by National Associations

The American Hospital Association and the National Association of Blue Shield Plans both utilize reserve requirements as part of their approval programs for Blue Cross and Blue Shield plans, respectively. The AHA Approval Standard Number 4 prescribes:

A plan shall maintain reserves adequate to protect hospital and subscribers' interests.

Adequate liability (a) admissions reported but not yet paid, and (b) unreported admissions, shall be provided for and shall be shown in a Plan's operating statement.

A Plan shall maintain an adequate reserve for contingencies over and above all liabilities. A Plan's reserves, exclusive of liability items including (a) and (b) above, shall be sufficient at least to meet *hospital and operating expenses for* a period of *three months.*

A Plan which does not meet this requirement, or which has not added at least *3% of gross income* to its contingency reserves during the preceding twelve-month period, exclusive of liability items including (a) and (b) above, shall produce *evidence satisfactory to* the . . . Board of Trustees of *the American Hospital Association* that its financial policies are sound. [Italics added.]

As a means of satisfying this standard, an association must submit detailed financial information to substantiate its reserve position.

Section 9 of the Membership Standards of the National Association of Blue Shield Plans states:

A. A Plan shall maintain such reserves as are legally required; they shall also be reasonably sufficient to protect subscribers' and physicians' interests. . . .

C. A Plan shall provide adequate liabilities for medical/surgical claims reported but not yet paid and unreported medical/surgical claims, and shall reflect these liabilities in its operating statement.

Plans having less than 1.25 months of average monthly medical/surgical claims expense in this liability account shall submit at the request of the Board of Directors satisfactory evidence that its liability account for claims outstanding is adequate.

D. A Plan shall maintain an adequate reserve for contingencies over and above all liabilities. A Plan's reserves, exclusive of liability items included in paragraph (C.) above, shall be sufficient to meet *medical/surgical and operating expenses for* a period of *three months.*

A Plan which does not meet this requirement, and has not added at least *2% of gross income* to its contingency reserves during the preceding twelve month period, exclusive of liability items included in paragraph (C.) above, shall produce *evidence satisfactory to the Board of Directors* that its financial policies are sound. [Italics added.]

The only difference between the Blue Cross and Blue Shield standards is that the latter prescribes a 2 per cent accumulation factor, while the former uses 3 per cent. The reserve formulas with which associations must comply in order to be approved have three features: an accrual factor, a minimum limitation, and an "escape clause." If claims and operating expenditures exactly equal premium income for a particular period, then a three months' figure for average monthly expenditures would be equivalent to a 25 per cent limit for gross subscription income. Still, there is a considerable difference between New York's statute, for example, and the Associations' requirements. New York imposes the accrual factor (of 2 per cent) first, and *then* specifies that the special fund be *no more than* 15 per cent of *net* premium income. The Associations prescribe, *first,* that three months of average expenditures shall be maintained. It should be noted that the three-month requirement is an initial *minimum,* while New York's 15 per cent figure is a *maximum.* New York's accrual factor is identical to the Blue Shield requirement of 2 per cent; the factor used by the Associations is based upon gross premium income, however, while New York uses net premium income as the base. There is no escape clause in New York's provision.

Except for the escape clause—which can nullify the other two requirements—Association standards are more exacting than are those contained in the New York law. This is true for most statutes which mention reserve limits. The different forms in which the minimum and maximum levels are imposed by states as opposed to the national associations seems to indicate that states are most concerned with the *reasonableness* of reserves. (That is, reserves must be kept from being too high or they will necessitate unreasonably high subscriber rates.) The Associations' reserve requirements, on the other hand, appear to be most concerned with the *adequacy* of reserves.

The American Hospital Association has seriously considered reducing reserve requirements from three months' to one month's hospital and operating expenses. As yet, no official action has taken place in this direction.

Appraisal of Reserve Requirements

The financial stability—and financial *instability* as well—of a Blue Cross or Blue Shield plan is affected by several elements. Paramount are the age of the association, rate of growth, nature of benefit structures and their changes, economic conditions in the association area, trends in costs for providing services and the degree to which an association can control these costs, and the ease and speed by which an organization may alter its rate structure.

The financial condition of a new Blue Cross or Blue Shield plan is more perilous because the organization may not have an adequate spread of subscribers to facilitate operation of the Law of Large Numbers for the medical care expense hazard. Then, too, its expenses are likely to be higher and possibly its management will be less experienced. Even though a relatively new organization may have had an adequate contingency fund based upon the needs of the period immediately past, a rapid growth rate could greatly reduce the proportion of assets offset by special reserves. Any association expanding its membership and obligations may face this situation. For example, an organization with a three months' reserve position will find itself with two months' reserve if it increases its membership by one half (assuming that the average claims and expense figures per member remain unchanged). Favorable claim experience, a decrease in benefits, or inclusion of a reserve factor in the rates are the only important ways to forestall this decline in reserve level.

Liberalizations in benefits or overutilization of existing benefit structures can also jeopardize reserve levels. If reserves were previously 25 per cent of average annual expenditures, and benefits are increased by 25 per cent without an accompanying rate change, the reserve level would decline to 20 per cent (25/100 versus 25/125).

Economic conditions may encourage utilization of benefits beyond what was anticipated. Unnecessary hospitalization and medical treatment, malingering, and similar events are more likely to occur when and where there is high unemployment. On the other hand, if reimbursements for hospitalization and doctors' services are soaring, an association will have to use some of its reserve funds unless projections in the rate structure properly anticipate the cost trend. When

hospitals and doctors have been committed to service benefits with stipulated reimbursement rates and fees, associations
do not have to absorb cost increases until the current schedules are terminated.

Finally, Blue Cross and Blue Shield plans that can secure
rate increases without undue difficulty are less likely to de-
plete their reserves. Lengthy rate hearings can occasion a reserve reduction because an association must continue to use
an inadequate rate during the delay. If rate increases are
granted automatically when necessary and in adequate
amounts, reserves are theoretically necessary only to protect
against unusual expenditures encountered before a rate
change can come to the rescue.

The reserve questions to be resolved include: are special
financial reserves necessary? If so, what should be the nature
of the reserve limits? If reserves are desirable, should they
be instituted by law, through the discretionary powers of
supervisory officials, or left to the national organizations or
the associations? Are uniform reserve standards possible
throughout the country?

The Desirability of Reserves. The function of a special
contingency reserve is to smooth out and stabilize any fluctuation between income and outgo. Financial reserves of this
type appear desirable. A considerable number of Blue Cross
plans and many Blue Shield corporations do not have guarantees from hospitals and doctors that services will be continued if funds are exhausted. Even where hospital and
physicians' guarantees have been obtained, they offer but
short-range relief. No hospital nor doctor could be expected
to provide services without compensation for an extended period. As a matter of fact, guarantees are given in most instances on the supposition that any decrease in reimbursements or fees will be repaid after the next rate increase.

It is true that . . . when Plans were being organized this guarantee was most important and the Plans were actually financially dependent upon member hospitals. However, in the opinion of your [NAIC] Committee, the situation meanwhile has

been reversed. The individual hospital is beset with its own problems of meeting the spiraling costs of nurses' salaries, supplies, equipment, etc. . . . Past experience has shown that member hospitals cannot afford to accept more than a minimum pro rating for a short period only. . . . In view of the foregoing, it seems unrealistic to your Committee to argue that an adequate surplus ratio is unnecessary on account of the pro rating agreements with member hospitals.[11]

An association will be edged toward a financial predicament if rates are consistently inadequate, regardless of its reserve position. Financial reserves help to provide stability, however, particularly if guarantees are nonexistent or if there are short-term cancellation periods on the contracts with participating hospitals and doctors.[12]

The fluctuating nature of claim costs and the fact that cost trends are generally adverse also stress the need for some form of financial reserves. The possibility that rate hearings will delay rate increases is an additional consideration. Then, too, epidemics are not a completely removed hazard even in the present day, and an association whose membership is largely confined to one city can be vulnerable in this respect.

Experience-rating techniques can modify the need for reserves on that portion of an association's business for which rates are self-adjusted, since experience rating is supposed to assure rate adequacy. In actuality, adequacy is guaranteed only in the case of *retrospective* experience rates.

The Nature of Reserve Limits. It is much more difficult to determine the exact form reserve requirements should take than to decide whether such limits are desirable. The various elements which influence the financial stability of an association make it inadvisable to state reserve requirements in terms of dollars. It is apparent, at least, that reserve provisions which have specific dollar requirements cannot con-

---

[11] *Proceedings of the National Association of Insurance Commissioners, 1953,* Vol. II, p. 533.

[12] AHA requires a ninety-day minimum termination period for hospital contracts as part of the Blue Cross approval program.

sider the environment and characteristics of individual Blue Cross and Blue Shield plans. It is slightly ludicrous to require, as in California for example, a $250,000 reserve for any and all associations, when some organizations pay out fifteen to twenty times that amount every month for subscriber benefits. At that, only one state which prescribes reserve limits in terms of dollars has a requirement higher than that of California. Most laws of this type have much lower minimum levels. There is but small additional value in varying the reserve by number of subscribers, because growth, benefits, and costs are not considered thereby.

The alternatives for ascertaining reserve levels when dollar stipulations are abandoned include a formula determination or an evaluation of the finances and circumstances of individual associations. A formula is more automatic and administratively convenient to apply. It is not likely many states have the funds or the staffs, even where associations pay for examination expenses, to determine the reserve each organization should maintain. If such examinations were possible, judgment would probably have to be backed by some rule of thumb or formula.

The exact extent of reserve limits is beyond the capabilities of this research to determine. However, cost trends and the desirability of benefit experimentation in such areas as coverages for the aged, extension of hospitalization day limits, and major medical coverages, would seem to press for a reserve of more than one month's average expenditures. A one-month figure allows approximately an 8 per cent variation in expenditures before the reserve is exhausted. Most executive directors feel the three-month level, as decreed in the approval programs, is proper.

Regardless of the extent of reserves or how they are determined, their effectiveness is controlled by the utilization of benefits and the adequacy of rates. No reserve formula will *furnish* a contingency fund unless a reserve factor is incorporated into an already adequate rate. Commissioners play a vital role in this respect. Inadequate rates not only fail to contribute to reserves but may also dissipate existing funds. It is natural for the spokesmen for subscriber groups, such as labor unions, to press for low rates. One means of forestalling rate increases, or temporarily lowering such increases, is not to include a factor for reserves; thus, subscriber groups customarily oppose reserves in general. This is one reason associations which have built up contingency funds dislike having them subsumed "surplus." The purposes of the excess funds are not evident and they become a source of subscriber misunderstanding.

As a general consideration, formulas should be influenced more by the operating financial requirements of an association than by its income. Reserves based upon expenditures will be lower when income exceeds outgo than if they are determined by receipts; the relatively higher income in such circumstances is a healthy factor which offsets the lower reserves. When they are based upon income, however, unexpectedly high expenditures find reserves at a lower level just at the time when income is insufficient.

Instituting Reserve Requirements. Reserves are too vital to be left to the discretion of individual associations. It is obvious that well-managed Blue Cross and Blue Shield plans want a financial backdrop; they are, nevertheless, put under pressure from subscriber groups to eliminate reserves when no legal requirements exist. Similarly, the reserve formula should not be left to the judgment of the regulatory authority, as he, too, is often subject to the same pressures and influences. With the reserve formula established in, and required by, an enabling act, a reserve factor is included in rates without associations and commissioners having to justify this action. Then, too, with statutory reserves as a *minimum*, commissioners can consider any unusual or special circumstances associations feel may warrant additional contingency funds.

Uniform Reserve Requirements. It is subject to conjecture whether reserve formulas should be applied uniformly throughout the country. The sheer improbability this uniformity will occur—even if desirable—might encourage one to abandon the question. Most commissioners who evaluated this issue stated uniformity is either not necessary or inadvisable. One supervisory official observed, "Due to different types of plans, benefits and coverages, a uniform reserve basis would not be practical." It is not likely, however, that the necessary examination and evaluation of each association will be conducted to determine the reserve which should be maintained. Thus, it would seem that reserve formula limits, at least within a range, *could* be applied in all states alike. It would require concerted action by the NAIC and commissioners to bring this about, of course. In the meantime, the only standards which will apply in the same manner in all states are those instituted by the national associations.

INVESTMENTS

It is common for enabling acts to prescribe that hospital and medical service associations may invest in only those media permitted for either life insurance companies or casualty insurance organizations. Twenty-four states so stipulate for Blue Cross, and twenty-five states do so for Blue Shield organizations. Two states limit investments to those allowed for savings banks while one jurisdiction uses the investments permitted for trust funds. Two states have set up special investment safeguards for associations. Nine states have no investment restrictions.[13]

New York, California,[14] Pennsylvania, and Illinois are among the areas whose statutes prohibit investments other than those permitted for life insurance companies.

New York allows associations, with the approval of the superintendent, to purchase real estate necessary for their principal offices or for convenient business operation. The aggregate amount of real estate owned, however, may not be more than 5 per cent of net premium income during the twelve months prior to the date on which approval for such a purchase is requested from the superintendent.

---

[13] Alaska, Colorado, Delaware, Missouri, Montana, Virginia, Washington, West Virginia, and Wyoming.

[14] The California law applies only to Blue Cross.

It is opportune only to outline generally the investment restraints imposed upon life insurance companies by the various states. These requirements have been broadly analyzed as follows:

> In general, the funds of life insurance companies must be invested in fixed-income corporate securities (bonds); real estate mortgages; obligations of the federal, state, and local governments (including certain Canadian obligations); and policy loans. Until recent years, most states have restricted the outright ownership of real estate to that (1) occupied by the company at its home office; (2) necessary for the convenient transaction of its business; or (3) acquired by legal process, such as by foreclosure of mortgage loans. . . . Within the last decade or so, some states have liberalized their laws to permit the investment of life insurance funds in housing projects. The New York law permits a company to invest up to 10 per cent of its admitted assets in such projects. A more recent development has been the liberalizing of state laws to permit the acquisition of certain types of commercial real estate for the production of income, subject to stated limitations and conditions. In New York, the aggregate investments of this type cannot exceed 3 per cent of a company's admitted assets.
>
> Common stock investments are prohibited entirely in a few states and are severely limited in all other states. Generally speaking, a life insurance company cannot own more than 10 per cent of the outstanding common stock of any corporation and cannot hold common stock, in the aggregate, in an amount greater than 5 per cent of its admitted assets or one third of its surplus to policyholders, whichever shall be the lesser. There is usually no overall limitation on the amount of preferred stock which can be held by a life insurance company, but the eligibility requirements with respect to the stock of a particular corporation are rather rigorous. In the aggregate, only about 2 per cent of life insurance companies' assets are invested in preferred stock.[15]

Cooperating regulatory officials were one short of unanimous in expressing the sentiment that the investment restric-

---

[15] Dan M. McGill, *Life Insurance* (Homewood, Ill.: Richard D. Irwin, Inc., 1959), pp. 760–61.

tions for life insurance companies are proper for associations and that no change in the laws is necessary. The dissenter felt that hospital and medical service organizations should have more liberal investment bounds than those applicable to life insurance companies.

EXPENSES

A lesser number of states have legislated regulatory controls over the expense portion of subscription fees than have granted approval powers for over-all rates. Twenty of the forty-four supervisory officials indicated their state laws grant some type of authority over at least a portion of the expenses of Blue Cross plans,[16] and nineteen so prescribe for Blue Shield plans.[17] Twenty-one states do not have any limitations of this sort; three statutes are in question, and six authorities did not reply. Among the states which include expense considerations in their statutes, some have restrictions on expenses in general while others have limitations on solicitation or acquisition costs and on administrative expenditures.

Thirteen of the twenty states which deal with expenses express their limitations in percentages. That is, expenses may not exceed a certain percentage of earned subscription, or gross, income. These limits range from a low of 7 per cent to a high of 35 per cent. The most common stipulation is 20 per cent. Some jurisdictions allow higher maximums during the initial years, such as 30 per cent of subscription income the first year an association is in business, 25 per cent the second year, and 20 per cent thereafter.

Six statutes simply mention that expenses are subject to the approval of the commissioner, while another prescribes that expenses must be "fair and reasonable."

The supervisory officials in six states impose expense re-

---

[16] Arizona, Arkansas, California, Florida, Georgia, Hawaii, Illinois, Iowa, Kansas, Kentucky, Massachusetts, New Jersey, New Mexico, New York, North Carolina, Oklahoma, Pennsylvania, South Carolina, South Dakota, and West Virginia.

[17] With the exception of Massachusetts, these are the same states as those which give control over Blue Cross expenses.

strictions in addition to those set forth by their respective enabling acts. Four of these are in areas where the enabling statutes do not mention expenses.

New York, California, Pennsylvania, and Illinois are among the states with legislative requirements concerning expenses for operating an association. New York proclaims:

> No corporation subject to the provisions of this article shall during any one year disburse more than ten per cent of the aggregate amount of the payments received from subscribers during that year as expenditures for the soliciting of subscribers, except that during the first year after the issuance of a permit, such corporation may so disburse not more than twenty per centum of such amount and during the second year not more than fifteen per centum.
>
> No such corporation shall, during any one year, disburse a sum greater than twenty per centum of the payments received from subscribers during that year as administrative expenses. The term, "administrative expenses," as used in this section, shall include all expenditures for non-professional services and in general all expenses not directly connected with the furnishing of the benefits specified . . . , but not including expenses referred to [above]. . . .
>
> If the Superintendent of insurance shall find that the disbursements of any corporation for either of the items specified in [the] paragraphs [above] . . . exceeds the amounts permitted thereunder, he may maintain proceedings to liquidate, rehabilitate or dissolve such corporation. . . .

The total expenses allowed for New York's Blue Cross or Blue Shield plans are thus 40 per cent during the first year, 35 per cent the second year and 30 per cent thereafter. Only one third of the ultimate 30 per cent maximum may be used to enroll subscribers.

The California provision for hospital service associations subjects all acquisition costs to the approval of the commissioner of insurance; the over-all expense limit, including solicitation expenditures, is 25 per cent of "the aggregate amount of rates, dues, fees and other periodic charges actually received during that year." Failure to remain within this figure may result in revocation of a Blue Cross plan's permit to operate in the state.

Only acquisition costs are mentioned in Pennsylvania's enabling acts, and these expenditures are subject to the commissioner's approval. There is no percentage stipulation, nor are requirements established for aggregate administrative expenses. This is also the situation for Blue Cross plans in Illinois. The expense restrictions imposed on the state's Blue Shield plans are identical to those used in New York.

The actual expenses incurred by associations are customarily far below the limits established by even the most restrictive laws. The combined operating-cost percentages for all Blue Cross plans in the United States have gradually declined in recent years. In 1952, for example, the over-all operating expense ratio was 7.43, while in 1961 it was 4.91.[18] Total expenses varied among hospital service associations from a low of 2.01 per cent of earned subscription income in the Canton, Ohio, plan to a high of 12.53 per cent in Great Falls, Montana. Both figures are atypical, as only four plans had expense ratios in excess of 10 per cent and the same number were below 3 per cent. Expenses vary generally by association size, with higher expenses to be expected in the smaller organizations.[19] The average expenses for all Blue

---

[18] Blue Cross operating expense as a per cent of earned income:

1961	4.91	1956	6.14
1960	5.04	1955	6.27
1959	5.40	1954	6.71
1958	5.92	1953	6.96
1957	6.00	1952	7.43

Source: Blue Cross Association.

[19] Operating expense percentages by size of plans:

Number of Subscribers:	Blue Cross (Dec. 31, 1961)	Blue Shield (Dec. 31, 1961)
More than 1,000,000	4.46	9.89
500,000–1,000,000	5.26	8.47
200,000–500,000	5.84	9.03
100,000–200,000	6.66	12.49
50,000–100,000	8.60	11.95
Less than 50,000	6.56	10.38

Source: Blue Cross Association, *Financial Report of Blue Cross Plans, Year of 1961*, pp. 4–6; Association of Blue Shield Plans, *Financial Reports, Blue Shield Plans, Year of 1961*, p. 10.

Shield plans on December 31, 1961 were 9.5 per cent of total income. The range of expenses was from 4.98 per cent of subscription income in Washington, D.C., to 21.94 per cent in Rockford, Illinois. The only other organizations with expenses in excess of 15 per cent of subscription income were the associations in New York City; Jamestown, New York; Sioux Falls, South Dakota; and Portland, Oregon.

REPORTS AND EXAMINATIONS

Reports

The primary manner state regulatory officials keep informed about the financial operations of associations is through periodic reports the organizations must submit. Information contained in these reports is verified by a public accounting firm in most cases. The only other means for ascertaining the correctness of figures is for representatives of a commissioner to conduct an examination of the books, operations, and personnel of an association.

Thirty-five states reported that plans are required to file annual financial statements with the appropriate state authority. Laws in six states do not necessitate reporting, and the exact stipulations of nine other areas are not known. Thirty-one of the thirty-five states have reporting procedures identical to, or more stringent than, those for health insurance companies.[20] Some state authorities require less detailed reports filed quarterly. Many associations voluntarily send their monthly operating statements to the commissioner in their state.

Blue Cross and Blue Shield plans in New York, Pennsylvania and Illinois, and Blue Cross plans in California, for example, must file financial statements with the state supervisory official on, or before, March 1, annually. These reports

---

[20] Arizona, Arkansas, California, Connecticut, Florida, Georgia, Hawaii, Illinois, Iowa, Kansas, Kentucky, Louisiana, Maryland, Massachusetts, Michigan, Minnesota, Nebraska, New Hampshire, New Jersey, New Mexico, New York, North Carolina, Ohio, Oklahoma, Oregon, Pennsylvania, Rhode Island, South Carolina, South Dakota, Virginia, and Wisconsin.

contain all information, as of the previous December 31, the regulatory official desires. The reports must be verified by at least two principal officers of the corporations.

The American Hospital Association and the National Association of Blue Shield Plans also require annual reports as part of their approval programs. Associations must file monthly statements when they fail to meet either the three-months stipulation for reserves or the accrual factor.

Examinations

As is customary for health insurance companies, most enabling acts specify examination of hospital and medical service organizations by members of the state insurance department once every three years. Thirty-six states are known to have so legislated; one jurisdiction requires an examination every two years; three states stipulate yearly examinations while one prescribes these once every four years.[21] An examination of association records is generally conducted, although interrogation of personnel may also take place to augment recorded information. The purpose of examinations is to verify or establish the financial condition of associations. The organizations examined often pay for the cost thereof, in which case no cost to the taxpayer is involved.

The New York statute is so worded that the normal regulatory provisions applicable to insurance companies generally apply to the nonprofit associations except where specifically stated to the contrary. Thus, the triennial examination requirements appropriate for companies also apply to Blue Cross and Blue Shield plans even though the enabling act does not mention examinations.

The provision in Pennsylvania's enabling act for examination of hospital service associations is typical of the requirements in other areas:

Every such nonprofit corporation shall be subject to examination not less frequently than every three years by the Insurance

---

[21] Six states did not submit information and three responding officials did not outline their examination requirements.

Commissioner, and his agents, who shall have free access to all books, records, papers and documents that relate to the business of the corporation, and the power to examine the officers, agents and members of the corporation under oath, in relation to the affairs, transactions and conditions of the corporation.

When a regulatory authority is granted discretion in timing examinations, such examinations are referred to as "visitations." Visitation-type provisions allow a commissioner to investigate any dubious conditions, even though it is not time for a required examination. Since most enabling laws allow visitations, the majority of commissioners do not feel additional inquisitive powers are necessary over Blue Cross and Blue Shield operations.

LIQUIDATION

When an association becomes involved in financial difficulties a commissioner may prescribe corrective measures. He may allow changes in rates or benefits, or he may institute liquidation procedures if he considers it in the public interest. Before a point of calamity is reached, it is likely an association would be under surveillance and assistance from one of the national associations.

If liquidation is necessary, as determined usually by the regulatory authority, it is common for the same provisions and procedures to apply to associations as are pertinent for insurance companies. Liquidation proceedings are under the supervision of the regulatory official.

New York and California are among the states which set forth in their enabling acts the conditions constituting insolvency. A New York association is insolvent if it, presently or prospectively, cannot fulfill its outstanding contracts and other liabilities and reserves. Insolvency exists in California if reserve-fund minimums are not maintained.

It is said that very few associations have "died"; rather, the impoverished organizations have merged with more healthy neighbors. For this reason merger procedures are prescribed in many enabling statutes.

chapter XIII

TAXATION

One historical point of conflict between health insurance carriers and Blue Cross–Blue Shield has been over the tax immunity of the associations. Competitors vilify this exemption because they feel it not only gives a cost advantage to the plans but in addition leads citizens to infer some sort of governmental sponsorship is behind these organizations. Because of the general exemption from taxes, the supposition is also commonly made that Blue Cross and Blue Shield plans enjoy a more liberal and less restrictive regulatory treatment than that imposed upon insurance companies. Previous chapters have indicated this is not a justified generalization.

A few association executives stated in connection with research for this book that they would prefer their organizations *be taxed*. Then, they say, associations could, among other things, be selective in their underwriting and it would not be necessary to take as many poor risks into the membership. A more "profitable" operation would result, and the incessant need for rate increases might be better controlled. The end result, of course, would be that associations would lose much of their social aura and at the same time assume more of the identifying features of insurance companies' operations. Also, less scrutiny of such aspects as rates, benefit structures, composition of the boards of directors, and so on, would be likely. The number of executive directors who would encourage Blue Cross and Blue Shield taxation, though, are definitely in the minority. Many executives do feel the tax advantages they enjoy do not furnish a sufficient competitive advantage to warrant their constant supervision, rate hearings, public scrutiny, and press coverage. Most of the associations' managements consider that with their relatively nonselective, community-type enrollment, they more than earn whatever tax savings they are granted.

The differential regulatory treatment accorded Blue Cross and Blue Shield plans was interpreted in a 1961 adjudication by Pennsylvania's insurance commissioner:

> The objects and purposes of Blue Shield become apparent when we recognize its origin and the legal basis of its continuing existence. The Legislature of Pennsylvania in enacting the Nonprofit Medical, Osteopathic and Dental Service Corporation Act intended that persons of *low income* should be provided . . . services at costs which they could reasonably afford through nonprofit enterprises acting for them in contracting with doctors to provide such persons with medical services for reasonable fees which doctors were certain to receive. . . .

> The Legislature went a step further and publicly subsidized these nonprofit enterprises by making them tax exempt. The Legislature was in effect stating that since the sole purpose of such organizations is to perform a public service free from all considerations of private gain, we will deny the Commonwealth of Pennsylvania and each of its political subdivisions the normal rights of taxation with respect to their income and properties.

> This action of the Legislature, beyond any doubt, vests in the public an unquestionable interest in the Pennsylvania Blue Shield Plan.[1]

CURRENT TAXATION OF INSURANCE COMPANIES

Justification for the taxation of insurance has long been recognized as resting almost solely on the procurement of revenue. Corporations of this type, with their great income and stores of funds, have presented an administratively simple and politically easy source for taxation. Thus, they have

---

[1] Adjudication, in the *Matter of Filing No. 1–H, 1960 of the Medical Service Association of Pennsylvania*, February 2, 1961, p. 4.

had almost every conceivable type of levy assessed against them. In addition to federal income taxation, insurance companies are often subjected to a variety of state-, and sometimes municipally, imposed general taxes. A special levy has also been created for insurance companies in the nature of a tax on premium income. States which use this method often grant deductions for reinsurance, returned premiums, unearned premium deposits, and policyholder dividends in arriving at the taxable premium income. Some states also permit local and state real estate and sales taxes to be subtracted. Still others allow deductions for increases in reserves. In many jurisdictions the premium tax takes the place of other state and local taxes. Usually where the premium tax is not used, insurance companies are responsible for one or more of several levies, including sales taxes, investment income taxes, real estate taxes, and business license fees.

The exemption from premium taxation enjoyed by Blue Cross and Blue Shield plans is one of two areas of differential treatment about which insurance companies are most vociferous. (The other area is that of hospital reimbursement schedules.) Insurance companies, though, do not pay taxes on *all* premium income. It is rather common for domestic premiums to be exempt, while nondomestic premiums are taxed. This is the situation on domestic health insurance premiums in at least eleven states, while four or more have reduced tax structures for domestic premiums. Not less than three others grant tax reductions if property or a certain portion of assets are held by a company within the state.[2] Some jurisdictions also treat mutual insurers more favorably than they do stock companies. It is not entirely proper, therefore, to assume that only Blue Cross and Blue Shield plans have advantageous tax positions.

---

[2] See the State of New York insurance department's booklet, *Fees and Taxes Charged Insurance Companies (Under the Laws of New York Together with Abstracts of Fees, Taxes and Other Requirements of Other States)*, or the *State Tax Guide* (New York: Commerce Clearing House, Inc.).

CURRENT TAXATION OF BLUE CROSS AND BLUE SHIELD

Twenty-three commissioners mentioned that the tax status of the Blues had not been litigated in their states. A 1943 case in California (*California Physicians' Service* v. *Garrison*) is one of the few important instances where the tax status of associations has been litigated. Taxation of the plan was denied in the California suit.

The most significant recent case resulted from an attempt by the city of Milwaukee to collect a property tax from the Wisconsin Blue Cross plan after the organization had constructed a new office building for its operations.[3] The plan paid the tax, but instituted a court action to force a refund. In May, 1961, the Supreme Court of the State of Wisconsin handed down a decision which reversed earlier rulings in the case and disallowed the tax. The issues involved in the Milwaukee litigation appear basically the same as those which would be associated with any dispute over the tax position of Blue Cross and Blue Shield organizations: Is tax exemption granted under the appropriate enabling statutes? If so, is such an exemption constitutional? If constitutional, what tests must be met to receive the exemption? The Wisconsin statute provided that:

Nonprofit corporations, that is corporations formed without capital stock, operated not for profit and exclusively for the purposes in this section set forth, and which declare no dividend, benefit or pecuniary profit, to be paid to or received by any of their members, directors or officers, may be organized, under this section for the purpose of establishing, maintaining and operating service plans, whereby hospital services may be provided to persons or groups of persons, subscribers to such plans, and their respective dependents, by hospitals with which such corporations may make a contract therefor. . . .

. . . Every such corporation is hereby declared to be a chari-

---

[3] *Associated Hospital Service, Inc.* v. *City of Milwaukee,* 109 N.W. 2d 271.

table and benevolent corporation, and its property, real, personal and mixed, its income, and property transferred to it, shall be exempt from taxation. . . . [This wording is similar to that of the model law.]

The statute in question clearly granted a tax exemption for the associations. The next issue was whether such exemption was constitutional. The court explained that even if there were no basis for classifying plans as "charitable" and "benevolent" in accordance with court decisions or dictionaries, this would not prevent the legislature from declaring certain corporations to be "charitable and benevolent." Furthermore, it was pointed out that the legislature could have simply declared hospital service associations tax exempt without mentioning they were "charitable and benevolent." The only bar to such an exemption would be if there were a reasonable basis for exempting one organization while a similar type of organization was not so treated: "To argue, that the act of attaching the label of "charitable and benevolent" in itself renders the entire exemption statute void, apart from the issue of reasonable classification, seems to us to be but a confusion of the issue."

The city of Milwaukee contended that the plan, as a matter of fact, engaged in no charitable or benevolent activities inasmuch as the association gave nothing away, and that the organization's activities did not relieve the state or local governments from expenses for hospital care. In this regard the court held:

. . . assertations by the city are not strictly true. The board of directors of the plaintiff consists of persons of great ability,—hospital administrators, physicians, attorneys, labor leaders, business executives and church officials. They donate the time which they devote to the operations and affairs of the plaintiff. There can be little doubt but that such donated time and effort results in better hospital service being rendered to the plaintiff's subscribers and their dependents, such as the insertion of more advantageous provisions from time to time in the subscribers' contracts. Furthermore, before the advent of hospital service prepayment plans, many people were unable to pay hospital bills who can now afford the modest monthly fees charged by the plaintiff. Nevertheless, the hospitals did not then turn such people from their doors but rendered service, and in many cases collected from local municipalities therefor on the basis that the patients were indigents. Without the coming and wide use of the plaintiff's Blue Cross coverage, the financial burden of the municipalities in providing hospital care for indigents would be greater than it is today.

An Ohio court has also declared a Blue Cross plan may be considered "charitable and benevolent."[4] The Milwaukee was particularly interesting with reference to eligibility for tax exemption, however, because the city maintained the Blue Cross plan conducted *ultra vires* acts which offered additional reasons for a rescission of its tax-exempt position. Thus, the city's contention was not only that the general activities of associations failed to qualify as "charitable and benevolent"—which the court refused to accept supra—but also that specific aspects of this plan's operation ought to result in a denial of its preferred status. Among the activities of the Blue Cross plan which were mentioned by the city as evidence it was not operating as a nonprofit organization were its support and participation in Health Service, Inc.; the possibility that a participating hospital might not be a nonprofit institution; and the fact that the association's income exceeded its expenditures for hospital service.

The court appeared to defend the plan's relationship with HSI even though the association had invested $10,000 in HSI capital stock (valued at the time at $23,000). (It was also declared that the city had no right to raise the issue of *ultra vires* activities inasmuch as statutes limited the raising of such an issue to three specific types of proceedings and the subject suit was not one of them.) The concern of the

---

[4] *Cleveland Hospital Service Association* v. *Ebright*, 1942, Ohio. App., 45 N.E. 2nd 157, 160 (affirmed in *Cleveland Hospital Service Association* v. *Ebright*, 1943, 142 Ohio St. 51, 49 N.E. 2nd 929).

city over a participating hospital's nonprofit status was similarly dismissed by the court.

We attach no significance to the fact that the nonprofit status of one of such participating hospitals is now in issue. This is because we must assume that when dissolution occurs the provisions of plaintiff's articles of incorporation for distribution of assets will be observed, and that such distribution will only be made to nonprofit participating hospitals.

The statute seems to assume that all associations will eventually be dissolved. Regardless of the validity of the assumption, the point being made is significant since proprietary hospitals are participating members of many associations. Such plans generally did not receive their initial financial contributions from the proprietary institutions, however, so upon a dissolution these institutions would not participate in the distribution of any surplus.

The court was very specific in the Milwaukee case about the income and reserve position of the association.

The City stresses a fact that the income of the plaintiff from the fees collected from its subscribers has exceeded the amounts that the plaintiff has disbursed to the participating and service hospitals for hospital service supplied to the subscribers and their dependents. Over the twenty year period of 1940–1959, inclusive, the claims paid by the plaintiff for hospital service have amounted to 91.1 per cent of the plaintiff's income.

The fact that plaintiff's income exceeds its disbursements does not necessarily destroy its nonprofit character. Whether dividends or other pecuniary benefits are contemplated to be paid to its members is generally the test to be applied to determine whether a given corporation is organized for profit. . . .

In the instant case the articles forbid any payments being made to the members. Furthermore, the fact that there is some margin of income over outgo does not militate against the objectives for which the plaintiff was organized, but rather promotes such objectives. This is because a hospital service corporation should build up reasonable reserves to guard against the contingency of future claims exceeding income. . . .

The brief of the City also points out that in 1959 the plaintiff realized from investments the sum of $160,000 income; and that it also receives approximately $300,000 income from Blue Shield, for acting as enrolling and billing agent for such organization. . . .

On the latter issue the court felt the legislature had contemplated that hospital service associations would have certain additional sources of income when it granted them tax exemption. The court was satisfied that: "All of such miscellaneous income is derived from activities which the directors in good faith deemed necessary, proper or incidental to carrying out of the general purposes of the plaintiff corporation."

State and Local Taxes

Information submitted in connection with this research indicates that associations in twenty states do not pay taxes of any kind, while Blue Cross and Blue Shield plans in twenty-two other jurisdictions are subject to some levies. Authorities from the following states reported taxes assessed as shown:

Alaska—2 per cent on premiums less losses.

Arizona—taxes on domestic real and tangible personal property.

Arkansas—state and county taxes only.

California—local real estate taxes only.

Florida—same taxes as for domestic companies. (There is no premium tax on domestic companies in Florida, however.)

Hawaii—real estates taxes.

Illinois—real estate and office-equipment taxes.

Iowa—taxes on property and funds held.

Indiana—same taxes as for mutual insurance companies.

Kentucky—property taxes only.

Louisiana—$250 annually.

Nebraska—premium tax of $\frac{4}{10}$ of 1 per cent.

Nevada—premium tax of 2 per cent.

New Jersey—real estate and equipment taxes.

New Mexico—real estate taxes.

North Carolina—$\frac{1}{3}$ of 1 per cent of gross annual membership dues.

Ohio—fees of $\frac{1}{10}$ of 1 cent per contract.

Oklahoma—ad valorem taxes only.

Rhode Island—municipal taxes on property owned and payroll taxes.

South Dakota—same as insurance companies ($2\frac{1}{2}$ per cent of premium income).

Virginia—$\frac{1}{20}$ of 1 per cent

Washington—business and occupational tax.

Definite information concerning the taxation of associations was not provided by the authorities in Alabama, Idaho, Maine, Mississippi, North Dakota, Tennessee, Texas and Utah. Secondary sources of information indicate associations are taxed in four of these states. Alabama and North Dakota stated in response to a 1956 survey that the organizations are subject to taxation.[5] Both the Blue Cross Association and the National Association of Blue Shield Plans have indicated in their financial statements that Mississippi imposes a premium tax of "approximately" 1.75 per cent on gross receipts, while Tennessee has a premium tax of 1.7 per cent.

The twenty states which have not been mentioned do not impose any kind of taxes on Blue Cross and Blue Shield plans.

New York legislation stipulates that "Every . . . [nonprofit medical and dental indemnity or hospital service corporation] shall be exempt from every state, county and municipal tax." The statutory wording precludes even real estate taxes. California's tax exemption provision is so stated that an association is "declared to be a charitable and benevolent institution and its funds shall be exempt from all and every State, county, district, municipal and school tax other than taxes on real estate and office equipment." The prohibition of taxes on "funds" prevents levying premium taxes in the state; real estate taxes, however, are imposed.

---

[5] "State Regulation of Blue Cross and Blue Shield," *Insurance Salesman* (January, 1956), p. 57.

In addition to prescribing that Blue Cross and Blue Shield plans are "charitable and benevolent institutions," Pennsylvania declares the "funds and investments" of hospital service associations and all "income, funds, investments and property" of medical service corporations exempt from all taxation of the state or its political subdivisions. The result is that no taxes of any sort are assessed against Pennsylvania associations.

The enabling act provision concerning taxation in Illinois is stated in terms similar to those of California's statute. Associations in Illinois are subject to real estate and office-equipment taxes.

The national enrollment organizations of Blue Cross and Blue Shield—Health Service, Inc., and Medical Indemnity of America, Inc.—are taxed exactly like other insurance companies, both as to state and federal taxes, because each is incorporated as a stock insurance company.[6]

Federal Income Tax

Except where organized as insurance companies, Blue Cross and Blue Shield plans do not pay federal income tax. Associations are included among the organizations listed in section 501 of the Internal Revenue Code of 1954 which are allowed exemption upon request. The actual release from taxation is granted under section 503 of the code.

THE FUTURE TAX POSITION OF BLUE CROSS AND BLUE SHIELD

It is a moot question whether in the long run there will be changes in the tax status of Blue Cross and Blue Shield plans. This will be influenced by modifications in the associations' characteristics and methods of operation as well as by alterations in their competitive and social environment. The more these organizations assume traits associated with insurance

---

[6] HSI is incorporated in Illinois and MIA in Ohio.

companies, the more likely it is their tax status will be reconsidered. The original position of associations tax-wise was established because their purpose was to operate a social-type **insurance scheme.** By so doing, Blue Cross and Blue Shield were considered to be taking over part of a problem that would otherwise have rested on the government. Associations were supposed to insure all elements in a community, including poor risks and those for whom group coverage was not available. If associations fall short in accomplishing this job there is greater likelihood of changes in regulatory—and tax—treatment in their respective areas.

Nine commissioners who evaluated the possibility of associations being taxed saw no future conditions which would jeopardize the current general exemption. Twelve officials listed possible circumstances which might cause this status to be reconsidered, including the failure to cover low-income groups and the aged, high expense ratios, and the use of insurance companies' tactics.

Currently, there is no reason to believe the nontaxed organizations will be subjected to state levies. This assumption rests on more than the nonprofit status of Blue Cross and Blue Shield plans. Associations which maintain and strengthen community enrollment motives that go beyond the advantageous subscriber groups will reduce the possibility of any serious reappraisal of the tax exemption. Reevaluation is also less probable where associations show they are socially oriented rather than instruments of hospitals and the medical profession. At the same time, the high proportion of subscription income disbursed directly for subscriber benefits will help to fortify conceptual and operational differences between Blue Cross–Blue Shield and insurance companies. Finally, associations which offer service benefits will be less subject to a reconsideration of their tax status than organizations which use the indemnity approach.

It is also not likely that associations will come under federal income taxation. Litigation was inaugurated in New York City against the Associated Medical Service (Blue

Shield in New York City) several years ago, but the case has never come to trial and apparently never will.

A further deterrent against taxation of the Blues may come from some insurance companies, as odd as this may seem. Many carriers are fearful of federal government encroachments both into the insurance business, such as through a federal program for the aged, and into the regulation of their areas of operation. There are several indications that companies recognize that Blue Cross and Blue Shield have helped to stave off these federal actions. Liaison groups between the associations and insurance companies for anti-federal lobbying and propaganda are indicative of this type of sentiment. Insurance companies thus have an oddly vested interest in seeing that associations cover the poor risks and those who present a social problem, unless the companies want to insure these individuals themselves.

Support of tax exemption for associations also comes from those domestic insurance companies which have preferential tax treatment. If Blue Cross and Blue Shield organizations located within a state were made subject to premium taxes, there is no reason to expect that domestic companies exempt previously from imposts would retain their position. They obviously want to see that associations are not taxed.

Finally, the very fact that commissioners generally do not desire any type of federal regulation will work toward a retention of associations' current tax status. If Blue Cross and Blue Shield plans were taxed, it is improbable they could be forced to enroll truly undesirable subscribers on a mass basis. Associations could then operate like insurance companies and utilize the latter's selection and underwriting procedures. Those elements of society excluded from protection thereby would look to the government, and probably the *federal* government, for coverage and relief. Increased federal activity in the insurance business and insurance regulation would probably result. State supervisory officials do not want to see this. It is understandable that they often are interested, therefore, in the continuation of prosperous, community-type Blue Cross and Blue Shield plans and the general retention of their exemption from levies by the state and its political subdivisions.

One commissioner stated that public acceptance of Blue Cross and Blue Shield has been so great that any change in tax status would create an uproar. The same factions which press for low rates at hearings would emotionally chastise attempts to tax the associations. "In some states it would be like trying to put a tax on the Social Security program," another regulatory official remarked.

All of these considerations seem to predict retention of the historical tax-exempt status of Blue Cross and Blue Shield for the next few years at least, and probably longer.

Part Three

GROWTH PROBLEMS AND CONCLUSIONS

chapter XIV

GROWTH PROBLEMS

The sources of problems, or problem areas, for Blue Cross and Blue Shield are found in their competition with insurance companies, the position they occupy as social-insurance-type organizations, and some difficulties in their internal operations.

The actual market positions of associations vary from less than pure competition to less than pure monopoly. The elasticity of substitution of service benefit contracts, for example, is not infinite (as would be required for pure competition); that is, all consumers do not view Blue Cross and Blue Shield coverages as completely interchangeable with policies issued by insurance companies. Neither do association coverages have a cross elasticity of demand of zero (which would be necessary for monopoly); for example, as the price of protection under Blue Cross and Blue Shield increases some subscribers shift to insurance company coverages. Thus, most associations are in continuous conflict with insurance companies. Problems concerning national enrollment, catastrophic medical care protection, liberalization of benefits, rating methods, and nongroup enrollment are a part of this struggle.

The second problem area in which Blue Cross and Blue Shield are involved arises out of their social nature. For instance, in most jurisdictions associations are considered so much in the public interest that the unimpaired use of supply-and-demand price determination is restricted. The social aspects of Blue Cross and Blue Shield are partially responsible for such problems as coverage of the aged, nongroup enrollment, rating methods, and governmental relations.

The sources of Blue Cross and Blue Shield problems are intertwined, as may be seen in the fact that some of the internal issues are either competitive problems or are concerned with the social nature of associations. This is true for national enrollment, nongroup enrollment, the composition of boards of directors, and the reserve levels to be maintained.

The influence of the following growth problems on the regulation of Blue Cross and Blue Shield has yet to receive final evaluation in this study: rising hospital and medical costs, liberalization of benefits, catastrophic medical care protection, coverage of the aged, and nongroup and nonqualified group enrollment.

RISING EXPENDITURES FOR MEDICAL CARE

The most common problem area for executive directors of Blue Cross and Blue Shield plans, as well as for insurance commissioners, is the increasing cost per member for medical care. Half of the association executives who cooperated in this research and one third of the state regulatory officials who assigned priorities to growth problems feel that rising hospital and medical costs constitute the major problems associations will encounter in the future.

Last year . . . the American Hospital Association figures it cost an average of $31.16 a day to keep each person bedded down. Five years earlier, per-day cost of the average patient was only $22.78. One authoritative forecast says hospital costs will rise 50% in the next 10-year period which began with 1958. Discussing that forecast recently, a hospital association official termed it "conservative."[1]

The mounting expenditures, as an average per member, are attributable to increased utilization by subscribers and

---

[1] *The Wall Street Journal,* September 7, 1960, p. 1.

to advances in the costs charged by those who render association services.[2] Rising average costs per subscriber create a problem because they endanger an association's financial condition. Several courses of action may be taken to avert such a crisis. Reserves may be accumulated which would be available in case of need. However, this is but a temporary solution because rising costs are more of a structural problem. A long-run solution, therefore, is required although short-run treatment is also desirable. Rate increases are an answer to the problem only if allowed periodically to offset the rising claim requirements. Even then, some subscribers may willingly, or unwillingly, give up their Blue Cross and Blue Shield membership because of the increased premiums.

Regulatory authorities who have considered this dilemma tend to feel a satisfactory solution can occur only by seeking to control cost increases. Their concern goes beyond the elimination of overutilization and leads to an attack on some of the causes which have motivated hospitals and doctors to raise their charges for rendering services to subscribers.

Increased Utilization

The Problem of Utilization. Utilization of Blue Cross benefits depends upon the proportion of subscribers hospitalized and the average length of hospital stay. These factors fluctuate widely even within a particular locale. Blue Cross plans in the United States had an annual range of from 98 to 249 hospital admissions per thousand members as of September 30, 1960. Fifty-six per cent of the associations had inpatient ratios from 127 to 159 per thousand. Thirty-one per cent of the organizations were above these bounds and 13 per cent below them. The median hospitalization rate for all Blue Cross plans in the United States was 150 per thousand, with a mean of 138.[3] The comparable mean for all

---

[2] Aggregate claim costs could increase merely because subscriber rolls have enlarged. Obviously, this is not the root of any problem concerning rising hospital and medical costs.

[3] Blue Cross Association, *Research and Technical Assistance Service Bulletin*, No. RT–60–1K, November 17, 1960, pp. 3–4.

individuals hospitalized in the United States during 1960 was 128.9.[4]

The average length of hospital stay also varied greatly among associations in the United States; the range was 3.75 to 9.37 days with a median of 6.98 days and a mean of 7.51 days. A mean of 7.6 days was the figure for all inpatients in the United States in 1960.[5]

A high hospitalization rate or a high average length of hospital stay can increase an association's claim costs tremendously. An annual rate of hospital admissions of 160 per thousand, for example, results in more than 12 per cent higher claim costs than does a rate of 130 per thousand, assuming identical lengths of hospitalization. In spite of a general decline in the average length of stay, the increase in hospital admissions has caused observers to predict an increase in over-all utilization of from 5 to 6 per cent in the next few years. (On top of this, medical care costs are expected to rise approximately 5 per cent annually, as has been discussed.)

The problem of utilization is most pressing for associations which offer service benefits; thus, rising costs are not as much of a dilemma, in general, for Blue Shield plans as for Blue Cross organizations. Medical service associations have required far fewer rate increases, on the average, in the past decade than have the hospital service plans.

Control of Utilization. Unwarranted utilization of benefits may be attacked in two directions. One is to institute various means of discouraging subscribers from abusing the benefits available. The second method is to work through, and in some cases exercise at least indirect control over, doctors and hospitals who provide services for subscribers.

Control of Utilization through Subscribers. The methods associations may institute to control the use of benefits include selective underwriting, benefit restrictions and con-

---

[4] Health Insurance Institute, *Health Insurance Data—1961* (New York, 1961), p. 61.

[5] *Ibid.*, p. 58.

tractual provisions which discourage the misuse of benefits, educational measures for subscribers, and experience rating.

A. Selective Underwriting. Selective underwriting involves screening prospective members for personal and environmental characteristics which encourage extensive use, if not outright abuse, of association benefits. This procedure includes attempts to determine if a prospective enrollee has any other hospital or medical-surgical coverage. "Overinsurance" exists when an individual has multiple coverage of a certain hazard such that he can receive more through insurance benefits than he will actually pay out or "lose" if the contingency occurs. Overinsurance converts the insurance scheme from reimbursement to "profit." When a gain of this nature is possible, an overutilization of subscriber or policyholder benefits is obviously encouraged. The Health Insurance Council determined in a 1958 survey that individuals with more than one hospital policy received an average reimbursement 44 per cent above their total hospital bills. The extent of excess reimbursement was greater where Blue Cross plans provided full service benefits.[6] The use of selective underwriting to correct these abuses, however, could violate the Blue Cross–Blue Shield principle of enrolling all elements of a community. Associations that use selective underwriting are often accused of having an insurance company type of operation.

B. Benefit Restrictions and Contractual Provisions. The second approach for discouraging subscribers from improper use of hospital and medical-surgical coverage is by benefit limitations, such as through deductibles, coinsurance, and other insurance provisions. Previous sections have elaborated these mechanisms. Association executives are looking upon these controls with more favor and regulatory officials are tending to encourage their use. When subscribers have a financial stake in personal medical expenses they are less likely

---

[6] Health Insurance Council, *A Survey of Multiple Hospitalization Coverage*, September, 1959.

to incur these expenditures unless absolutely necessary.[7]

Overinsurance or other insurance provisions would help to reduce overutilization only among subscribers with more than one contract. Stipulations of this sort also require extensive claim-investigation facilities. Overinsurance provisions are beneficial, however, in at least discouraging some individuals who would try to profit by duplicate coverage.

Benefit structures can also be widened to include coverage in nursing homes and outpatient treatment, both of which are less expensive than actual hospitalization. On this point the insurance commissioner in Pennsylvania has remarked: "I wish to particularly commend the thinking of the Blue Cross administrative personnel . . . for placing in their subscriber contracts, or proposing as changes in such contracts, features which will tend to reduce utilization. . . ."[8]

C. Subscriber Education. Regulatory officials point out that associations are going to have to accelerate their attempts to educate the public regarding cost levels, unwarranted utilization, and the like. The public should know that in actuality subscribers and those who provide medical care determine the rates, not associations or commissioners. A truly broad educational program will entail increased advertising expenditures, which are also under regulatory purview.

Control of Utilization through Hospitals and Physicians. In spite of various measures to encourage or stimulate subscribers not to abuse their rights to medical care benefits, current emphasis is being directed more toward hospitals and doctors as sources for reductions in unnecessary use of benefits. Regulatory officials, as well as association managements, are behind this trend. Doctors particularly are being looked to for controls on the frequency of hospitalization and the length of hospital stay inasmuch as the physicians usually

---

[7] Surprisingly enough, many subscribers do not mind the deductible or coinsurance provisions, or at least they prefer them to relatively higher rates. In Philadelphia, for example, over half of the Blue Cross members voluntarily switched to a new coinsurance-type contract ("co-pay comprehensive") during the first year it was available.

[8] Adjudication, Pennsylvania, April 15, 1958, pp. 9–10.

determine which subscribers will be hospitalized, the services that will be provided, and the time at which patients will be discharged.

Pennsylvania's regulatory authority stated in 1958:

I do not believe that everything has been done by hospital administrators, by the Blue Cross organizations, and by the medical profession to eliminate unnecessary admissions and to reduce protracted hospital stays. In fact I believe, with few exceptions, very little has been done. I do believe, however, unless action is taken immediately in both of the above regards, the whole scheme of prepaid medical care through the Blue Cross system will be irreparably injured at the expense of millions of citizens of Pennsylvania resulting in severe personal and financial hardship and suffering.[9]

The sentiments of the supervisory official in Maryland are also pertinent to the problem:

Maryland's Insurance Commissioner F. Douglass Sears . . . declared that if unnecessary hospital use were cut by a cooperative effort of the Blue Cross, doctors and hospitals, it would save the state's hospitalization subscribers more than $1 million a year. . . .

The Maryland commissioner scaled down the rate increase sought by the Blue Cross after he received the results of a survey of 222 doctors interviewed by Opinion Research Corporation of Princeton. More than three-fourths of the doctors believed "hospital facilities sometimes are used in an unnecessary or uneconomical manner." About 80% said they had patients who had requested hospitalization when it wasn't necessary, in most cases to take advantage of insurance. About 11% of the doctors admitted that "one fifth or more of their own hospitalized patients are admitted for diagnostic procedures that could be performed in a doctor's office or under hospital out-patient service." About one-third of the doctors said that unecessarily prolonged hospital stays are "frequent."

Though Mr. Sears was critical of some of the methodology of the survey, he commented, "Nevertheless . . . I felt that there

---

[9] *Ibid.*, p. 5.

emerged a picture of a sufficient amount of unnecessary hospital use by a sufficient large segment of the population and *countenanced by a sufficiently large proportion of physicians to* warrant immediate action on my part."[10]

Hospitals themselves are being questioned in some areas as to their objectivity in retaining patients. The Columbia Report stated, for example:

It is a paradoxical but well known fact in the hospital field that when a hospital is crowded, the medical staff will "police" itself against unnecessary admissions and undue lengths of stay; but when occupancy is low and the financial stability of the institution is threatened, the administrator hopes for an increase in admissions and is under no pressure to get patients out, especially if they have health insurance.[11]

New York's superintendent of insurance outlined in connection with a 1960 adjudication some steps taken to control utilization and costs:

The American Medical Association has established a Commission on the Cost of Medical Care charged with the study of all medical care costs including doctors' fees, hospital charges, nursing costs, drug expenditures and health insurance premiums.

In New York, the Greater New York Hospital Association, through its Sub-Committee on Utilization, is engaged in a broad inquiry into both managerial and professional aspects of hospital operations with the aim of improving efficiency and controlling excessive utilization.

Surgical tissue committees have long been established in accredited hospitals. To a far lesser extent, hospital admissions and chart review committees have been set up. Such techniques have begun to provide an effective sanction against deviational practice—judgment of a professional by a group of his peers. The mere existence of a functioning mechanism of professional review is a potent deterrent of abuse. . . . Discipline, where appropriate, is the responsibility of hospital boards, medical societies and the Board of Regents.

---

[10] *The Wall Street Journal,* October 12, 1960, p. 1.

[11] School of Public Health and Administrative Medicine, Columbia University, *Prepayment for Hospital Care in New York,* p. 192.

The Columbia Report recommends that every hospital have a utilization committee. . . .[12]

Efforts to correct abuses of hospital and medical service benefits have assumed an ever-increasing urgency since 1958, and they have come from many sources:

Perhaps the most effective [procedure] to date is a program launched two years ago by the Associated Hospital Service of Philadelphia [Blue Cross in Philadelphia].

It set up a Physicians' Review Board to study the abuse problem and to screen questionable Blue Cross claims. The board consists of 36 physicians, all generally regarded as among the leaders in their profession. Once a month the group gathers and divides into six or seven examining boards to consider questionable claims.

In 1959, the first full year of its work, the board looked over 1,073 "questionable" cases referred to it by Blue Cross, involving 708 doctors in the Philadelphia area. The board advised Blue Cross not to pay the bill in 563, or 52% of the cases, contending that hospitalization was not properly required under the Blue Cross contracts. The worst offenders were three doctors who had six rejected cases apiece.

In the first half of [1960] . . . the board reviewed 861 cases and rejected 508, or 59%. "If you judge our work so far by the number of 'arrests' we've made," says Dr. Hugh Robertson, cochairman of the Philadelphia board, "then you can't prove too much. But if you look at it from the point of view of the influence we've had on doctors generally, then I think it can be said we're making a lot of progress." Dr. Robertson believes that every rejected case may have influenced doctors to forego "10 or 11" potential hospitalization claims.[13]

By mid-1960 the Blue Cross–Blue Shield organizations in seventeen cities had patterned review boards after the one used in Philadelphia, while a similar number of areas had them in the planning stage.[14] The Philadelphia Blue Cross

---

[12] Adjudication of Thomas Thacher, Superintendent of Insurance, State of New York, in the *Matter of Two 1960 Applications of Associated Hospital Service of New York,* August 3, 1960, pp. 20–21.

[13] *The Wall Street Journal,* October 12, 1960, p. 20.

[14] *Ibid.*

has also organized a "hospital administrators' board," which functions somewhat like the physicians' review board. The new group concentrates on appraising the lengths of stay in member hospitals, while the physicians' review board is primarily concerned with whether various hospital admissions are appropriate.

The use of control or review procedures over doctors and hospitals is by no means widespread since these are relatively recent innovations. The pioneering development in Pennsylvania occurred as a result of a directive from the insurance commissioner. The adjudication of a rate-increase request in 1959 prompted the commissioner to note: "Testimony admitted into the record of the Philadelphia hearings shows conclusively that hospital administrators and their medical staffs can substantially reduce the abuse of hospital care."[15] The commissioner stated thereafter:

It is further determined that *no additional rate increases will be* entertained or *granted* by me, as Insurance Commissioner, unless the Nonprofit Hospital Plan requesting such increases submits substantiating evidence that it has fulfilled all of the following directives in a satisfactory manner:

1. The administrative officials of each Blue Cross Plan shall collectively or singly thoroughly review the program instituted at the Sacred Heart Hospital in Allentown[16] for reducing unnecessary hospital utilization and shall disseminate all information so obtained to each member hospital.

2. Each Blue Cross Plan is hereby directed to notify each member hospital that the Insurance Commissioner will *condition his*

---

[15] Adjudication, Pennsylvania, April 15, 1958, p. 7.

[16] "A Committee on Admissions, Conduct and Discharges was formed by Sacred Heart Hospital to work out and execute disciplinary procedures and rules and regulations to correct abuses. Each morning for two months this Committee reviewed admissions made during the past twenty-four hours. To shorten the stay of patients simple regulations were adopted such as requiring that x-ray and laboratory tests be ordered before noon on the day of admission; requiring that consultation requests be answered immediately; and requiring that doctors authorize a patient's discharge on the day before he is to leave. By these and other rules, with the full cooperation of the medical staff and hospital administrators, the average patient-stay in Sacred Heart Hospital has been decreased by one-half day." (*Ibid.*)

approval of any hospital reimbursement formula between Blue Cross and such hospital upon the actions of such hospital in inaugurating the beneficial features of the Allentown Hospital Plan into such hospital's internal administration. Any existing approval of a reimbursement contract with a member hospital will be subject to withdrawal where a member hospital fails to cooperate in this effort.

3. Each Blue Cross Plan, subject to these Adjudications, is hereby directed to allocate as an item of administrative expense, to be defrayed from existing reserves, a sum of money sufficient to maintain constant vigilance over the progress of hospitals in instituting reforms to eliminate abuses in the use of hospital care.

4. From the item of expense so allocated, each Blue Cross Plan is directed individually or collectively with other Blue Cross Plans within the Commonwealth of Pennsylvania to make further researches into methods and means of eliminating abuses in utilization of hospital care. . . .

5. Each Blue Cross Plan shall expressly request the assistance of the county medical societies for the counties served by such Plans in resolving the abuses in hospital utilization. . . . Reports on the action taken under this recommendation and the progress attained thereunder shall be made to the Insurance Commissioner on a bi-monthly basis. . . .[17]

Blue Shield plans have been reticent to become involved in the overutilization problem whenever it concerns doctors. A recent adjudication in Pennsylvania presented a part of this situation:

Blue Shield has been formally advised by its legal counsel that because of the provisions in Section 8 (b) of the Blue Shield Regulatory Act, it cannot conduct studies regarding diagnosis or treatment with a view to imposing a restriction on utilization. . . . Section 8 (b) of the said Act provides, inter alia, "A nonprofit medical, osteopathic and dental service corporation shall impose no restrictions on the doctors of medicine, doctors of osteopathy and doctors of dental surgery who administers to its subscribers, as to methods of diagnosis or treatment."

---

[17] *Ibid.*, pp. 10–11. Italics added.

It is my firm conviction that . . . within the framework of the law . . . there is ample latitude for Blue Shield to do much more than it has in cooperating with Blue Cross Plans, medical societies, hospitals, and the public in lessening necessary utilization of Blue Shield services. With the exception of diagnostic and emergency services provided in doctors' offices, practically all Blue Shield services are rendered in hospitals. If unnecessary *hospital* utilization is reduced, it would follow that a substantial amount of unnecessary utilization of Blue Shield services would also be reduced. . . .

I do not believe that the confidential nature of medical records would be a bar to such cooperation, since the accumulation of such facts need not identify doctors or patients. . . .

Blue Shield can encourage its practicing doctors to establish admissions committees within hospitals. Such action by Blue Shield would in no manner restrict doctors as to their methods of diagnosis or treatment.[18]

The commissioner went on to direct, among other things, that Pennsylvania Blue Shield conduct discussions with physicians and representatives of medical societies to determine how doctors' records can help in reducing overutilization.

Increased Hospital and Medical Costs

Factors Associated with Medical Care Costs. Even control of unwarranted utilization will not curb rate increases when medical care costs rise continually. Supervisory officials have no intention of trying to restrain "normal" inflationary increases. They are also tolerant of certain elevations in the pay scales of nurses, who in times past have been compensated at a level below that of occupations of a similar caliber. Costs, however, can be affected by institutional efficiency. This is particularly important since about 70 per cent of hospital expenditures are for wages. Regulatory authorities are also concerned about the lack of cooperation among hospitals in

---

[18] Adjudication, *in the Matter of Filing No. 1–H, 1960, of the Medical Service Association of Pennsylvania,* February 2, 1961, pp. 10–11.

utilizing joint purchasing and sharing specialized equipment. In addition, the failure of many institutions to adopt uniform accounting methods prevents an accurate evaluation of their cost situation. Then, too, there is the perennial question of whether the position of doctors (and, to a lesser extent, hospitals) allows some to "overcharge" the ailing, and thus the associations, since a return to good health is so all-important for the sick.

Attitudes and Edicts for Controlling Costs. The associations' supervisory official in Pennsylvania has also declared he will not grant rate increases for Blue Cross unless the organizations comply with the following directives:

. . . 2. Each Blue Cross Plan subject to these Adjudications shall individually or collectively solicit the assistance and co-operation of hospitals served by them, hospital councils, and other interested persons, in exploring all areas of hospital administration to determine where economies can be made.

3. The studies in hospital administration required by recommendation #2 shall encompass previous studies that have been made in the field by experts such as Dr. C. Rufus Rorem. . . . The studies under recommendation #2 should consider among other things— (a) The adoption by all member hospitals of uniform accounting methods and practices; (b) Utilization of joint purchasing practices, with special emphasis in the fields of drugs and pharmaceuticals; (c) The sharing of specialized equipment; (d) Standardization among hospitals of those costs which hospitals can control; (e) More efficient utilization of beds and diagnostic and treatment facilities; (f) More effective use of professional and institutional personnel; (g) Establishment outside the in-patient department of rooming facilities for certain patients requiring protracted stays.

4. The Blue Cross Plans shall disseminate the results of their studies to each member hospital; and . . . the Insurance Commissioner will condition his approval of any hospital reimbursement formula . . . upon the actions of such hospital in putting into effect the plans and methods recommended to it by Blue Cross. Any existing approval of a reimbursement contract

with a member hospital will be subject to withdrawal where a member hospital fails to cooperate in this effort. . . .[19]

The use of regional committees, composed of representatives of various groups, organizations, and professions concerned with medical care, has been suggested by the Columbia Report. In addition to the over-all consideration of medical care costs, these committees would ascertain the desirability of proposed hospital additions and new hospitals. Several major cities have already established hospital planning councils to perform functions of this type.

Eventual Solutions to the Problem of Rising Costs and Utilization

The problem created by rising medical care costs and utilization presents a very complex regulatory issue and the fact that so many parties are involved makes it much more elusive of regulatory treatment. The attack on costs and utilization obviously calls for more than legal requirements and constant scrutiny from supervisory officials. It necessitates action on the part of associations, doctors, hospital personnel, and subscribers. The cooperation of these individuals is often difficult to obtain since some have opposing interests.

Blue Cross and Blue Shield plans must look at the mechanism they have developed for financing medical care and see how it facilitated abuses—both by subscribers and by those rendering services to subscribers. At the same time, hospital administrators, their boards of directors, and medical doctors must do some soul searching to see how they can modify their own attitudes and practices. An insurance commissioner cannot legally control hospitals and doctors directly but he can "reach" them through the payments made by associations for medical care services. In addition, the quotations included in this discussion indicate that at least some regulatory authorities feel Blue Cross and Blue Shield must take an active part in controlling over-all cost increases if they want

---

[19] Adjudication, Pennsylvania, April 15, 1958, p. 16.

to survive (that is, if they want rate increases and if they hope to avert governmental programs of medical care).

LIBERALIZATION OF BENEFITS

The liberalization of benefits is a regulatory problem not only because the benefit structures in most states must have the supervisory official's approval but also because extensive changes in benefits can require rate increases. While most Blue Cross and Blue Shield plans would undoubtedly like to broaden their coverage, liberalizations are restrained because an increasing number of subscribers become unwilling or unable to pay for protection as rates are altered upward. At the same time, associations must consider the claim costs incurred if new benefits are added to the coverage. This requires actuarial determination of the increased hazards involved since when service benefits are provided the appraisal of the hazards can be even more vital than for indemnity coverage—unless a "blank check" is to be given to subscribers.

Most regulatory authorities will allow broadened benefit structures if they are convinced the rates are both adequate and reasonable. Prior to the time definite experience is available for determining the proper rate factor, commissioners often grant permission for an association to use a new benefit structure in connection with a portion, or all, of its group subscribers on an experimental basis. Nongroup members are usually the last to receive benefit liberalizations.

It is vital that insurance commissioners recognize their responsibilities with respect to benefit liberalizations. Pressures for "reasonable" rates—which are often interpreted to mean no rate increases—should not override desirable extensions in medical expense protection. An indication this has occurred in at least one area may be seen in a recent report by the New York Joint Legislative Committee on Health Insurance Plans:

Your Blue Cross plan [Buffalo] is congratulated on providing a broad spectrum of hospital care services. . . . But even more comprehensive measures—such as the inclusion of coverage for mental illness in the basic contract—would have been possible at least on an experimental basis if requests for premium rate increases had been approved, when requested, in years gone by, by Insurance Department Superintendents serving with previous State administrations. What appeared then to be politically inexpedient—an adequate premium rate increase—would in the long run have been a major economy and a big step forward in social progress.

Important modifications in Blue Cross benefits in the not too distant past have included private-room credits and hospitalization in nonmember institutions. One important liberalization is for an association to expand its use of service benefits, even if modified by a deductible. The lengthening of the number of days of hospitalization hospital service associations will provide is among the trends in benefit changes. (Some executives feel that if the period of eligible hospital service is extended sufficiently, such as to 365 days, there will be no real need for catastrophic medical coverages. This view is not widely accepted, though.) Many Blue Cross plans are also considering nursing-home care coverage. Benefits of this type have been allowed in New York since 1959 when the legislature granted permission for associations to offer nursing-home benefits immediately after discharge from a hospital. The inclusion of nursing-home care in Blue Cross coverage is an additional factor which will help move plans from their status as an "arm" of the hospitals.

There is some inclination on the part of hospital service associations to include outpatient treatment under specified circumstances, although this movement has not gained great momentum as yet. Coverage of the aged is a benefit extension which will be treated in a special section of this chapter.

The discussions in Chapter III indicated that the scope of included services is increasing in most Blue Cross plans. For instance, it is now possible to obtain limited coverage for men-

tal illnesses in many associations. A Joint Legislative Committee in New York held hearings in 1958 and 1959 on the
issue of coverage for mental disorders, and the statistics and
opinions presented seemed to indicate this benefit was not as
difficult to include as many had previously felt:

> Dr. Louis Reed of the Sloan Institute of Hospital Administra-
> tion, Cornell University, presented figures to show that Blue
> Cross plans could cover mental illness on the same terms as other
> plans with an increase of only 2% to 3% in cost.
>
> Carl Metzger, president of Hospital Service Corporation of
> Western New York [Blue Cross], Buffalo, said it is offering a
> rider at an increased premium of 15¢ a month for individual and
> 25¢ for family, to provide 10 days of hospitalization for mental
> illness. He contended that there is no public demand for broad
> coverage, only "agitation from professionals," and said that
> when there is enough public demand and enough community
> psychiatric service available, the voluntary plans will provide
> this coverage.[20]

Medical benefit structures can be liberalized by increasing
the number of doctors' visits which will be covered or for
which reimbursement will be made. Surgical benefit liberalizations for the many Blue Shield plans with indemnity certificates involve an increase in the reimbursement level, bar-
ring a switch to service-type benefits. Service contracts are
liberalized by raising the income limits whereby more subscribers become eligible for service benefits. Blue Shield
plans point out, however, that a change in these limits almost
always requires an elevation of the doctors' fees as set forth in
the fee schedules. This, in turn, necessitates rate increases.

The national organizations for the associations are among
the forces behind benefit liberalizations. The National Association of Blue Shield Plans, for example, is steadily working toward the adoption of service benefits by all medical
service plans, with X-ray and radiology included and a
$6,000-income limit. This group feels that the only exception
to service benefits should be maternity coverage.

---

[20] *Employee Benefit Plan Review,* January, 1959, p. 52.

With reference to benefit liberalizations, one executive of a national organization to which associations belong remarked, "Blue Cross and Blue Shield must aim toward broadening their services; there will otherwise be continuous pressure for the government to step into the area of medical care coverage."

CATASTROPHIC MEDICAL CARE PROTECTION

The question of whether Blue Cross and Blue Shield should offer coverage against catastrophic medical expenditures presents another philosophical issue. The associations traditionally have been associated with "first-dollar" coverage. Deductibles and/or coinsurance provisions, however, are deemed necessary to keep premiums for major medical expense contracts within allowable ranges; a deductible of course compromises the first-dollar principle. For this reason, and because major medical is often thought of as an insurance company technique, some plan executives have looked askance at catastrophic medical coverage. As standards of living rise, however, this attitude should become increasingly questionable. The purpose of any insurance-type device, including Blue Cross and Blue Shield coverages, should be to help individuals and families avert financial catastrophes. If an important portion of the population can bear the first dollars of medical care expenses themselves, without being financially imperiled, then associations should certainly consider adopting some type of catastrophic expense contract. Only in this manner can the best use be made of subscriber dollars. In addition, it was pointed out previously that the first-dollar concept is not an inherent feature of the service approach.[21]

About forty Blue Shield plans and a similar number of Blue Cross organizations now have contracts which provide catastrophic medical care protection. Seventeen of the Blue

---

[21] See page 87.

Cross plans use the term "major medical" to identify this type of coverage, while twenty other associations use such terms as "master medical," "extended benefit," and "long-term illness."[22] The latter certificates are generally similar to contracts known as "major medical." Many associations have chosen not to use the term "major medical" because of its close identification with insurance companies.

As of December 31, 1961, about one million Blue Cross subscribers were covered under major medical or "comprehensive extended-benefit" certificates. An example of Blue Cross catastrophic medical expense coverage may be seen in the group "extraordinary medical expense" contract offered by the Philadelphia plan. (The Philadelphia coverage could well be the forerunner of similar group, as well as nongroup, protection. This was true of the Philadelphia "co-pay comprehensive" contract which led the way for many deductible certificates throughout the country.) For a subscription charge of $1 a month from single subscribers and $2 from families, coverage is granted for expenses up to $15,000. The amount of a subscriber's medical care expenses not covered under the basic contract during a given year is reduced by a deductible of 4 per cent of his annual income or $500, whichever is lower. The "extraordinary" contract pays for 80 per cent of the remainder, up to the $15,000 maximum.

Health Service, Inc., is also offering major medical coverage which is quite important in the Blue Cross system inasmuch as HSI is the enrollment organization for national groups. The HSI major medical protection is a supplemental-type contract with a twelve-month benefit period and a $5,000 maximum benefit. There is a $100 deductible provision and a 75 per cent coinsurance requirement.

Regulatory authorities in general do not oppose the use of catastrophic medical expense benefits by associations. They look upon service benefits with much the same attitude as

---

[22] Blue Cross Association, *Blue Cross Guide, January, 1962* (Chicago: 1962), pp. 15–317.

they view community rating; the modification of either of these will not change the regulatory position of Blue Cross and Blue Shield provided the public interest and the purpose for which the associations were organized are better served.

Major medical does not require a complete abandonment of the service approach. Associations can continue contractual relationships with hospitals and doctors. Service in member institutions and from contracting physicians can still be provided after the deductible provisions have been met.

One factor spearheading the use of catastrophic medical care benefits by Blue Cross and Blue Shield is the concern that insurance companies with this type of coverage will capture an increased share of the group and nongroup market.

COVERAGE OF THE AGED

The problem of paying the medical care expenses of aged individuals is so vital that it has become one of the most talked-about issues of social and private insurance. In 1900, one person out of every twenty was over age sixty-five; one out of every eleven individuals is currently in this category. The aged population increased 35 per cent in the 1950–60 decade alone. More than 17 million persons aged 65 or over are now in the United States, and this group has an annual net increase, on the average, in excess of 400 thousand.[23]

The rising number and percentage of the elderly constitute a problem with great dimensions because a significant proportion of these individuals have meager earning capacities and savings with which to cope with potential medical care expenditures—and the risk is increasing in terms of dollars. About one fifth of the aged are in the labor force.[24] The 1960 census found that 52 per cent of those over age sixty-five (who are not in institutions) have annual incomes of less than $1,000, while the median income for all of the

---

[23] "New Population Facts on Older Americans, 1960," a staff report to the Special Committee on Aging, United States Senate, May 24, 1961, pp. 1–2.

[24] *Ibid.*

aged is $950.[25] The statistics are not altered significantly when the elderly are categorized as to those who live alone, husband and wife over age sixty-five, etc. A medical bill in excess of $500 can be paid out of savings by only four out of every ten aged persons.[26]

Unlike insurance companies, associations have traditionally allowed subscribers to retain their Blue Cross or Blue Shield coverage after reaching age sixty-five. A few regulatory officials and many executive directors feel that if insurance companies had used a similar approach the current problem with the aged would not be so pronounced. Insurance companies are making great strides in this direction at the present time, however. Many insurers are urging extension of group insurance plans to retired people, and employers are being solicited to do their share. Considerable encouragement is to be found in this type of progress.

In addition to allowing a continuation of coverage after age sixty-five, most Blue Cross and Blue Shield plans have no age limit on their regular *group* enrollment. Fifty-six Blue Cross plans and fifty-one Blue Shield plans either have no age limit for nongroup enrollment or have special "senior certificates" for nongroup members enrolling initially after age sixty-five.[27] Almost all associations will have coverage available for the elderly by early 1963. In 1960, only twenty-nine hospital service associations and thirty-four medical service organizations offered nongroup coverage to those over age sixty-five enrolling for the first time.

While it is generally agreed the Blues have done more in covering the aged than have insurance companies, most associations do not have the same proportion of the aged enrolled as they do of the general population. Plans cover

---

[25] "Health Insurance for Aged Persons," a report submitted to the Committee on Ways and Means, House of Representatives, by the Secretary of Health, Education, and Welfare, July 24, 1961, pp. 14–15.

[26] Ethel Shanas, *Meeting Medical Care Costs Among the Aging* (New York: Health Information Foundation, 1960) , p. 8.

[27] Chapter IV discussed additional details concerning the enrollment eligibility of the aged.

about four and one-half million people over age sixty-five, which accounts for approximately 30 per cent of the aged population. Many observers think it only right that Blue Cross and Blue Shield have a greater relative share of those over age sixty-five on their rolls inasmuch as one of their purposes—and a reason for their tax exemption—is to cover those for whom commercial coverage is not available. To this extent it is also important for associations to have subscription charges at a sufficiently low level so that at least a significant portion of the aged can afford the coverage.

The regulatory concern with medical care coverage for the aged goes beyond humanitarian reasons. Supervisory officials know the federal government will become involved more than ever in the insurance realm if an adequate, voluntary system of protection for the aged does not evolve. This is one reason some commissioners have not approved requests for special contracts for the aged if they felt the benefit structure fell short of what should and could be provided. In refusing to approve a "senior citizen agreement" for Blue Shield, the regulatory authority in Pennsylvania remarked:

> . . . the testimony is also clear that generally the income of senior citizens is significantly lower than the income of the subscribers covered by Plan A. If it is true that persons in higher income categories should pay more to Blue Shield in order to provide service benefits to such subscribers (Plan B), does it not follow that persons in lower income categories should pay less to Blue Shield for service benefits?

> The net result of the filing before me is to propose Senior Citizen Coverage which is the same as the Standard Nongroup Plan with an increase in premium. It is apparent that no consideration has been given to the special needs of older persons with respect to income, benefits or rates.[28]

The commissioner is also of the opinion that not only should hospital service associations within the state cooperate

---

[28] Adjudication of Francis R. Smith, insurance commissioner of the Commonwealth of Pennsylvania in the *Matter of Filing No. 2–H, 1960, of the Medical Service Association of Pennsylvania,* February 2, 1961, p. 5.

to provide a uniform contract for the aged but that Blue Cross *and* Blue Shield organizations should participate in the same coverage. "In my opinion, the development of health-care coverage for our older citizens must be accomplished on a state-wide rather than a heterogeneous basis. Coverage for hospital services and coverage for medical and surgical services are inextricably combined and related."[29]

Coverage of the aged involves difficulties beyond enrollment and benefit adequacy. The fact that those over age sixty-five use about two and one-half times the number of hospital days as those under this age presents a problem of rate determination that seems almost insurmountable to some associations. There is a similar picture of utilization for aged subscribers of Blue Shield. If these individuals were placed in a separate rate class only a small portion would be able to afford the premiums. Yet when they are included in the general classifications (individuals, two-member units, and family units), the premiums for each class become out of proportion with group rates. These dilemmas were considered in the chapter on rates where it was suggested that a factor for the aged should be included in group subscribers' rates if pensioners are not retained as members of the group.

Both Blue Cross and Blue Shield have recently announced plans for nationwide coverage of individuals over age sixty-five, without regard to their current state of health. The proposed Blue Cross hospital expense protection, co-sponsored with the American Hospital Association, would provide seventy days of service benefits in rooms with three or more beds. The benefits would include the usual general nursing services, use of operating room, and drugs and medicines, as well as anesthestics (under certain conditions), X-rays and electrocardiograms. When other accommodations are used, as in the case of a private room, the program would provide up to 85 per cent of the average semiprivate room charges. Up to ninety days of nursing home care would be

---

[29] *Ibid.*, p. 6.

allowed after hospitalization, depending upon the length of confinement. The problem of financing this program has not been resolved. Blue Cross has announced it hopes to have the federal government finance the arrangement.

The Blue Shield program for the aged, sponsored by the National Association of Blue Shield Plans and the American Medical Association, would cost participants approximately $3 monthly. No governmental assistance is contemplated in the financing. The program would provide medical and surgical treatment on a service basis for individuals with annual incomes not in excess of $2,500 and couples whose annual incomes do not exceed $4,000. Those with incomes above these limits would receive indemnity benefits.

In spite of the rapid development of contracts for those over age sixty-five who previously were not eligible for coverage, many regulatory authorities think financial support from the federal government is going to be necessary before a major portion of the medical bills for the aged can be paid by insurance-type organizations. The sizeable proportion of those over age sixty-five who have very meager incomes seems to suggest the eventuality of governmental involvement. An alternative is a universal community rate for medical care coverages whereby the younger and better risks would contribute to the financial hazards presented by the aged. This would require a complete revamping of the rate regulation of associations and insurance companies, as well as a reeducation of subscribers and subscriber groups. As long as either insurance carriers or Blue Cross–Blue Shield use experience-rating techniques, there will be an insufficient number of select risks left in the community-rating scheme to bring the over-all rate down to a point where most of the aged can afford to pay it. Since the outlawing of experience rating is not likely, the inclusion of a factor for the aged in group rates is one method to protect the general "community"-rate level and still cover a portion of the aged. The remainder of those over age sixty-five will be covered only when governmental funds are available.

NONGROUP AND NONQUALIFIED GROUP ENROLLMENT[30]

In addition to the aged, the major coverage problems for Blue Cross and Blue Shield concern those in rural areas, the self-employed and groups too small to obtain group coverage, college students, and migratory workers. Each of these is a challenge to the educational and promotional efforts of the associations. Only the migratory workers present a seemingly unsolvable problem.

It has been estimated that 35 per cent of the civilian population in the United States is in the nongroup classification. One of the latest surveys of this segment was in 1954 when Blue Cross had approximately 8.6 per cent of the nongroup population enrolled and insurance companies accounted for about 17 per cent.[31] Currently, only two Blue Cross plans and two Blue Shield plans fail to have nongroup enrollment.[32] Most associations allow prospective nongroup members to enroll initially at least up to the age of sixty-five.[33]

One reason given for the failure of associations to cover a larger percentage of the citizens who are not members of a group is that enrollment representatives have concentrated on group enrollment. Nongroup subscribers have generally enrolled through the mail or by voluntarily appearing at the Blue Cross or Blue Shield office. Contributing to the smaller proportion of nongroup members is the fact that enrollment representatives are customarily paid on a salary basis. Commission-compensated salesmen are more aggressive in reaching less-accessible individuals and areas, such as those in farming locales.

---

[30] This entire area is extensively reviewed in Sol Levine, Odin W. Anderson, and Gerald Gordon, *Non-Group Enrollment for Health Insurance* (Cambridge: Harvard University Press, 1957) .

[31] Levine, Anderson, and Gordon, *op. cit.,* p. 14.

[32] *Agnes W. Brewster, Nongroup Enrollment under Blue Cross and Blue Shield Plans for Older Persons, Early 1960,* U.S. Department of Health, Education, and Welfare, Research and Statistics Note No. 12, 1960, p. 5.

[33] Chapter III discussed nongroup eligibility requirements in detail.

A survey of Blue Cross plans by the Health Insurance Foundation listed several barriers to nongroup enrollment.[34] The associations ranked these factors in the order of their importance, from one to three. The following list shows the combination of all rankings.

Difficulty in reaching or contacting the nongroup population   90 per cent
Insufficient knowledge about Blue Cross by the nongroup population   52 per cent
Cost of acquisition   52 per cent
Difficulty in obtaining an adequate cross section of the population   51 per cent
Cost of protection   34 per cent

The same study determined 73 per cent of the Blue Cross plans have continuous nongroup enrollment.

Enrollment of non-employee groups is regarded as the most effective method of reaching the rural farmer by 47 per cent of the respondents [Blue Cross plans]. . . . Continuous over-the-counter enrollment and periodic plan-wide campaigns are regarded as the most effective means of reaching the aged and retired. . . . For enrolling the self-employed, in general, and those working in small groups, over-the-counter enrollment is again more highly favored than any other approach. Apparently, this approach is regarded as the best to cover diverse, unorganized segments.[35]

Several regulatory problems are associated with nongroup enrollment. If associations are to fulfill their objective of covering segments of the population for whom medical coverage is not otherwise available at "reasonable" rates, such nongroup classes as the aged and those in rural areas must be considered. The expenses of obtaining nongroup members are considerably higher than for group enrollment. This feature along with the greater loss experience for non-

---

34 Levine, Anderson, and Gordon, *op. cit.*, p. 42.
35 *Ibid.*, p. 109.

group members generally necessitates higher rates for these subscribers.

Even though nongroup enrollment is not considered a major problem for Blue Cross and Blue Shield plans at the present time, the issue does relate to important dilemmas such as rating methods and rising subscriber costs. In addition, some observers believe that if associations are to enroll nongroup members successfully it will involve higher average expenses, incentive wages for enrollment representatives, and selective underwriting. Each of these factors could bring Blue Cross and Blue Shield closer to resembling insurance companies.

chapter XV

CONCLUSIONS

The regulation of Blue Cross and Blue Shield plans involves an unusual ring of complications inasmuch as the
regulatory apparatus must encompass legal requirements,
supervisory attitudes, competitive techniques, *and* a social
philosophy. The outer "ring" may be characterized as the
philosophy which surrounds hospital and medical service associations and is involved in the continual extension of social
thinking in the United States. There is an increasing acceptance of the concept that the mass should care for the
needy—not on a charity basis but rather in a manner which
preserves individual dignity. With reference to the study at
hand, this means medical care *will* be available to a greater
percentage of the nation's citizens. The conclusion is also
supported by the rising standard of living in this country,
which encourages a greater consumption of services such as
hospitalization and treatment from physicians.[1] The proportion of the population that can afford to pay for its own medical care, however, is expanding at a slower pace than the
concept that medical care must be available regardless of
individual ability to pay for it.

The purchase of medical care basically involves two parties:
the afflicted, and those who render services—hospitals and
doctors. Economic circumstances, however, add other parties
to this relationship, since a high percentage of citizens would

[1] A rising standard of living means that more goods and services are available per capita. The marginal propensity to consume various goods decreases
as the standard of living rises. This increases the purchase of services as a
proportion of each dollar spent. Medical care would be high on the list of
these services.

310

find it inconvenient, if not extremely difficult, to pay for large medical bills out of current income or financial savings. One intermediary is the Blue Cross–Blue Shield plan. Associations and insurance companies have, in turn, necessitated the intervention of a fourth party—the regulatory authority—to oversee the citizens' interests.

The current position of the four parties (consumers, hospitals and doctors, Blue Cross–Blue Shield organizations, and supervisory officials) varies by individual states. Thus, the purpose of the research on which this publication is based was to ascertain the current regulatory status of Blue Cross and Blue Shield plans, analyze the associated problems, and suggest possible solutions.

THE REGULATORY STATUS OF BLUE CROSS AND BLUE SHIELD PLANS

Contrary to common opinion, it is not unusual to find associations treated like health insurance companies in many aspects of their operations, even though most states have enacted special laws for the plans. The regulatory areas in which both types of organizations receive nearly identical treatment include permits to commence operation, approval of benefit structures, investment limitations, advertising procedures, and reporting and examination requirements. Blue Cross and Blue Shield are generally regulated less stringently than insurance companies in the areas of taxation, capital and surplus requirements, reserve standards, and licensing of sales representatives. Tax exemption is, obviously, a very notable difference. Associations are supervised more closely as to their subscriber rates than are health insurance companies, which generally do not have their premiums reviewed by insurance commissioners. This, again, is an important dissimilarity since rates are often thought the heart of an insurance-type transaction. In addition, some Blue Cross and Blue Shield plans have been subjected to public hearings on rate changes, benefit modifications, reimbursement and fee schedules. Then, too, associations must often confine their operations to specified territorial boundaries and conform to certain expense limits, as well as meet requirements for representation on their boards of directors. Rarely do these restrictions apply to insurance companies. (Reimbursement and fee schedule approval would not be appropriate for insurance companies since they do not offer service benefits.)

In addition to meeting the statutory and administrative requirements in their areas of operation, Blue Cross and Blue Shield organizations must also comply with the provisions of approval programs administered by national associations. In many instances, such requirements are more strict than those imposed by supervisory laws and officials.

These considerations point to the unfairness and inaccuracy of any generalization which implies Blue Cross and Blue Shield plans are nonregulated or not regulated to the same extent as their competitors. Only when specific areas of regulation are discussed can a proper, over-all statement be formulated. Even then, a generalization must be qualified in order to apply to specific states.

PROBLEMS CONCERNING REGULATION OF BLUE CROSS AND BLUE SHIELD

Parts II and III dealt with the specific problem areas hospital and medical service associations are facing. Probably the most important of these issues concern[2] representation on boards of directors, reserve levels, reimbursement schedules, rating methods, rising cost of medical care protection, coverage for the aged, and national enrollment. Associated problems involve the questions of whether Blue Cross plans within an area should be merged in order to serve the public better; whether similar action is necessary for Blue Shield organizations; and whether it is desirable to combine Blue Cross and Blue Shield operations.

---

[2] Not listed in order of importance.

Representation on Boards of Directors

Composition of the governing boards for Blue Cross and Blue Shield is a fundamental regulatory concern because of the social nature of these organizations. This issue would not arise if plans were regular health insurance companies. The competitive aspect of insurance companies, and their nature as private-enterprise operations, prescribe that a firm's stockholders or policyholders be allowed to select those who will represent them on a board. Since no contracts are made by insurance companies with hospitals or doctors, those associated with the hospital and medical fields do not have a vested interest in the operation of insurance companies. Just the opposite is true for Blue Cross and Blue Shield plans, inasmuch as institutions and individuals who provide medical care are often committed to offer services for the associations. Then, too, the organizations are not supposed to be motivated by profit or competition but rather by broad social considerations in medical care protection.

Where service benefits are provided, hospital representatives must constitute an important portion of the representation on the association's board, and the same should be true for doctors on the boards of Blue Shield plans which have service certificates. While associations which offer indemnity contracts also need hospital representatives or doctors on their boards of directors, it is not as vital these individuals be given such an important voice as where service benefits are available. In all Blue Cross and Blue Shield plans, regardless of the manner in which they provide benefits, representatives of the public should comprise a majority on the governing boards to help guarantee the organization acts in the best interests of the subscribers and the area's citizens as a whole. Only in this manner can it be assured that the governing board is not more concerned with the interests of those who stand to profit from the activities of the organization—doctors and hospitals—than with the interests of the members of the community.

State regulation in all areas is currently inadequate to bring about the type of board representations suggested above. To this extent, then, the appropriate regulatory statutes should be modified to require a majority of the governing board at any official meeting not represent the vendors of medical care services. At the same time, hospital trustees should not be permitted to act as lay representatives unless evidence is produced to the satisfaction of the insurance commissioner that it is not possible to obtain others qualified to represent the public.

Reserves

Regulation is also inadequate at the present time in the area of contingency reserves (or "surpluses"). Even when hospitals and physicians guarantee they will provide services for subscribers of an association if funds are not available to pay for them, it is not an adequate substitute for financial surpluses. Guarantees are effective only for the contract period—often ninety days and sometimes less—and are made on the assumption that subsequent rate increases will be sufficient to reimburse for any services provided without compensation.

The possibility of epidemics, the advancing medical care costs, and the increasing utilization of Blue Cross and Blue Shield benefits combine to necessitate financial surpluses which can be used when rates (and the projection factors in rates) are inadequate. The need for an emergency surplus would be circumvented if hospital and physicians' guarantees were effective until rate increases could be obtained or if there were assurance the regulatory authority would grant rate modifications as soon as the previous rate structure was shown inadequate. Neither of these developments is likely to occur.

Contingency reserve requirements should be specified in the enabling legislation of the various states. In this manner the regulatory authority will be spared many pressures from various groups concerned with low rates and thus with low reserves.

The precise nature of the reserve requirement is an actuarial-accounting consideration beyond the limits of this study. Such a stipulation should be made on a formula basis, however, rather than in terms of a specific number of dollars. Currently, less than 20 per cent of the statutes applicable to Blue Cross and Blue Shield specify a reserve formula. Still a formula provides a sounder adjustment in reserves as financial variations occur in the associations. It seems apparent that a surplus requirement should be above one month's claims and expense needs, as a one-month figure allows for an above-normal fluctuation of only 8 to 9 per cent annually. The minimum requirement should probably be close to a three-month level for claims and expenses.

Reimbursement Schedules

While the parties to a reimbursement or fee schedule should be allowed to negotiate the contractual conditions, regulatory officials must be given the power in enabling legislation to approve or disapprove the arrangements decided upon. Only half of the states grant their insurance commissioners this approval power. In Blue Cross, for example, more than 80 per cent of the subscription income is disbursed in accordance with the provisions of these schedules and they vitally affect the adequacy of rates (as do the benefit structures and their utilization). The proper regulatory control of rates, therefore, necessitates a supervision of reimbursement and fee schedules.

Enabling statutes should not specify the nature of the schedules for hospitals, that is, whether they are to be on a costs, retail charges, or per diem basis. In many cases there are but shades of difference between the types and even then the name given to a particular schedule depends upon the definition used. In addition, the relationship between costs and charges varies considerably by area; in some locales for instance, the medically indigent are cared for in special institutions and in others they are treated in regular hospitals. The regulatory official is in a position to determine whether a base for reimbursement and the rates of reimbursement in a particular area are appropriate. This regulatory procedure will also allow changes in methods of reimbursement as more sophisticated accounting techniques are developed and adopted.

It does seem to be currently desirable in most areas to relate reimbursement to hospital costs, particularly where an association is covering a large segment of those who, if Blue Cross protection were not available, would be recipients of "free" care. Provision of medical care for the needy is really an obligation of the entire citizenry and not just those with insurance or Blue Cross–Blue Shield coverage. It is proper for the cost basis to relieve an association from assuming part of the burden of free care when the Blue Cross organization is already contributing toward the reduction of the medically indigent. At the same time, the cost basis acknowledges the large-scale purchase of hospital accommodations by associations and the fact that payment is virtually guaranteed for services provided to subscribers.

Regulatory supervision will help to assure that neither subscribers nor hospitals and/or doctors are being abused by the schedule arrangements.

Rating Methods

The conceptual enigma presented by experience rating is being resolved largely by competitive factors. While about one third of the associations still utilize a community rate exclusively, the stigma against those using experience modifications in their rating methods is not as strong as formerly. Even the regulatory climate is now generally favorable for experience rating. Most enabling statutes do not need amending to permit the use of merit rating since the wording of these laws does not preclude such techniques. In addition, most regulatory officials have come to look more kindly upon the use of merit rating for groups above a certain size.

It is probably true that if insurance companies and associations were prevented from using experience rating it might be possible to cover a larger portion of those with a relatively high utilization of medical care benefits. Nevertheless, since insurance companies are permitted to modify a rate through consideration of individual experience, there is no alternative, it seems, but to allow the use of such rate alterations by Blue Cross and Blue Shield plans. If the latter organizations are prevented from adjusting the rates of groups with favorable loss experience, these groups will obtain their health protection programs from insurance companies. The loss of favorable groups will leave Blue Cross–Blue Shield with a higher over-all loss ratio; rates will have to be increased; other groups with individually lower loss ratios than that of the community rate will switch their coverage to insurance companies; and the cycle will continue. The end result is that many nongroup subscribers will not be able to afford the steadily advancing community rate, and the basic goal of associations to cover a large segment of the population, particularly those for whom commercial coverage is not available at reasonable rates, will be thwarted.

While Blue Cross and Blue Shield plans should be allowed to experience rate, groups which enjoy this advantage but do not permit pensioners to retain their group coverage should make a contribution to offset the high loss ratios of the aged under the community rate. This is the only proper way to prevent the community rate from bearing the entire burden of the aged who were group members prior to being pensioned.

Rising Cost of Medical Care Protection

The increasing cost of medical care and the expanding utilization of subscriber benefits present an intricate and dominant regulatory problem. These two factors determine the financial obligations of Blue Cross and Blue Shield organizations. Unless restrictions are placed on these elements, supervisory authorities will be continually forced to allow rate increases if associations are to survive over the long-run. Contingency surpluses are only short-run stabilizers which will not solve a structural problem of this type.

There are indications that insurance commissioners in at least the larger states are starting to grapple with this problem through offensive, rather than defensive, tactics. Only a few direct changes in legislation can be made to assist regulatory officials in controlling the rising costs and utilization, other than giving them powers of approval over reimbursement and fee schedules as well as over rates and benefits. Since the medical care field goes beyond the considerations of insurance protection, insurance commissioners cannot, and should not, be given *direct* powers over hospitals and doctors. There is good reason, though, for commissioners to impose indirect restraints on the vendors of services, and direct controls on associations, when the entire system of medical care protection appears endangered by abuses and spiraling costs.

Control of utilization can take place first through measures to discourage subscribers from misusing Blue Cross and Blue Shield benefits. While selective underwriting will help, particularly where overinsurance is involved, it must not hamper the extension of benefits to the community as a whole. Regulatory officials should insist, therefore, upon use of contractual provisions and benefit restrictions which will help control unnecessary utilization. Supervisory authorities can accomplish this by approving only benefit structures incorporating the desired features. Most states give the insurance commissioner approval power over benefits, but many officials have not used their authority to bring about changes which would discourage the misuse of benefits. Subscriber educational programs which elaborate on why rates are increased will assist in the reduction of improper utilization, as will experience-rating techniques.

The second approach to controlling unwarranted use of

benefits is through the hospital and medical professions. Supervisory officials should require the use of review boards which examine, among other items, hospital admissions and the length of hospital confinements. This can be accomplished if a commissioner advises he will not honor any requests for rate or schedule changes unless the review facilities are functioning. Several choices are available for the composition of review boards. In a 1961 query of insurance commissioners on this issue, the attitudes of the respondents were as follows:

	Number of commissioners
Committee made up of hospitals' medical staffs	7
Joint committee representing hospitals, physicians, Blue Cross, and/or the public	7
Health department or other state agency	5
Blue Cross physicians review committee	2
Medical society	1
Other	5
Total	27

It is going to be very difficult for insurance commissioners to stem the rise of medical care costs. Much of the increase in expenses is necessary if the quality of medical care is not to be impaired and advantage is to be taken of advances in medical science. At least one aspect of the rising-cost picture which needs regulatory attention, however, is the construction of unneeded hospital facilities. An investigation by New York State's Joint Legislative Committee on Health Insurance Plans in the fall of 1961 pinpointed the problem. Results of the study were published in "letters to the editors" of papers in regions where the hearings took place. The following comments were among those included in the letters from the committee:

The . . . community, which has undertaken the support of construction of the 100 acute and 30 chronic hospital beds now being planned, should understand that their completion and availability in the area will mean an increase in utilization, an increase in Blue Cross costs and inevitably Blue Cross rates.

With an effectively functioning regional hospital planning council, Blue Cross in this area, as elsewhere, must be concerned as to the extent of new hospital construction. Even granting the difficulty of predicting, with accuracy, just how much new hospital beds in any area will add to Blue Cross costs, every additional bed will inevitably be filled with a patient and these additional cases will mean more Blue Cross claims, adding to Blue Cross costs and eventually making higher Blue Cross premium necessary. It is essential to let the public—especially those who are Blue Cross subscribers—know how their Blue Cross premium rates are going to be affected by new hospital bed construction. This should be done at the time the new bed construction is first discussed—not months or years later, when premium rates must be raised.

The New York Joint Legislative Committee also pointed out the need for cooperative and cost-conscious attitudes by hospitals.

It was disquieting to learn that two hospitals within three miles of each other in the . . . area, intend to expand as separate institutions instead of amalgamating into one. Such an amalgamation would avoid duplicating such facilities as dietary, laundry, heating plant, etc., and provide a single hospital of 125 to 130 beds instead of two eighty-seven bed facilities. This determination to ignore expert hospital regional planning advice will result in some twenty beds for the area in excess of actual need. Estimating cost of construction of a single hospital bed at $20,000, it appears that the citizens of this area will be saddled with a cost of $400,000 for construction only. (Maintenance will be a constantly recurring additional cost.) This expense will necessarily have to be shared out of the tax funds now available to these two institutions as well as by the Blue Cross and other patients who use the new facilities. They will be an important part of the increased costs which Blue Cross will probably have to recover at sometime in the future by increased premium rates.

No one assumes regulatory officials alone can control general inflationary pressures in the field of medical care. Unnecessary cost increases can be averted, however, by efficiency measures, including uniform accounting, central purchasing and hospital planning techniques, and a general reappraisal of charges and fees, particularly by those in the medical care field. An insurance commissioner can "encourage" cost-control devices by refusing to approve schedule and rate changes until he is satisfied progress is being made toward the levels of efficiency he feels possible.

Coverage for the Aged

Blue Cross and Blue Shield plans customarily continue the coverage of a subscriber who has reached age sixty-five— the point after which the term "aged" traditionally applies. Contrary to the practice of many health insurance companies, group members have generally been given conversion rights when employers would not continue their protection upon termination of employment. Many observers feel associations have tried to do their share in giving the aged coverage against medical care expenses. If insurance companies had granted conversion privileges to pensioners, a considerable portion of the current problem of medical care for the aged might have been alleviated. (Companies are *currently* making rapid progress in allowing conversion, as well as encouraging employers to continue the coverage of retired employees.)

In addition to allowing most pensioners to continue their protection, it seems in keeping with the aims of Blue Cross and Blue Shield to offer membership to those over age sixty-five enrolling for the first time. Most associations do so for group members and over one third of the organizations offer initial nongroup membership to the aged. Supervisory officials should encourage use of "senior certificates" adapted to the particular needs and circumstances of pensioners.

It has been suggested that any group not retaining coverage for pensioners should be required to contribute to a special fund to help offset the high loss ratios of the aged. This procedure would recognize that groups or insurance organizations which use experience-rating techniques owe some responsibility to pensioners, and others should not be expected to bear the financial burden presented by the aged accepted as group insureds prior to age sixty-five. This contribution to a fund for the aged would help bring the coverage into the financial range of more in this category. Still, unless experience rating is prohibited for both associations and insurance companies—a highly unlikely occurrence— many aged will not be able to pay the cost of medical care coverage. The eventual solution to the entire problem will undoubtedly require federal government involvement. This conclusion has been accepted more and more widely as the medical care expense problem matures into an issue with great national significance. The New York Joint Legislative Committee on Health Insurance Plans noted in late 1961, for instance: "The problems of [the community] serve to demonstrate the possible inevitability of some form of governmental subsidy of hospitals, since apparently costs are rapidly outrunning the ability of most people to pay them, regardless of the mechanism by which payment is achieved. Such subsidy exists in virtually every other civilized country in the world and may well be the only practical solution to a problem which grows increasingly serious in America." If a subsidy is required, it is hoped it will be provided within the framework of existing insurance institutions.

National Enrollment

National enrollment has been a problem for Blue Cross and Blue Shield because it requires the cooperation of many, if not all, of the associations, each of which is an autonomous and basically independent organization. A partial solution evolved when a large number of the associations agreed to cooperate in the Local Benefit Agreement for National Accounts. However, this merely made selling and accounting processes more flexible in procuring coverage for national organizations. It was not until Health Service, Inc., and Medical Indemnity of America, Inc., were organized that machinery was available for offering uniform benefits and rates throughout the country. While employers with multistate operations need deal with only one organization to procure countrywide protection from Blue Cross and Blue Shield, some administrative and sales difficulties still give insurance companies the competitive edge in covering non-local groups. Most of these are internal problems for the associations, rather than direct regulatory issues for insurance commissioners. However, state laws which prevent associations from cooperating in HSI and MIA arrangements should be modified to permit local plans to accept the national group members located in their areas and with rating methods and benefit structures established at the national level.

Involvement of the Federal Government

Failure to resolve many issues previously discussed could result in the much-feared involvement of the federal government in the medical care field. Governmental intervention could take several forms: a governmental program of medical care for the aged;[3] direct regulation of the associations by the federal government; or utilization of Blue Cross and Blue Shield plans by the federal government as a means of providing medical care coverage for the aged[4] (possibly in conjunction with insurance companies). In the latter case, associations could provide hospital and medical-surgical protection for those over age sixty-five on a cost-plus basis and be reimbursed with tax funds.

Since regulatory authorities are convinced a workable program of medical care protection for the aged requires federal subsidies, the problem of governmental relations is certain to assume ever-widening importance.

It is possible that any major change in the regulation of insurance companies could affect the supervision of Blue

---

[3] The possibility of the government taking over the responsibility of the aged does not bother associations as much as does the likelihood that once this occurs the government would encroach on the other areas of coverage.

[4] A state program of this sort is currently in operation in Colorado. See William T. Reich and Odin W. Anderson, *Colorado's Medical Care Program for the Aged,* Health Insurance Foundation Perspectives Number a2 (New York: Health Insurance Foundation, 1960).

Cross and Blue Shield, inasmuch as many phases of their operations are treated in a similar manner. (The threat of such changes has been evidenced by the recent Senate Judiciary Antitrust Subcommittee investigation of state regulation.)

THE POSITION OF BLUE CROSS AND BLUE SHIELD ORGANIZATIONS

It is apparent the characteristics of Blue Cross and Blue Shield organizations have undergone changes during their three decades of existence. This was inevitable, if only because competitors arose to challenge the position of associations in the medical care field. Political and economic changes have altered the operational environments, as well. The years have seen the associations adopt some techniques of competing insurance companies, often by necessity. Still, many original principles and some identifying marks of Blue Cross and Blue Shield remain intact. For this reason several basic features of their regulation, including tax exemption, have been retained while other regulatory aspects have been modified considerably. Generally, their operations have come under more and more regulatory supervision, and this trend is certain to continue. As one executive remarked, "Regulatory bodies have become more conscious of the widespread acceptance of the plans by the public and will be more inclined to closely observe the plans' fulfillment of their avowed purposes." It seems appropriate in this final section to reiterate some of the purposes and to philosophize generally as to the position associations should maintain.

The starting point for any evaluation and justification of the Blues must be that the goals with which the associations were identified in the 1930's are of continuing urgency in the present day. Urbanization and weakened filial responsibilities have, in many cases, adversely affected the accessibility of medical care for individuals. Although standards of living have risen, the financial liquidity of individuals—through which medical care expenses are paid—has not seen much relative improvement in recent years. At the same time, methods of medical care have been vastly improved and extended and the costs of such treatment have increased drastically. Then, too, there still remains an important portion of the population for whom adequate protection against such expenses is not available at rates they can afford to pay.

Plans need to reaffirm their traditional aim of providing protection against the expenses of medical care for the broadest possible segment of the citizens in their respective areas. Blue Cross and Blue Shield must recognize their position is a "nongovernmental form of social insurance" rather than a "nonprofit form of private insurance."[5]

A second assertion can be made concerning the position of associations: it is both proper and beneficial for Blue Cross–Blue Shield plans and health insurance companies to live side by side, even though the former are identified as social insurance organizations while the latter are private-enterprise operations. Competition, when properly supervised, is desirable in medical care protection as well as in other areas of insurance. Probably more extensions of Blue Cross and Blue Shield benefits have resulted from insurance company competition than from any other factor. Blue Cross and Blue Shield operations have had a similar influence on the benefits offered by insurance companies; in fact, associations provided the impetus that brought insurance companies into the medical care field. Plans must go beyond competitive influences, however, and serve citizens who cannot obtain coverage from health insurance firms. Thus, the extent of competition needs to be supervised. It should never be so intensive that coverage, in terms of people or benefits, is restricted (such as when obsession with low rates results in unduly selective underwriting by an association) or financial stability is adversely influenced.

It is in keeping with the purposes of governmental super-

---

[5] This distinction in terminology and concept was originally developed by Dr. C. Rufus Rorem.

vision in a democratic society to ensure competition is on a fair basis. Associations which enroll segments of the population with high loss ratios should be granted special regulatory treatment, such as exemption from taxation, since health insurance companies are not obligated to cover the adverse elements and these special considerations help retain the competitiveness of Blue Cross and Blue Shield plans.

Regulatory authorities can both assist and prod the nonprofit organizations toward achieving their proper place as social insurance mechanisms whose basic concern is to help the general citizenry pay for their medical care expenses. Supervisory officials can assist, for instance, by seeking the passage of legislation which will prevent improper competition from health insurance companies. One area of concern in this respect is rating. As has been discussed, experience-rated groups which do not retain pensioners should contribute to a special contingency "fund" for the aged, in the absence of a legislative or administrative prohibition of merit rating. A legislative requirement for guaranteed renewability of coverage or paid-up types of policies might also be considered.

Insurance commissioners can prod associations toward their proper goals through approval powers over formation of plans, reimbursement and fee schedules, benefit structures, and rates. Broad enrollment objectives, experimentation in benefit structures with the intention of liberalizing benefits, and adequate public representation on boards of directors are a part of the aims hospital and medical service associations should adopt. Failure to channel activities in these directions should brand a Blue Cross or Blue Shield plan as a nonprofit form of private insurance, and such organizations should be treated as health insurance companies for purposes of regulation, including taxation.

Possible solutions or alternatives to the problem areas of Blue Cross and Blue Shield were discussed in individual sections of this book. In some instances the solutions were obvious from current trends. In other cases, judgment—with its limitations—was the source of determination. There may be no *one* path desirable to the exclusion of all others in solving these problems but the selection and support of one approach may at least prompt a more extensive consideration of dilemmas that have defied resolution in the past.

By self-regulation, as well as through statutes and supervisory officials, Blue Cross and Blue Shield associations must unceasingly continue the quest to eliminate gaps in medical care coverage and benefits. Only in this manner can the Blues justify and fortify their future existence.

APPENDIXES

THE REGULATION OF BLUE CROSS AND BLUE SHIELD PLANS

I. REGULATORY LAWS AND DEPARTMENTS
   A. What state agency, or agencies, has supervisory authority over Blue Cross and Blue Shield Plans?
      Insurance department only ( ).
      Insurance department in conjunction with another state division ( ).
      If so, what division?
      Department, other than the insurance department, called the:
   B. If there is no special legislation in your state applicable to Blue Cross and Blue Shield Plans, under what statutes do the plans operate?
II. REGULATORY PROCEDURES REGARDING PLAN OPERATIONS
   A. Admission of plans:
      1. Do the laws of your state require that a certain percentage of physicians participate in a medical service plan before it is approved? Yes ( ). No ( ). If yes, is this requirement in the public interest, in your opinion? Why, or why not?
      2. Do the state laws require that a certain percentage of the board of directors for a plan be representatives of any profession or group?
         Hospital service plans:
            physicians .... _____%
            hospital representatives .... _____%
            representatives of the public .... _____%
            others .... _____%

Medical service plans:

physicians .... _____%

lay representatives .... _____%

others .... _____%

3. What are the capital requirements a plan must meet to commence operation?

4. Do you foresee any reason why such capital requirements would need to be changed? If so, why?

B. Enrollment representatives: what limitations, if any, do state regulations place on the method of compensation for enrollment representatives?

C. Approval:

1. Must benefit provisions and certificate forms be approved by the state regulatory authority? Yes ( ). No ( ).

Prior approval? Yes ( ). No ( ).

2. Is approval required for:

Hospital reimbursement schedules? Yes ( ). No ( ).

Participating physicians' fee schedules? Yes ( ). No ( ).

D. Advertising:

1. What limitations does the state law place on advertising expenditures?

2. Has the interest of the Federal Trade Commission in insurance advertising caused any new state laws or regulatory practices regarding advertising and representations by the plans? If so, what is their nature? (Citations?)

III. Regulatory Procedures Regarding Financial Requirements for Plans

A. Reserves:

1. What does the state law stipulate as reserve requirements for:

Hospital service plans?

Medical service plans?

2. Does the regulatory authority have any rule-of-thumb regarding reserves which should be maintained by either of the foregoing types of plans?

3. Is there a desirable reserve basis and level which

could be uniformly applied to plans throughout the country? If not, what should be the determinants in developing a reserve basis within the state?

B. Investments:
   1. What investment limitations does state law place on plans?
   2. What additional limits, if any, do you feel should be imposed, or should there be no such restrictions?

C. Expenses:
   1. What expense limits, if any, are imposed by state law for the plans?
   2. Does the regulatory authority stipulate any other expense restrictions?

D. Reporting:
   1. What reporting and examination requirements are placed on hospital and medical service plans by state laws or administrative rulings?
   2. How do these requirements differ from those for health insurance companies?
   3. Do you feel there is a need for additional inquisitive powers over these plans? Please explain.

IV. RATE REGULATION OF BLUE CROSS AND BLUE SHIELD PLANS

A. Do state laws or administrative ruling require prior approval of rates before they become operative? Yes ( ). No. ( ).

B. Do you feel that a "community rate" is desirable for the majority of Blue Cross and Blue Shield subscribers? Yes ( ). No ( ). Comment:

C. Is an "experience" or "merit" rate inconsistent with the basic rating philosophy of the Blue Cross–Blue Shield movement, in your opinion? Why?

D. What criteria are applied in determining whether a request for a rate change should be approved?

E. In your opinion, are rate hearings a desirable feature in rate regulation? Why, or why not?
   Do you feel these hearings will become more widespread? Yes ( ). No ( ).

F. Has a rate change request by a Blue Cross or Blue Shield Plan been declined in the past year? In the past two years? Please explain.

G. Please outline in general terms the regulatory procedure utilized in processing a rate request by a plan, including the supporting statistics required, etc.

V. TAXATION

A. To what type of taxes are nonprofit plans subjected in your state?

B. Has the tax status of the plans been litigated in your state? Please give citations.

C. What developments do you feel could jeopardize the tax status of the plans? (For example, if a plan failed to cover a sizeable portion of the low-income groups, might its tax position be reappraised, etc.?)

VI. GROWTH PROBLEM AREAS: The following problems have been suggested as among those which Blue Cross and Blue Shield Plans will face in the next few years. Which of these do you consider to be most pressing? What changes in regulatory laws or standards may be required?

A. Coverage of the aged:

B. National enrollment:

C. Catastrophic illnesses:

D. Liberalization of benefits:

E. Experience rating:

F. Rural enrollment:

G. Others:

VII. REGULATORY METHODS: Which of the following methods of regulating Blue Cross and Blue Shield Plans do you consider to be most important? In your comments would you please identify any particular type which has importance for a specific area of regulation.

A. Regulatory laws:

B. Regulatory officials:

C. National Association of Insurance Commissioners:

D. Courts:

E. Self-regulation (that is, by the plans, themselves, and their national organizations—the Blue Cross Association and the National Association of Blue Shield Plans) :

VIII. CHARACTERISTICS

A. To what extent has each of the following characteristics influenced current regulatory procedures and attitudes:

1. Nonprofit status?

      2. Community sponsorship?

      3. Service approach?

      4. Community-rating procedure?

      5. Prepayment principle?

  B. Do you feel each is a current characteristic of the plans?

  C. Do you feel that Blue Cross and Blue Shield Plans are sufficiently similar to health insurance companies for both types of organizations to be treated alike by regulatory authorities? Yes ( ). No ( ).

     If, in your opinion, these plans are different from insurance companies, please indicate the areas of variance: (purpose of the plans, method of organization, method of operation, type of benefits, or what?)

IX. What possible changes in attitude toward Blue Cross and Blue Shield by regulatory authorities do you see in the future?

Thank you very much for the thought and time necessary to complete these questions!

MODEL LAW TO ENABLE THE FORMATION OF NON-PROFIT HOSPITAL AND/OR MEDICAL SERVICE PLANS, PROPOSED BY THE BLUE CROSS COMMISSION

SCOPE 1. Any corporation organized not for profit under the General Corporation Act of the State of ...... for the purpose of establishing, maintaining and operating a non-profit corporation, whereby hospital and/or medical service may be provided by a group of hospitals and/or physicians, with which such corporation has a contract for such purpose, to such of the public as become subscribers to said corporation under a contract which entitles each subscriber to certain hospital and/or medical care, shall be governed by this act and shall be exempt from all other provisions of the insurance laws of this state, unless otherwise specifically provided herein.

INCORPORATION 2. The articles of incorporation of every such corporation, and amendments thereto, shall be submitted to the Department of Insurance, whose approval thereof shall be endorsed thereon before the same are filed with the Secretary of State; provided, however, that if the articles of incorporation of any such corporation shall have been filed with the Secretary of State prior to the effective date of this statute, the approval thereof by the Department of Insurance shall be evidenced by a separate instrument in writing filed with the Secretary of State.

DIRECTORS 3. The Directors of such corporation must at all times include representatives of the following groups: administrators or trustees of hospitals which have contracted with such corporation to render medical service to the subscribers; general public exclusive of hospital representatives and physicians. (The committee recognizes that the proportions of the groups mentioned may vary with the special character of the program offered by each corporation established under this legislation.)

CONTRACTS 4. Such corporation may enter into contracts for the rendering of hospital and/or medical service to the subscribers only with hospitals approved for participation by the Department of Insurance and with licensed physicians. (The corporation may include in the conditions for hospital participation certain professional and administrative standards, subject at all times to approval by appropriate regulatory bodies, such as the Health or Welfare department in consultation with the Department of Insurance.)

All contracts issued by such corporation to the subscribers shall constitute direct obligations of the hospitals and/or physicians with which such corporation has contracted for hospital and/or medical service. The rates charged to the subscribers for hospital and/or medical service and the rates of payment by such corporation to the contracting hospitals and/or physicians at all times shall be subject to the approval of the Department of Insurance.

LICENSURE 5. A corporation subject to the provisions of this act may issue contracts only when the Department of Insurance has by formal certificate or license authorized it to do so. Application for such certificate of authority or license shall be made on forms to be supplied by the Department of Insurance, containing such information as it shall deem necessary. Each application for such certificate or license shall be accompanied by copies of the following documents: (*a*) certificate of incorporation; (*b*) by-laws; (*c*) proposed contracts between the corporation and participating hospitals and/or physicians showing terms under which hospital and/or medical service is to be furnished to subscribers; (*d*) contracts to be issued to subscribers showing the benefits to which they are entitled; (*e*) a table of the rates to be charged to the subscribers; (*f*) financial statement of the corporation, including the amounts of contribution paid or agreed to be paid to the corporation for working capital and the name or names of each contributor and the terms of each contribution.

The Department of Insurance shall issue a certificate of authority or license upon payment of a fee of $ .... and upon being satisfied on the following points:

(*a*) That the applicant is established as a bona fide non-profit hospital and/or medical service corporation.

(*b*) That the contract between the applicant and the participating hospitals and/or physicians obligate each hospital and/or physician party to render service to which each subscriber may be entitled under the terms and conditions of the contract issued to the subscribers.

(*c*) That the rates to be charged and benefits to be provided are fair and reasonable.

(*d*) That amounts provided as working capital of the corporation are repayable only out of earned income paid and payable for operating expenses and hospital and/or medical expenses, and such reserve as the Department of Insurance may deem adequate.

(*e*) That the amount of money actually available for working capital be sufficient to carry all acquisition costs and operating expenses for a reasonable period of time from the date of the issuance of the certificate.

REPORTS 6. Every such corporation shall annually on or before the first day of March file in the office of the Department of Insurance a statement verified by at least two of the principal officers of said corporation showing its condition on the 31st day of December, then next preceding, which shall be in such form and shall contain such matters as the Department shall prescribe.

VISITATION 7. The Department of Insurance may appoint any Deputy or Examiner or other person who may have the power of visitation and examination into the affairs of any such corporation and free access to all of the books, papers and documents that relate to the business of the corporation, and may summon and qualify witnesses under oath to examine its officers, agents or employees or other persons in relation to the affairs, transactions and conditions of the corporation.

The Insurance Department shall conduct an examination of each such corporation, at least every three years, and the costs of such regular or other special examinations shall be borne by the corporation.

EXPENSES 8. All acquisition and administrative expenses in connection with such hospital and/or medical service corporation shall at all times be subject to control by the Department of Insurance.

INVESTMENTS 9. The funds of any corporation subject to the provisions of this act shall be invested only in securities permitted by the law of this state for the investment of assets of life insurance companies.

DECISIONS 10. Any decision and finding of the Department of Insurance made under the provisions of this act shall not be any bar to constituted legal procedure in a court of competent jurisdiction.

DISSOLUTION 11. Any dissolution or liquidation of a corporation subject to the provisions of this act shall be conducted under the supervision of the Department of Insurance which shall have all power with respect thereto under the provisions of law with respect to the dissolution and liquidation of insurance companies.

TAXATION 12. Every corporation subject to the provisions of this act is hereby declared to be a charitable and benevolent institution, and the corporation shall be exempt from every state, county, and municipal tax.

Source: Louis S. Reed, *Blue Cross and Medical Service Plans* (Washington, D.C.: Federal Security Agency, U.S. Public Health Service, 1947) , pp. 294–96.

NAIC ADVERTISING CODE

Rules Governing Advertisements of Accident and Sickness Insurance

WHEREAS the insurance laws of this State and particularly (refer to specific sections of law) prohibit the transmission of information in the form of advertisements or otherwise in such a manner or of such substance that the insurance buying public may be deceived or misled thereby; and

WHEREAS said insurance laws establish only general standards by which advertisements in the field of individual, group, blanket and franchise accident and sickness insurance should be prepared, disseminated and regulated; and

WHEREAS it is considered proper and desirable to implement and interpret the general statutory standards and to adopt proper procedures to expedite enforcement thereof by this office, now therefore

IT IS ORDERED that the following standards for advertisements of such accident and sickness insurance as well as the administrative and enforcement procedures here-after enumerated be and are hereby adopted as a formal and official rule (ruling) of this Department:

Section 1. *DEFINITIONS*

A. *An advertisement* for the purpose of these rules shall include:

    (1) printed and published material and descriptive literature of an insurer used in newspapers, magazines, radio and TV scripts, billboards and similar displays; and

    (2) descriptive literature and sales aids of all kinds issued by an insurer for presentation to members of the public, including but not limited to circulars, leaflets, booklets, depictions, illustrations, and form letters; and

    (3) prepared sales talks, presentations and material for use by

agents and brokers, and representations made by agents and brokers in accordance therewith.

B. *Policy* for the purpose of these rules shall include any policy, plan, certificate contract, agreement, statement of coverage, rider or endorsement which provides accident or sickness benefits, or medical, surgical or hospital expense benefits, whether on a cash indemnity, reimbursement, or service basis, except when issued in connection with another kind of insurance other than life and except disability and double indemnity benefits included in life insurance and annuity contracts.

C. *Insurer* for the purpose of these rules shall include any individual, agent, broker, corporation, association, partnership, reciprocal exchange, inter-insurer, Lloyds, fraternal benefit society, and any other legal entity engaged in the advertisement of a policy as herein defined.

Section 2. *ADVERTISEMENTS IN GENERAL*

Advertisements shall be truthful and not misleading in fact or in implication. Words or phrases the meaning of which is clear only by implication or by familiarity with insurance terminology shall not be used.

Section 3. *ADVERTISEMENTS OF BENEFITS PAYABLE, LOSSES COVERED OR PREMIUMS PAYABLE*

A. *Deceptive Words, Phrases or Illustrations*

Words, phrases or illustrations shall not be used in a manner which misleads or has the capacity and tendency to deceive as to the extent of any policy benefit payable, loss covered or premium payable. An advertisement relating to any policy benefit payable, loss covered or premium payable shall be sufficiently complete and clear as to avoid deception or the capacity and tendency to deceive.

Explanation:

(1) The words and phrases "all," "full," "complete," "comprehensive," "unlimited," "up to," "as high as," "this policy will pay your hospital and surgical bills" or "this policy will replace your income," or similar words and phrases shall not be used so as to exaggerate any benefit beyond the terms of the policy, but may be used only in such manner as fairly to describe such benefit.

(2) A policy covering only one disease or a list of specified diseases shall not be advertised so as to imply coverage beyond the terms of the policy. Synonymous terms shall not be used to refer to any disease so as to imply broader coverage than is the fact.

(3) The benefits of a policy which pays varying amounts for the same loss occurring under different conditions or which pays benefits only when a loss occurs under certain conditions shall not be advertised without disclosing the limited conditions under which the benefits referred to are provided by the policy.

(4) Phrases such as "this policy pays $1,800 for hospital room and board expenses" are incomplete without indicating the maximum daily benefit and the maximum time limit for hospital room and board expenses.

B. *Exceptions, Reductions and Limitations*

When an advertisement refers to any dollar amount, period of time for which any benefit is payable, cost of policy, or specific policy benefit or the loss for which such benefit is payable, it shall also disclose those exceptions, reductions and limitations affecting the basic provisions of the policy without which the advertisement would have the capacity and tendency to mislead or deceive.

Explanation:

(1) The term "exception" shall mean any provision in a policy whereby coverage for a specified hazard is entirely eliminated; it is a statement of a risk not assumed under the policy.

(2) The term "reduction" shall mean any provision which reduces the amount of the benefit; a risk of loss is assumed but payment upon the occurrence of such loss is limited to some amount or period less than would be otherwise payable had such reduction clause not been used.

(3) The term "limitation" shall mean any provision which restricts coverage under the policy other than an exception or a reduction.

(4) *Waiting, Elimination, Probationary or Similar Periods*
When a policy contains a time period between the effective date of the policy and the effective date of coverage under the policy or a time period between the date a loss

occurs and the date benefits begin to accrue for such loss, an advertisement covered by Section 3B shall disclose the existence of such periods.

(5) *Pre-existing Conditions*

    (*a*) An advertisement covered by Section 3B shall disclose the extent to which any loss is not covered if the cause of such loss is traceable to a condition existing prior to the effective date of the policy.

    (*b*) When a policy does not cover losses traceable to pre-existing conditions no advertisement of the policy shall state or imply that the applicant's physical condition or medical history will not affect the issuance of the policy or payment of a claim thereunder. This limits the use of the phrase "no medical examination required" and phrases of similar import.

Section 4. *NECESSITY FOR DISCLOSING POLICY PROVISIONS RELATING TO RENEWABILITY, CANCELLABILITY AND TERMINATION*

An advertisement which refers to renewability, cancellability or termination of a policy, or which refers to a policy benefit, or which states or illustrates time or age in connection with eligibility of applicants or continuation of the policy, shall disclose the provisions relating to renewability, cancellability and termination and any modification of benefits, losses covered or premiums because of age or for other reasons, in a manner which shall not minimize or render obscure the qualifying conditions.

Section 5. *METHOD OF DISCLOSURE OF REQUIRED INFORMATION*

All information required to be disclosed by these rules shall be set out conspicuously and in close conjunction with the statements to which such information relates or under appropriate captions of such prominence that it shall not be minimized, rendered obscure or presented in an ambiguous fashion or intermingled with the context of the advertisement so as to be confusing or misleading.

Section 6. *TESTIMONIALS*

Testimonials used in advertisements must be genuine, represent the current opinion of the author, be applicable to the policy advertised and be accurately reproduced. The insurer, in using a testimonial, makes as its own all of the statements contained therein, and the advertisement including such statements is subject to all of the provisions of these rules.

Section 7. *USE OF STATISTICS*

An advertisement relating to the dollar amounts of claims paid, the number of persons insured, or similar statistical information relating to any insurer or policy shall not be used unless it accurately reflects all of the relevant facts. Such an advertisement shall not imply that such statistics are derived from the policy advertised unless such is the fact.

Section 8. *INSPECTION OF POLICY*

An offer in an advertisement of free inspection of a policy or offer of a premium refund is not a cure for misleading or deceptive statements contained in such advertisement.

Section 9. *IDENTIFICATION OF PLAN OR NUMBER OF POLICIES*

A. When a choice of the amount of benefits is referred to, an advertisement shall disclose that the amount of benefits provided depends upon the plan selected and that the premium will vary with the amount of the benefits.
B. When an advertisement refers to various benefits which may be contained in two or more policies, other than group master policies, the advertisement shall disclose that such benefits are provided only through a combination of such policies.

Section 10. *DISPARAGING COMPARISONS AND STATEMENTS*

An advertisement shall not directly or indirectly make unfair or incomplete comparisons of policies or benefits or otherwise falsely disparage competitors, their policies, services or business methods.

Section 11. *JURISDICTIONAL LICENSING*

A. An advertisement which is intended to be seen or heard beyond the limits of the jurisdiction in which the insurer is licensed shall not imply licensing beyond those limits.

B. Such advertisements by direct mail insurers shall indicate that the insurer is licensed in a specified state or states only, or is not licensed in a specified state or states, by use of some language such as "This Company is licensed only in State A" or "This Company is not licensed in State B."

Section 12. *IDENTITY OF INSURER*

The identity of the insurer shall be made clear in all of its advertisements. An advertisement shall not use a trade name, service mark, slogan, symbol or other device which has the capacity and tendency to mislead or deceive as to the true identity of the insurer.

Section 13. *GROUP OR QUASI-GROUP IMPLICATIONS*

An advertisement of a particular policy shall not state or imply that prospective policy-holders become group or quasi-group members and as such enjoy special rates or underwriting privileges, unless such is the fact.

Section 14. *INTRODUCTORY, INITIAL OR SPECIAL OFFERS*

An advertisement shall not state or imply that a particular policy or combination of policies is an introductory, initial or special offer and that the applicant will receive advantages by accepting the offer, unless such is the fact.

Section 15. *APPROVAL OR ENDORSEMENT BY THIRD PARTIES*

A. An advertisement shall not state or imply that an insurer or a policy has been approved or an insurer's financial condition has been examined and found to be satisfactory by a governmental agency, unless such is the fact.

B. An advertisement shall not state or imply that an insurer or a policy has been approved or endorsed by any individual, group of individuals, society, association or other organization, unless such is the fact.

Section 16. *SERVICE FACILITIES*

An advertisement shall not contain untrue statements with respect to the time within which claims are paid or statements which imply that claim settlements will be liberal or generous beyond the terms of the policy.

Section 17. *STATEMENTS ABOUT AN INSURER*

An advertisement shall not contain statements which are untrue in fact or by implication misleading with respect to the insurer's assets, corporate structure, financial standing, age or relative position in the insurance business.

Special Enforcement Procedures for Rules Governing the Advertisement of Accident and Sickness Insurance

(1) *Advertising File:* Each insurer shall maintain at its home or principal office a complete file containing every printed, published or prepared advertisement of individual policies and typical printed, published or prepared advertisements of blanket, franchise and group policies hereafter disseminated in this or any other state whether or not licensed in such other state, with a notation attached to each such advertisement which shall indicate the manner and extent of distribution and the form number of any policy advertised. Such file shall be subject to regular and periodical inspection by this Department. All such advertisements shall be maintained in said file for a period of not less than three years.

(2) *Certificate of Compliance:* Each insurer required to file an annual statement which is now or which hereafter becomes subject to the provisions of this rule (ruling) must file with this Department together with its annual statement, a certificate executed by an authorized officer of the insurer wherein it is stated that to the best of his knowledge, information and belief the advertisements which were disseminated by the insurer during the preceding statement year complied or were made to comply in all respects with the provisions (of the insurance laws of this State as implemented by this rule —ruling) (of this rule—ruling). It is requested that the chief executive officer of each such insurer to which this rule (ruling) is addressed acknowledge its receipt and indicate its intention to comply therewith.

Effective date of this rule (ruling) 90 days from date hereof.

Dated this ____ day of _____, 195__.

Signature _____

Index

INDEX

A

Adjudications, 112
Advertising
  codes, 161–62, 311, 340–46
  financial limits, 162
  litigation concerning, 160–61
  by plans, 162
Aged
  hospital utilization, 221, 305
  incomes, 216, 306
  medical care coverage
    continuance of coverage, 303, 321
    conversion, 32, 37–38, 51, 168–69,
      171, 211, 221, 321
    eligibility, 303, 321
    enrollment, 304
    governmental involvement, 216,
      306, 322–23
    number of plans offering, 303–05
    rate-making problems, 216, 221,
      284
    regulatory attitudes, 304
  national programs
    Blue Cross–American Hospital
      Assn., 305–6
    National Assn. of Blue Shield
      Plans–American Medical
      Assn., 306
  proportion of, 302
  savings, 303
American Hospital Association; *see
  also* Approval programs
  administration of approval pro-
    gram, 61, 125–26
  coverage for aged, 305–6
  early influence on plans, 11
  participation in the research, 6
  Principles of prepayment of hos-
    pital care, 185, 193–94
  relations with Blue Cross Associa-
    tion, 125, 127–28
  responsibilities assumed from Blue
    Cross Commission, 61
  self-regulation through, 121, 125–
    27, 129

American Life Convention
  attitude toward cost-based reim-
    bursement, 193, 202–3
American Medical Association
  appointment of directors of Na-
    tional Assn. of Blue Shield
    Plans, 73, 125
  coverage for aged, 306
  current relations with Blue Shield,
    70–74, 76, 125, 127–28
  role in Blue Shield development,
    16–17, 70–72
  self-regulation through, 121, 125,
    127
Annual reports; *see* Reports
Approach of the study, 5
Approval programs
  Blue Cross
    administration by American Hos-
      pital Association, 61, 125–26
    board of directors, requirements
      concerning, 141
    compensation of enrollment rep-
      resentatives, 159
    early requirements, 11
    hospital participation require-
      ments, 134
    nature of, 126, 312
    reports, 265
    reserve requirements, 251–53
  Blue Shield
    administration by National
      Assn. of Blue Shield Plans,
      74, 126
    board of directors, requirements
      concerning, 141
    compensation of enrollment rep-
      resentatives, 159
    early role of American Medical
      Assn., 70
    nature of, 126, 312
    physicians' participation, re-
      quirements, 135
    reports, 265
    reserve requirements, 252–53

349

This book has been set in 11 and 10 point Baskerville, leaded 2 points, Part numbers are in 30 point Eden Light; part titles in 18 point Lydian Bold. Chapter numbers are in 18 point Eden Light; chapter titles in 14 point Lydian Bold. The size of the type page is 24 x 42 picas.